The "Chirping" Crickets
Yngwie Malmsteen's Rising Force
Perpetual Flame
Eric Clapton
Apache–Man of Mystery–The Stranger–F.B.I.
mono
The Shadows to the Fore
Columbia
Tony
Dire Straits
"Sultans of Swing"
"Eastbound train"
Buddy Guy: A Man & The Blues
The Colorful Ventures
MC5
Teen Age Lust
Rory Gallagher
Live!
Earl King
Hard River to Cross
The Surfaris
Wipe Out
Point Panic • Surfer Joe • Waikiki Run
livefromaustintx
Eric Johnson
Austin City Limits
F.B.I
Midnight
Man of Mystery
The Stranger
The Shadows
Richard Thompson
Eric Clapton
Slowhand
The Soul of Ike & Tina
Nils Lofgren
Old School
Yngwie J. Malmsteen's
Rising Force
Ritchie Valens
Anson Funderburgh & The Rockets
"Talk to You by Hand"
"Tore Up"
"Walking Dr. Bill"
"That Will Never Do"
"This Should Go On Forever"
Show & Dance
S'Wonderful
Jeff Beck
Emotion & Commotion
The Shadows
Apache
Tony
Fifty Sides of
The Beach Boys
Their Story
Mark Dillon
Rory Gallagher
Against the Grain
Sexual Telepathy
Sam Myers
Anson Funderburgh
Yngwie J. Malmsteen
Trilogy
The Surfaris play...
Wipe Out
Point Panic
Waikiki Run
Surfer Joe
and 8 others
Jeff Beck
Live and Exclusive
From the Grammy Museum
Lucky Peterson
Lucky
Strikes!
The Meteors
Featuring their smash hit
Big Little Katie
Joe Louis Walker
Blue Soul
The Shadows Vocals
The Shadows
Tony
Kingfish
Live 'N' Kickin'
Stevie Ray Vaughan
Couldn't Stand the Weather
So Little Time
Yngwie Malmsteen
High Impact
John Mayer
Heavier Things
Eric Clapton · Just One Night

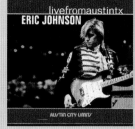

BYRON FRY
COMBUSTIBLE
DAVE ALVIN
ASHGROVE
dIRE sTRAITS Live
love Over gold / Solid rock
DEEP PURPLE
made in japan
THE SHADOWS
mono
COLUMBIA
The Shadows
BACHMAN-TURNER OVERDRIVE
You Ain't Seen Nothin' Yet
Free Wheelin'
SONNY LANDRETH
Robert Cray Band
Yngwie Malmsteen
relentless
NILS LOFGREN
Cry Tough
DUARTE GROUP
SILVERTONE
SUGAR
TEXAS
JEFF BECK WIRED
BACHMAN-TURNER OVERDRIVE
FLAT BROKE LOVE
HEY YOU
THE SHADOWS
SONNY Landreth
MISSISSIPPI BLUES
Eric Clapton
Rising Force
eric johnson
ERIC CLAPTON JUST ONE NIGHT
DAVE SPECTER BARKIN' BILL SMITH
BLUEBIRD BLUES
RONNIE EARL
ROBERT CRAY
I WAS WARNED
RONNIE EARL
THE BEST OF ERIC CLAPTON
DICK DALE
RONNIE EARL & THE BROADCASTERS
Deep Blues
STEVIE RAY VAUGHAN
SOUL TO SOUL
THE ROBERT CRAY BAND
THIS TIME
F.B.I
MIDNIGHT
MAN OF MYSTERY
THE STRANGER
THE SHADOWS
THE CREAM OF
CLAPTON
MAGIC SLIM & THE TEARDROPS
JOE CARTER WITH SUNNYLAND SLIM
that ain't right
HUBERT SUMLIN
HEALING FEELING
RONNIE EARL
DARRELL NULISCH
U. P. WILSON
Booting
'Strong, bad to the bone'
GEORGE THOROGOOD
JSP
Family Style
THE FANTASTIC SHADOWS
ROBERT CRAY STRONG PERSUADER
Tommy Castro
Can't Keep A Good Man Down
U.P. Wilson
Boogie Boy!
JSP
CD 255
IAN MOORE
HUBERT SUMLIN
Produced by WILLIE DIXON
OTIS RUSH
1956-1958
Cobra
RECORDINGS

THE FENDER STRATOCASTER

THE LIFE and TIMES OF THE WORLD'S GREATEST GUITAR and ITS PLAYERS

DAVE HUNTER

FOREWORD BY RANDY BACHMAN

Fender
VOLUME
TONE
TONE

CONTENTS

FOREWORD

BY RANDY BACHMAN

THERE ARE TWO ICONIC GUITARS that shaped the blues and rock 'n' roll—the Gibson Les Paul and the Fender Stratocaster. They each have their own distinctive look and sound, and because they are opposites in every way, every guitar player has to have both of them.

The Strat was and still is the most recognizable image, sound, and pioneering guitar to ever make music. The first time I saw a Strat was with Buddy Holly & the Crickets on *The Ed Sullivan Show*. At the same time, I got a copy of *Out of the Shadows* from England and saw my first red Strat. The sound had me hooked.

The Stratocaster is the most versatile and durable guitar ever made. The ability to interchange different Fender guitar necks, bodies, pickups, etc., made all Fenders in demand. No airline has ever destroyed one of my Fender guitars. To demonstrate their toughness, I have thrown a Strat off the roof of a house, climbed down, picked it up, and played it—and it was still in tune.

They are the workhorse of most guitar players. In my early days, I had a '59 Black Strat that I customized by stripping off the paint (stupid move), reversing the innie guitar jack to be an outie (smart move), sanding the back of the neck to be more like a violin, putting a '59 Tele pickup at the bridge and a Ricky pickup at the neck, and adding three off-on pickup switches and a T-wang bar arm. I was set for anything. This guitar was known as The Legend by many guitarists and fans as it was the guitar I played through the Guess Who years, into the Brave Belt years, which became the Bachman-Turner Overdrive years. Unfortunately, it was stolen, and my heart still aches when I think of that. There should be a death penalty for guitar thieves! If you've had one stolen, you'll agree.

I have quite a collection of Strats now. My favorite is an Olympic White 1954, serial number 0717, that sounds so clear on the top end, it's like a pedal steel.

It would not be out of line to change the "T" to a "D," and call this model of guitar a "Stradicaster." The Fender Stratocaster is truly the Stradivarius of guitars.

Stay tuned,
Randy Bachman
The Guess Who
Bachman-Turner Overdrive
Ringo Star All Star Band '95
Bachman & Turner

Randy Bachman, Bachman-Turner Overdrive, and a Fender Strat rock the bad old '70s. *David Redfern/Redferns/Getty Images*

The Sparkletones loved their Fender Stratocasters and picked those Strats to a big 1957 hit with "Black Slacks."

Leo Fender at his drafting table in his later years. *Bob Perine*

The Fender factory on Santa Fe Avenue in Fullerton, California, circa 1950.

PART I

HISTORY

WHAT A FEELING, to live in an age when simple old rock 'n' roll seemed at the forefront of a cultural revolution, and a curvaceous new solidbody electric guitar with unprecedented features seemed about as radical a work of design-art as could be imagined. We like to think that things move fast in our current age: "The iGizmo 4 came out just last year, and *already* they're releasing the iGizmo 5!" Certainly iProgress, and the consumer products that go hand in hand with it, has ramped up to a heady pace here in the second decade of the twenty-first century. And yet, briefly consider how fast things were moving in an earlier age—a predigital age, pre-"information" age, sure, but one in which an early–Cold War Western world was jogging swiftly toward a level of technical innovation in everyday life that was staggeringly advanced over what was known just a couple of decades before. Now apply that to the world that is of immediate concern to us—which is to say, guitarists and fans of guitar history—and the mid-twentieth century really does appear to have been the dawn of a brave new world, and one in which the advances in how we made music came on fast and furious.

Rickenbacker was one of the pioneers of electric-guitar technology. The California company's solidbody Hawaiian—such as this 1931 "Frying Pan" lap steel—and Spanish semi-solidbody and hollowbody guitars were among the first available on the market. *Nigel Osbourne/Redferns/Getty Images*

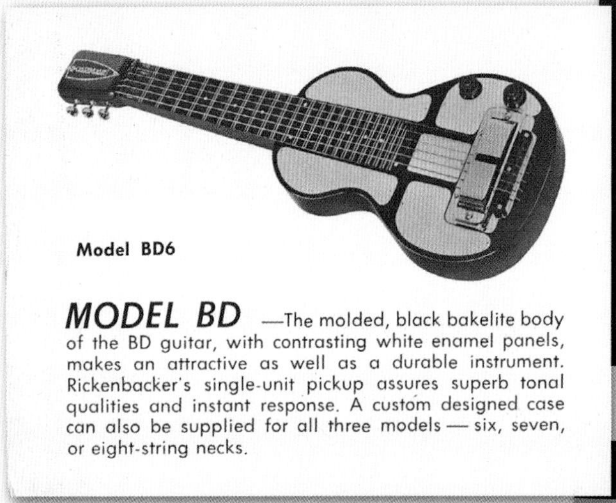

Model BD6

MODEL BD —The molded, black bakelite body of the BD guitar, with contrasting white enamel panels, makes an attractive as well as a durable instrument. Rickenbacker's single-unit pickup assures superb tonal qualities and instant response. A custom designed case can also be supplied for all three models — six, seven, or eight-string necks.

Rickenbacke
The World's Most Distinguished Name in Guitars, Amplifiers and Acces
HAWAIIAN
STEEL GUITARS

There's nothing for it but to admit that the sublimely sexy and superbly versatile Stratocaster, released in 1954, was a quantum leap from the bare-bones Esquire and Broadcaster that had come out four years before (the guitar soon and forever after known as the Telecaster). Even if you are first and foremost a Telecaster fan, and there remain several great reasons to be one, you can't deny that the Stratocaster took the electric guitar into an entirely different plane of existence design-wise. Early on in *The Fender Telecaster: The Life and Times of the Electric Guitar That Changed the World*, I described the Tele as "a total redrawing of the blueprint" of the guitar as it had previously been known. Fender's debut electric might not look terribly radical now, but considered in light of the deep-bodied, fully acoustic electrics that had come before—with its slim maple bolt-on neck, stylized body, and integral bridge and pickup unit—it represented a groundbreaking leap in design. Well, examining in hindsight what came along four years later, you wouldn't think a new bridge design with a few springs in an additional body cavity, an extra pickup, and some sultry new horns and contours and curves would make such a difference, but they sure enough did. Compared to the Telecaster, even today, the Stratocaster appears a bold departure in the form; at the time, it must have looked like a music machine from another planet. Or at least from another generation—one capable of putting the frights into the knife-creased slacks of the generation that came before.

With the Stratocaster, Leo Fender finally left behind any semblance of what our common conception of "guitar" had been just a half dozen years before, other than in the six strings and

E-A-D-G-B-E tuning. From out of the slab-bodied, two-pickup, hardtail twanger had grown an extremely versatile performance machine with the looks to match its revolutionary sonic capabilities. Yet we still need to begin our history of the development of this amazing new guitar at a time that precedes the predecessor, if you will, in order to fully appreciate Fender's development toward the most groundbreaking guitar ever created. In light of its humble origins, the Stratocaster is all the more impressive, coming, not from a large, established maker with several decades of success in the industry, but from one self-driven man with a hatful of great ideas, a few maverick helpers, and a willingness to thoughtfully examine the true needs of musicians of the day.

Leo and the Birth of Fender

Clarence Leonidas Fender was born on August 10, 1909, to orange growers Clarence and Harriet Fender in what was then the farmland of would-be greater Los Angeles, California, not far from the eventual home of his Fender factory in Fullerton. Leo, as he would be known, enjoyed a childhood that was in no significant way out of the ordinary for the time, although he did show a great interest in both electronics (radios and amplification in particular) and music from a relatively young age. He learned to play the saxophone and piano and built a guitar from scratch in his mid-teens, but he never truly learned to play the guitar or ever undertake any formal training in electronics. Leo did, however, apparently learn a significant amount from an uncle who was skilled in radio repair and developed his talent the old-fashioned way, building and repairing radios himself throughout his time at Fullerton Union High School and, following his graduation in 1928, while studying accounting at Fullerton Junior College.

The "tinkering" persisted, to the point where Leo started making a name for himself as a builder and repairman of just about all things tube-amplification-related. He was even asked by local bands to build public address (PA) systems in his spare time while working as a bookkeeper in the early 1930s. Even when this blossomed into a thriving little sideline, building, renting out, and maintaining PAs used at musical and sporting events around the Orange County area, the young accountant didn't seem to consider shifting his career to music electronics until he lost his job at a tire company in nearby San Luis Obispo that cut its entire accounting department in 1938. Unemployment inspired Leo to move with Esther, his wife since 1934, back to his home environs of Fullerton, take a loan for $600, and open his own business: Fender's Radio Service. This prewar venture proved the modest beginning to a steadily upward climb for Fender, and the first mild bleat from what would become one of the loudest voices in the musical instrument industry.

Upon its debut in 1949, Gibson's three-pickup ES-5 was the premier guitar of the day. Still, the ES-5 was truly just an acoustic guitar with pickups screwed on. *Michael Dregni*

Early Fender lap steel guitars and accompanying amplifiers. The construction of these guitars led the way to building solidbody Spanish electric guitars. *John Peden*

For several years, though, "upward" certainly must have felt like "uphill." Initially a one-man shop, things at first moved at a slow yet steady pace at Fender's Radio Service. Leo branched out from selling records and repairing radios and gramophones to, once again, building PA systems and musical-instrument amplifiers for sale and rent, and before long, dabbled in designing the magnetic pickups that these instruments required in order to be amplified in the first place. In the early 1940s Leo teamed up with musician and inventor Clayton Orr "Doc" Kauffman, and the pair developed an original pickup design together in 1943 (which was granted a patent in 1948), as well as a precision 45-rpm record changer to which they sold the design and manufacturing rights for $5,000. With what then would have seemed a hefty chunk of seed money in hand, in 1945 Kauffman and Fender formed the K&F Manufacturing Company, which produced three types of tube amplifiers and six models of Hawaiian lap steel guitars to be played through them, before the partnership's early demise later that year.

Moving from Repairing to Manufacturing

Kauffman's main concern about the business involved Leo's desire to move more wholly into manufacturing than repair. It would seem, with hindsight, that such concerns couldn't have been more ill-founded (would we have eventually seen "a K&F Stratocaster" otherwise?), but Fender did have some lean years before the whole thing boomed. In 1946, Leo established the Fender Electric Instrument Co. and pushed forward with his production of lap steel guitars and the amplifiers they were played through. The latter were particularly successful—or relatively so, given the Fender company's modest means at the time—on a scene where that technology might have seemed to be lagging behind the musical times. Leo Fender's vast experience in repairing commercial radios and related products gave him great insight into both the virtues and flaws in many such designs, which he applied to his designs for musical instrument amplifiers. As a result, as young as his company was, Fender amps were generally sturdier and more roadworthy than almost anything else on the market by the late 1940s and yielded volume levels and a quality of tone that were equally elevated. As Fender told *Guitar Player* magazine in 1971, "I guess you would say the objectives were durability, performance, and tone." Extrapolating from that, his stated belief was that a product that would be easy to repair would also be easier to manufacture; the tone factor relied upon how you put those low-maintenance ingredients together.

If the amps arguably proved Leo's greatest early success, his formative years of building lap steel guitars, and learning from the musicians who played them, would be crucial in helping to distinguish Fender's eventual electric Spanish guitars from anything else that was already on the scene. Leo's goals of durability, ease of maintenance, and ease of manufacture would be transported from the amp line to the guitars, but the sonic goals of "performance and tone" would be more directly derived from the input of musicians who primarily played "hillbilly" and western swing. They wanted instruments that were bright, firm, punchy, and feedback-resistant, and Fender already knew how to deliver, even before the Broadcaster hit the scene. Essentially, Fender guitars were not designed to sound like amplified versions of traditional guitars, but to be very much an evolution of the existing Hawaiian lap steel guitars—which displayed these characteristics in abundance—that could be played fretted in the "upright" Spanish style, in standard tuning.

As a result, while more traditional makers such as Gibson, Epiphone, Gretsch, and a few others already had the template for the electric guitar in hand in the form of their existing archtop acoustic guitars, and approached the task mainly from the perspective of amplifying these, Leo

Long before developing his first Esquire, Leo Fender made his own add-on pickup for guitars and patented it. This 1940 Martin 000-42 was modified by Leo at his Fender Radio Service workshop shortly before or after World War II with one of Fender's early pickups. It was originally owned by Fred Clay, who performed with Bob Stacks and the Nighthawks in southern California. *John Peden*

went at it tone-first, abandoning all preconceptions of the form and designing his guitar from the ground up. He already knew the sound and how to get it; he just needed a playable and visually acceptable instrument to produce it.

Fender's—and the World's—First Production Solidbody

Leo nailed the "playable" part of the equation in 1950 with the release of a guitar that was briefly called the Esquire, then Broadcaster, and eventually and forever after, Telecaster (the name I will use for ease of reference). From the start of the Telecaster's production, players lauded the fast, comfortable feel and easy playability of Fender's guitar necks, and this characteristic would form a significant component of their reputation going forward. As for the "visually acceptable" component, well, that wasn't quite there yet, in many people's view at least.

Whether or not you're a fan, you have to acknowledge that today the Telecaster is considered an undeniable classic, an iconic piece of midcentury-modern guitar design, so elegant in its simplicity that it's hard to conceive of it causing any offense. When they first set out to get the Telecaster into the guitar stores, though, Fender's salesmen encountered some resistance from players and merchants who derided it as a "plank," a "canoe paddle," and worse. In short, the Tele was far from traditional, but that was exactly the point. For forward-looking players in search of a much-needed new tool to play a sonically demanding new form of music, the Tele fit the bill exactly.

In 1984, Leo Fender told *Guitar Player* magazine of taking a guitar, early in the new solidbody's existence, to the Riverside Rancho Dance Hall in Riverside, California, for up-and-coming country virtuoso Jimmy Bryant to check out. Bryant took it up on stage with Little Jimmy Dickens and his band and started playing, and, as Leo told it, "Pretty soon the band stopped, everybody on the dance floor stopped, and they all gathered around Jimmy when he played." If the solidbody electric guitar is "old hat" now—a thing that we feel has always been with us—this window into one of the new creation's first public appearances in 1950 hints at just how revolutionary it must have appeared and sounded. Clear, bright, cutting, sustaining, and feedback-free at higher volumes, Fender's guitar proved exactly what Bryant had been looking for and soon proved to be the sharpest tool in the box for plenty of other players besides. The simple fact was, plank or not, this thing boasted qualities that the hollowbody archtop electrics by Gibson, Epiphone, and so many others just couldn't claim for themselves, and it established that essence known as "the Fender sound," defined by a sonic personality that Leo would seek to repeat in all his guitars.

Among the other early adopters of the new Fender solidbody—in addition to Jimmy Bryant—were several significant artists of the era, even if their names mean little to anyone today other than country music historians. Spade Cooley was one of the most

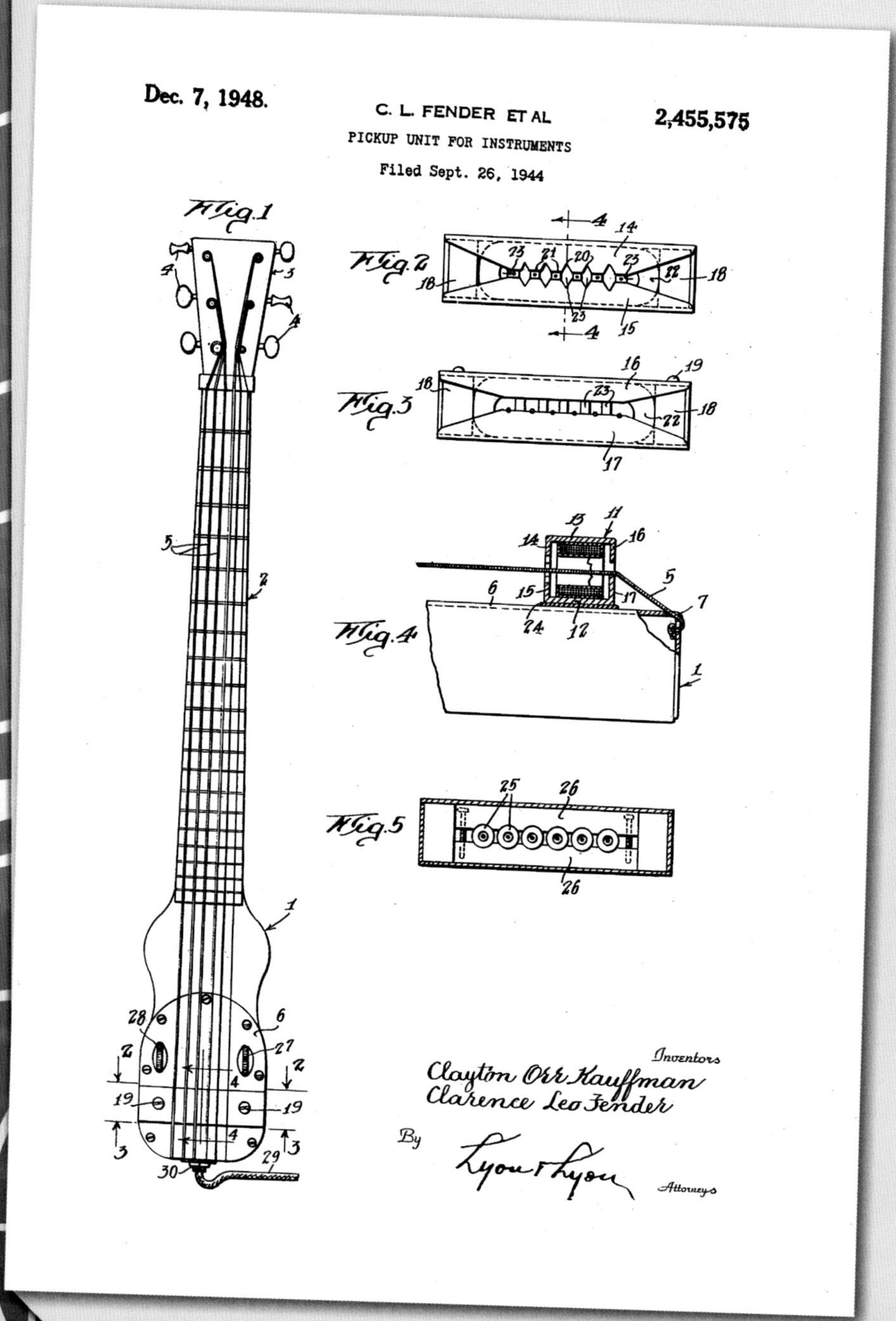

The 1944 patent drawing for Leo Fender's early electric lap steel.

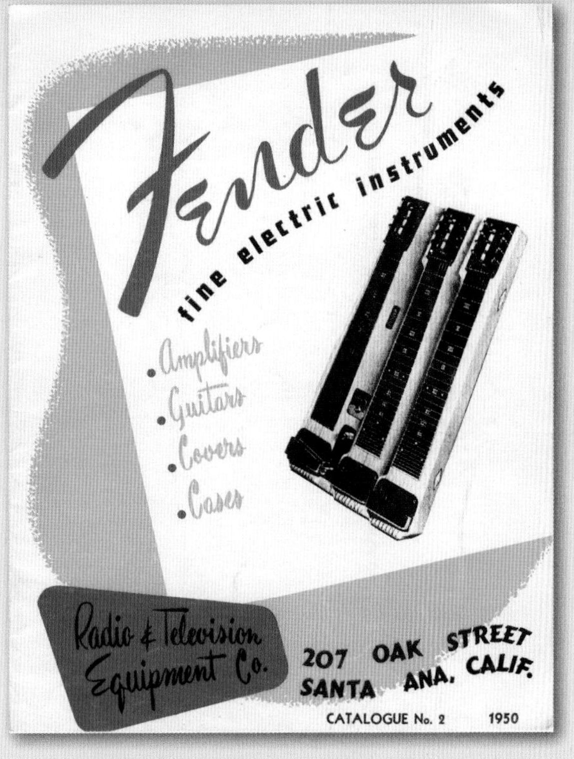

1950 Fender catalog.

significant bandleaders on the western swing scene of the late 1940s and early 1950s, and his star steel player, Noel Boggs, was already a Fender endorser when the new solidbody came out, so it was an equally big deal when Cooley's six-stringer, Jimmy Wyble, endorsed an Esquire in an ad released in May 1950. The names of the Broadcaster- and Esquire-playing guitarists in the Silver Spur Boys, Fender endorsers from 1950 to 1952, seem lost to the annals of time, and that of the up-and-coming Native American guitarist Tawnee Hall, who played a Broadcaster in Lefty Frizell's band for a couple of years, is little remembered due to Hall's death from an unknown illness at the age of just 25 on November 21, 1952. Bill Carson, who played in the bands of Eddy Kirk and Hank Thompson, is somewhat better remembered, but that might be for the part he was to play at Fender in 1953–54. Alongside him, Eldon Shamblin, guitarist for Bob Wills and His Texas Playboys, might have been Fender's biggest endorsee of all—except for the fact that he patently refused to play Leo's plank-bodied Tele. Either way, the Fender brand was more and more in the sites of Spanish-style guitarists on the Western scene, and Leo was priming the rig lure in even those who weren't entirely enamored of the first solidbody out of the gates.

Riffing Toward a Radical New Solidbody

To win an even greater following, though, Fender needed a somewhat different and more versatile addition to the lineup, and with the Telecaster doing relatively well in its first years, it made sense to expand the range anyway. Leo must have seen the sense in this himself. He had already logged another major first in 1951 with the release of the Precision Bass, the Fender amplifier line was growing apace, and another classic of the steel-guitar lineup was launched in the form of the Stringmaster in 1952. The development of a new and even more radical second Fender solidbody six-string would apparently be even more of a team effort, bringing in a new design talent, a Tele endorsee who seemed to never have been entirely happy with the design, and ultimately winning over a major name who outright rejected the slab-bodied single-cut. Just exactly when it all happened, though, and precisely who was at the drawing table (or was holding the pen, at least), seem to be points of debate that will never be entirely settled.

Even if you don't know his name, or know it only from other books on Fender history that you might have read, you will have heard at least one example of Freddie Tavares's steel-guitar playing on countless occasions, in the form of the iconiclap steel glissando that opens the theme tune to vintage *Loony Tunes* cartoons. Tavares was a far more skilled and accomplished player than even this novelty example might imply, though, and he had a background that would seem primed to be bent to the will of a growing Fender company. He was born on the Hawaiian island of Maui in 1913, one of twelve children born to Portuguese immigrant Antone Tavares and his wife, Julia Akana, who was of Hawaiian, Chinese, English, and Tahitian-Samoan descent. He took up the guitar at the age of 12 when his older brother left his own instrument behind upon heading to law school at the University of Michigan, and in 1934, at the age of 21, joined Harry Owens and the Royal Hawaiians, the famed house band at the Royal Hawaiian Hotel in Waikiki. The Royal Hawaiians, with Tavares on the steel, frequently toured the United States over the course of several years and recorded numerous sides and movie soundtracks in Hollywood in the process. Tavares, his wife, and two young sons eventually settled for good in the Los Angeles area, where he dedicated himself mainly to session and radio work—avoiding extensive touring to remain home with the family—and performed on recordings by the Andrews Sisters, Deanna Durbin, Dean Martin, Bing Crosby, Sons of the Pioneers, Spike Jones and the City Slickers, and even Elvis Presley.

In addition to his playing achievements, Tavares had taught himself electronics and other mechanical crafts and had built his own steel guitars and amplifiers. While playing at LA's Cowtown Club with the Ozark Mountain Boys in 1953, Tavares was introduced to Leo Fender by fellow steel guitarist Noel Boggs. Legend has it (as detailed in a story by Shanon Wianecki, *Hanahou* magazine, September 2012) that Tavares set about pointing out several faults in Fender's amps—in answer to which Leo Fender pulled out a screwdriver, removed the back panel from Tavares's own homemade amp, checked the work inside the chassis, and then offered him a job in the Fender development lab on the spot.

Most credible accounts of the development of the Stratocaster indicate that Tavares's job, from day one at Fender, was to concoct the body shape and general design of the new guitar, which was but a basic concept in Leo's mind at the time of Freddie's arrival

Grand Ole Opry
TAKES DELIVERY
OF TWO NEW
Bigsby Guitars
Billy Robinson and Grady Martin, featured guitarists with the Red Foley-Prince Albert unit of the Grand Ole Opry, are shown as they play their new Bigsby guitars at Los Angeles Shrine Auditorium during brilliant one-night performance of famous radio troupe.
Bigsby
ELECTRIC GUITARS
8114 E. PHLOX ST., DOWNEY, CALIF. TOpaz 2-5036

MERLE TRAVIS

MERLE TRAVIS

at the factory in spring 1953, shortly after Fender had moved to a new, larger factory on Pomona Street in Fullerton. In his book *The Fender Stratocaster* (Hal Leonard, 1994), A. R. Duchossoir quotes Tavares as saying, "The first real project that I had was to put the Stratocaster on [the] drawing board. It was about April or May 1953 and Leo said, 'We need a new guitar,' and I said, 'How far apart are the strings at the nut, how far [at] the bridge?' I got those parameters and I said, 'What's the scale?' Then I knew where the strings are and we started from there."

Leo Fender was himself quoted as saying that he was already working on elements of the Stratocaster's design in 1951 and 1952, and it seems some players—Bill Carson among them—were asking for a new and more deluxe solidbody electric, and particularly one with a built-in vibrato unit, perhaps as early as this. No clear records exist, however, of drawings or prototypes or dated accounts of Stratocaster R&D going on as early as this, and, while Leo wasn't afraid to take his time and get things right, most new models were moving more quickly from prototype to production by this time than the ponderous three years that Leo's account implies. Ultimately, as with some other things, it might be that Mr. Fender's memory was a little hazy by the time he stated such things in interviews.

It seems we are unlikely to ever know precisely who concocted exactly what detail and when, and that there was input to a greater or lesser extent from each of several individuals, including Fender employees Tavares and George Fullerton, performers Bill Carson and Rex Galleon, Fender sales director Don Randall, and of course Leo Fender himself. A look at what *is* known of the development of different aspects of the Stratocaster, however, even if the credit given—or claimed—is sometimes apocryphal, should bring us closer to an understanding of what a groundbreaking undertaking it was in its day.

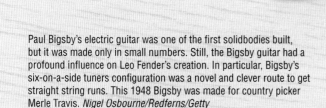

Paul Bigsby's electric guitar was one of the first solidbodies built, but it was made only in small numbers. Still, the Bigsby guitar had a profound influence on Leo Fender's creation. In particular, Bigsby's six-on-a-side tuners configuration was a novel and clever route to get straight string runs. This 1948 Bigsby was made for country picker Merle Travis. *Nigel Osbourne/Redferns/Getty*

The Salesman Drives a Revolution

While we bicker and argue over who designed the Stratocaster, it can often be too easy to ignore the role played by the man at Fender who very likely asked for this new model in the first place and was in position to see it fit into the new and growing market. Don Randall was the general manager of Santa Anna electrical parts wholesaler Radio and Television Equipment Company (RTEC) when Leo Fender launched his own brand in 1946, and he quickly saw the benefit of undertaking exclusive distribution of this upstart's new products. "The idea of getting involved in a product where we controlled the brand name seemed exciting," Randall told *Music Trades* magazine in 1996. That Fender quickly proved to be the most creative new maker in a rapidly booming industry certainly made the entire venture still more exciting.

As the man on the ground, the head of the team responsible for getting Fender guitars and amplifiers into the stores, Randall was the single biggest hub for receiving consumer feedback from dealers and players and directing it to where it would do some good. As such, he was clearly adept at translating that into features that Leo and the design team could use to make the products more saleable. Several reports indicate that it was Don Randall who urged Leo to include a truss rod in the Esquire/Broadcaster neck design—an essential ingredient carried over to the Stratocaster and all subsequent Fender guitars—after he received damning feedback on the truss-rod-less necks of two prototypes, which he took to the NAMM show in summer 1949 to test the waters. Similarly, Randall had input on several other features of Fender guitars over the years, details that would either appeal to players, thus making the instruments easier for RTEC reps to sell to dealers, or that might prevent warranty nightmares that would cost the company money. Adjustable bridge saddles, adjustable pickups, multiple pickups and switching, and stylistic elements involving body and headstock shapes might all seem the purview of the guitars' designers, but as often as not these were concocted at the direct urging of Randall and his sales team.

In addition to his influence on designs in the lab, Don Randall had an even more direct impact on the public perception of Fender products that were floated onto the guitar market. Randall named the Broadcaster for the dominant form of media at the time of the guitar's release, and, in a genius stroke of foresight, renamed it the Telecaster in spring 1951 for the likely power of that growing new medium, after the Gretsch company objected to the first model name's similarity to its "Broadkaster" drum kit. Randall, a licensed pilot, would also be the man to take the next major Fender guitar into the stratosphere in 1954 with an appropriately thrusting name.

In June 1953, RTEC's exclusive deal with Fender was terminated with the formation of Fender Sales Inc., of which Don Randall was made president, while also being taken on as Leo's partner in Fender Electronic Instruments itself. The change brought Randall even more firmly into the Fender fold and secured a partnership that would power Fender from strength to strength right up until the CBS takeover of 1965. In addition to remaining an essential conduit between Leo's R&D and Fender's growing dealer network, Randall was the driving force behind Fender promotion and would eventually be the man to sign off on an advertising campaign that was arguably the hippest seen from any significant guitar manufacturer of the era. But we're getting ahead of ourselves. For now, it's merely important to remember that Randall, as head of the sales team, provided input that was crucial—and perhaps central—to the development of the Stratocaster, even if he never put router to wood, as well as urging Leo to add another guitar to the lineup, so his men in the field would have something else to sell.

The Team Puts the Pieces Together

The easiest way to see how much the new Stratocaster brought to the table might be to start with the Telecaster as a template—which is certainly how the Fender team, and the players and sales reps who influenced them, would have perceived the venture—and examine what was changed or added to the formula. The neck, of course, remained virtually the same, other than gaining a larger headstock shape, purportedly at Don Randall's request, to more proudly display the Fender logo. The body was still crafted from solid swamp ash, and the pickups were still of a thin single-coil design, employing individual Alnico rod-magnet pole pieces with a coil wound around them. Other than these, though, virtually every detail of the new guitar was entirely different.

Radical new elements in the Stratocaster design included the following:

- a more comfortable body shape, with contours where it met the player's ribcage and right forearm.
- a broader sonic range, courtesy of three individual pickups.
- a more ergonomic control layout, along with a recessed jack for accidental pull-out safety.
- a built-in vibrato unit.
- not least of all, superbly stylish new looks.

Added together, the sum result was arguably the most comfortable feeling and versatile performing guitar on the market at the time, anywhere, and this just four years after Fender had entered the Spanish-electric guitar market in the first place. The impressive thing is that none of these ingredients, so ubiquitous today that we largely take them for granted, came about merely by whim or chance. All were enacted for one good reason or another, and they coalesced toward a spectacular whole from sometimes disparate points of origin.

Guitarist Bill Carson seems to have been looking for changes to the Telecaster design from the start, or at least from the time he made Leo Fender's acquaintance around mid-1951. Carson has said in several interviews that he often suggested Fender build a guitar with a built-in vibrato. He is also frequently credited with coming up with the ideas to contour the Stratocaster's body. As Carson told A. R. Duchossoir in 1988 in interviews for his book *The Fender Stratocaster*, "The thing I didn't like about the Telecaster was the discomfort of it, because I was doing a lot of studio work at the time on the West Coast and sitting down its square edges really dug into my rib." Clearly Leo Fender had long been receptive to such suggestions from the players who plied their trade on his instruments too.

In one of his own interviews with Carson, gleaned from his years as a writer and editor of *Guitar Player* magazine and reprinted in his excellent tome *The Stratocaster Chronicles: Celebrating 50 Years of the Fender Strat*, Tom Wheeler quotes Carson as saying, "Leo was receptive to a musician just walking in off the street to talk to him. He seemed to want to pick the head of every player who came around. He'd ask all kinds of questions and be very friendly and make you feel comfortable right away." That said, Leo himself has also been quoted as saying, in interviews with both Wheeler and Duchossoir, and elsewhere, that the contouring notion came from local guitarist Rex Galleon before it was suggested by Carson. Either way, it's likely that multiple recommendations from respected performers helped the idea to achieve a sort of critical mass with Leo, and resulted in the two bandsaw swipes for the tummy and forearm contours that produce the extremely comfortable feel of the Stratocaster body as we know it today.

As for the development of what might arguably have been the Stratocaster's most innovative advancement on the form, the built-in vibrato bridge, well, it seemed this one required quite a bit more effort. While Carson has also, via several sources, claimed responsibility for suggesting this one, the vibrato unit was unlikely to have been his idea alone, or even first. Leo knew not long after the Telecaster started gaining acceptance that he would need to build a guitar with a vibrato, to fend off competition from the guitar Paul Bigsby originally designed and built for picker Merle Travis, a solidbody that preceded the Esquire and Broadcaster's release. In addition, the Bigsby vibrato unit that soon showed up retrofitted to Gibson and Gretsch guitars was gaining momentum. It is likely that Don Randall had urged the inclusion of this feature, as with so many other things, because it would have been a major feature upon which to sell the new guitar. Nevertheless, a player like Carson still helps us understand the appeal of this piece of hardware. "Steel guitar played a large part in country and western swing bands," he told A. R. Duchossoir. "When I was doing studio sessions with a foot control [volume pedal] that Leo made me, I could use a vibrato and do steel guitar things and I would sometimes get paid double for the session." For the musicians, it was all about the functional tool, and that was something Leo Fender had understood—and gotten right—from the start.

While the concerned parties at Fender pretty much knew the new model would at least carry a vibrato, well before either the shape of the vibrato or the guitar itself were anything close to final conception, tackling that task would prove more time consuming than all other elements of the new design. According to George Fullerton, as quoted in an interview in Tom Wheeler's *The Stratocaster Chronicles*, "The vibrato was the new guitar's last piece. . . . We already had the body contouring, pickup design, third pickup . . . the new headstock shape, the tooling—everything except that vibrato had already been accepted."

New Pickups and Electronics

Whereas Gibson largely used the same pickup design throughout the model range from the late 1940s to the mid-1950s, Fender went with three different pickups for its flagship Spanish-electric guitars in the space of just a few years. All might have shared some similarities in that they were relatively narrow single-coil pickups with individual rod magnet segments for pole pieces, but each was unique regardless. The Telecaster carried quite different pickups in its bridge and neck positions, with a wider, longer coil in the former than in the latter, and Leo had determined that something different still would be needed for the new model.

As discussed earlier, treble content—which aided brightness, clarity, and cutting power—was valued highly at the time, and Leo sought the same in his new pickup. In order to achieve an adequate blend of bite and body, Fender settled on 42 AWG copper wire wound in a narrow coil around six individual pole pieces cut from Alnico V rod magnets, all supported by thin fiber top and bottom plates. This was essentially the same construction used in the Telecaster's bridge pickup at the time, wound into a slightly narrower coil with a little less coil wire, although the earliest Broadcaster bridge pickups, and ongoing Telecaster neck pickups, used a finer 43 AWG wire. The result was a pickup with slightly less beef in the tone than that of the Tele's bridge pickup, for a bright, cutting sound in the bridge position, and a fat and warm, yet clear and articulate, tone in the neck position.

All Fender pickups were noted for their excellent string-to-string articulation, a feature enhanced by the individual pole pieces cut from actual magnets, and the Strat certainly retained this desirable characteristic. To further enhance the string-to-string balance, Fender also used magnets of staggered heights on the new Stratocaster pickups, with lower magnets on the louder strings for a comparable overall output across all six.

The inclusion of three of these new pickups on the new guitar would also prove a feature the sales team could brag about, and the trio sure looked impressive up against what was available in the day. Even if the three pickups didn't give the Stratocaster, with its three-way switch, any more tone selections than the Telecaster already possessed, the ones it did have were arguably already more usable (see the "Tone & Construction" section for further discussion of these points). The Stratocaster's switching and control complement didn't yet tap the full potential of the trio of pickups and their various combinations; it was more versatile than many guitars of its day. The use of a master volume control with direct routing of the bridge pickup from switch to volume, along with individual tone controls for the bridge and middle pickups, yielded a clear, crisp tone from each of the three switch positions (fulfilling that Fender objective yet again), where the Telecaster still retained a pre-set "bassy sound," with the neck pickup wired through a small capacitor network in the forward switch position, a tone that many players found virtually useless.

In addition to the wiring schematic beneath them, the positioning of the switch and controls themselves was arguably more ergonomic than that of any production electric guitar seen before. The Fender team very consciously placed the master volume control within easy access of the player's right-hand "pinky" finger for easy, on-the-fly volume swells, while the three-way switch was equally accessible for quick pickup changes. The result was a guitar that, from head to tail, would be deemed by many musicians to be more playable and sonically versatile than any to have come before it.

Pickups were an early area of expertise for Leo Fender, who had successfully filed a patent for an original pickup design in September 1944 (granted in December 1948) and included his own designs of great-sounding pickups on K&Flap steel guitars from 1945 onward. It seems it was no great struggle achieving a satisfactory Strat pickup—more a matter of narrowing down the variables to arrive at the ideal unit for that particular guitar—yet Bill Carson attributed a perceived flaw in these pickups to a supposed failure of one of the prototypes that he had taken to test at a performance prior to the guitar going into production. As Carson reported in an interview with Tom Wheeler for *Guitar Player* magazine, "One of the early failures we had were the first pickups. They just didn't make it. I don't know what happened, but they seemed to lose a lot between when Leo made them at the shop and when I took them out on the job. The sound had a rapid decay and a somewhat banjo-like tone." As the team in the lab would soon discern, though, nothing was wrong with the pickups themselves. An early bridge design, on the other hand, was letting the prototype down, and badly.

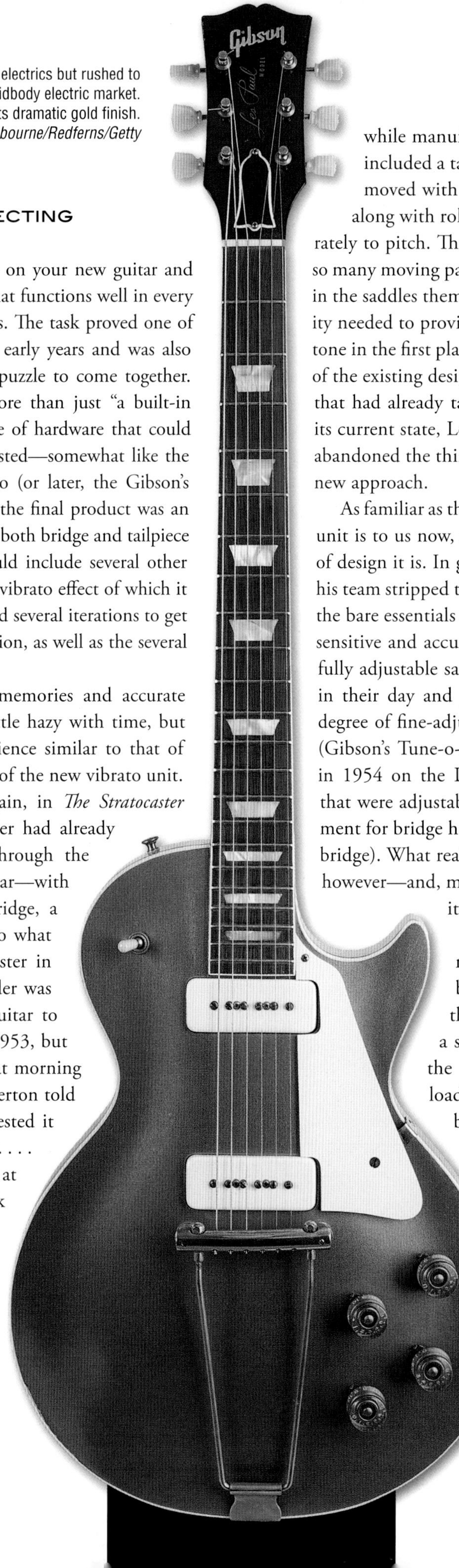

Industry leader Gibson had a full range of archtop electrics but rushed to follow Fender's Esquire and Telecaster in the solidbody electric market. Still, this 1954 Gibson Les Paul stood out with its dramatic gold finish. *Nigel Osbourne/Redferns/Getty*

Prototyping and Perfecting the Fender Vibrato

Deciding you need a built-in vibrato on your new guitar and actually developing an original unit that functions well in every respect are clearly two different things. The task proved one of the greatest undertakings of Fender's early years and was also the slowest piece of the Stratocaster puzzle to come together. Note, too, that this unit was far more than just "a built-in vibrato." Rather than a separate piece of hardware that could be added behind whatever bridge existed—somewhat like the Kauffman Vib-Rola or Bigsby vibrato (or later, the Gibson's Maestro Vibrola or Burns Vibrato)—the final product was an entirely new design that encompassed both bridge and tailpiece in one unit. The eventual result would include several other major innovations, in addition to the vibrato effect of which it was capable, but it took some time and several iterations to get the "all-in-one-unit" part of the equation, as well as the several details within it, just right.

Again, we have to accept that memories and accurate chronologies might have grown a little hazy with time, but George Fullerton reported an experience similar to that of Bill Carson with an earlier rendition of the new vibrato unit. Speaking to Tom Wheeler once again, in *The Stratocaster Chronicles*, Fullerton said that Fender had already started putting 100 Stratocasters through the line—and had completed one guitar—with the first "final" rendition of the bridge, a unit that, by all reports, was close to what eventually ended up on the Jazzmaster in 1958 after further refinements. Fender was making a major effort to get the guitar to the summer NAMM show in June 1953, but it was not to be. "I couldn't wait that morning to get the first one off the line," Fullerton told Wheeler. "I grabbed that one and tested it out, and it was terribly bad sounding. . . . I rushed to the lab, Leo and I looked at it, and we called Freddie over to look at it. That vibrato sounded like a tin can. We all agreed it wasn't going to work, so we shut down the line. It was a sad day. It was then that Leo went back to the drawing board."

This "first final" rendition of the important new component, while manufactured to be an all-in-one, drop-in unit, included a tailpiece that was separate to the bridge and moved with the player's depression of the vibrato bar, along with roller saddles to help the strings return accurately to pitch. The main problem, it seemed, was that with so many moving parts, as well as some side-to-side movement in the saddles themselves, the unit lacked the mass and solidity needed to provide adequate sustain and to achieve a solid tone in the first place. Rather than continue to address details of the existing design to correct its faults, extending an effort that had already taken several months to get the vibrato to its current state, Leo, Freddie Tavares, and George Fullerton abandoned the thing altogether and started in on an entirely new approach.

As familiar as the final rendition of the Stratocaster vibrato unit is to us now, it's easy to overlook what a brilliant piece of design it is. In going back to the drawing board, Leo and his team stripped this thing down to what we can now see are the bare essentials for an all-in-one bridge and tailpiece with sensitive and accurate vibrato functions *and* individual and fully adjustable saddles. The latter alone were revolutionary in their day and provided players with an unprecedented degree of fine-adjustment of intonation and playing action (Gibson's Tune-o-matic bridge, which also hit the market in 1954 on the Les Paul Custom, had individual saddles that were adjustable for intonation, but only global adjustment for bridge height via thumbwheels at either end of the bridge). What really made Fender's new vibrato work right, however—and, more importantly, *sound* right—lay beneath its relatively simple surface components.

To compensate for the lack of body mass in the string anchoring of the vibrato bridge (a situation created by anchoring the strings to a moving part), Leo devised a steel inertia block that he mounted below the vibrato's base plate. The strings were loaded through holes drilled through the block and, as a result, were anchored with the mass needed for satisfactory tone and sustain. The inertia block also served as the connection point for the springs (up to five), which were anchored at their other end at a "spring claw" screwed into the body, at the far end of a channel routed into the guitar's back. The steel bridge base, with bent-steel saddles above and inertia block

Les Paul plays his self-electrified Epiphone archtop. *Library of Congress*

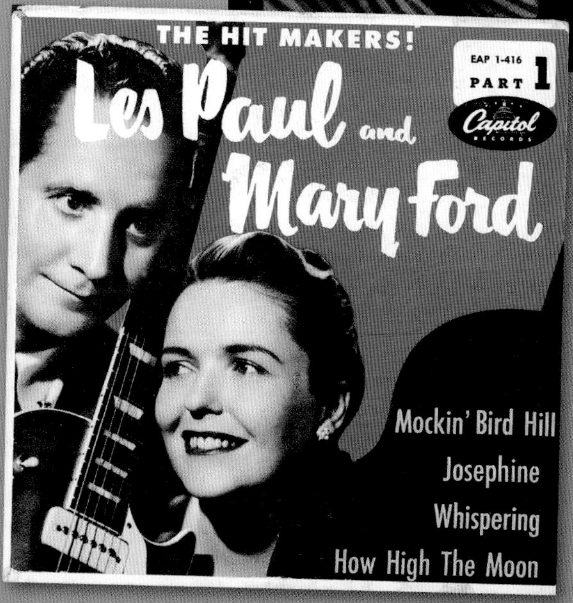

The first prototype of the Esquire was believed completed in 1949. The early production Esquires from 1950 did not have truss rods; they were added late that year. By 1952, when this Telecaster was made, the features of Fender's solidbody electric were set. *Fretted Americana*

THE TELECASTER AND ESQUIRE MODELS

The "Telecaster" dual pickup and "Esquire" single pickup guitars are something entirely new in the electric Spanish guitar field. These instruments feature a new style construction which vastly improves their usability. A new type one piece neck is reinforced with an adjustable tension rod which provides a means for keeping the neck perfectly straight. This new slender neck is a great aid to easy fretting and fast action, and it is replaceable by the owner in a matter of a few minutes—thus eliminating costly and time consuming repairs. The body of these outstanding instruments is designed to provide easy accessibility to the entire length of the neck thereby making it possible to play full chords up to the very end of the fret board. Because the bodies of these guitars are solid there is no acoustic cavity to resonate and to cause the troublesome hown known as feedback, and can be played at extreme volume for this reason. The pickups on these guitars are fully adjustable allowing one to get any desired tone response and in addition to this there is a full range tone control. A three position tone change switch is provided which allows instantaneous changes from a sharp ringing "take off" or "lead" tone to a very soft "rhythm" tone. These guitars feature the new adjustable Fender bridge which is the answer to every guitar player's desire to be able to change the action and intonation of his instrument. With this new bridge the player can adjust each string for height from the fret board and for length thereby obtaining perfect intonation and affording each player his own individual touch. The necks of these guitars are made of clear hard maple and the body is made of fine clear blond hardwood. The instrument is trimmed with a black pick guard and all of the metal parts are heavily chrome plated. Each guitar is furnished with a beautiful top grain adjustable leather strap.

The Fender "Telecaster" and "Esquire" guitars are truly great instruments and ones which all guitar players will want.

Case—Molded, plush lined, covered with Dupont "Hair Seal." very rich appearance.

Bag—Plastileather, padded guitar bag, durable and serviceable.

1954 Stratocaster.
Chicago Music Exchange, www.chicagomusicexchange.com

below, had knife-edge fulcrum points in its six mounting holes, which anchored against hardened steel screws to minimize friction while in motion. The end result was a unit that moved fluidly and returned to pitch well but still provided a solid strings-to-body anchor, with a good, ringing tone and impressive sustain.

It might have put the development of the new model as a whole back by a good six months or so, but the new vibrato really was a wonder of engineering. The lack of "dead" string space between a tailpiece and the bridge saddles, and the fact that the strings didn't need to slide over the saddles to produce the unit's pitch fluctuation, meant far fewer tuning instabilities than experienced in some other vibrato units. In addition, the ingenious inertia block proved a wondrously simple solution to a problem that had threatened to sink the entire enterprise in the final hour.

Although Fender dubbed the new unit the "Synchronized Tremolo Action" when it released the Stratocaster and billed it as one of the new guitar's top features, it was, of course, a "vibrato" and not a "tremolo." Tremolo more accurately describes the modulation of volume, rather than frequency or pitch. A vibrato, on the other hand, modulates pitch, which is exactly what Fender's "Synchronized Tremolo" does. Conversely, Fender also usually referred to the genuine tremolo effect on many of its amplifiers as "vibrato,", even though it did not fluctuate the pitch of the guitar signal in any way, but pulsated the volume. Fender repeated the misnomer on his patent application for the new "Tremolo Device for Stringed Instrument," filed August 30, 1954, and granted a little less than two years later.

Prototype Turns to Production

For all the work that went into pulling together the Strat's revolutionary new ingredients—including having prototypes in the field for testing by mid-1953, and the ongoing development of new components—we have far fewer verifiable reports or photos of genuine Stratocaster prototypes than we do of Telecaster prototypes. In his book *Fender: The Sound Heard Round The World*, Fender historian Richard Smith published photos taken by Leo Fender of a supposed Stratocaster prototype from 1953. The photos showed a "breadboard" guitar of sorts, with a black fiber pickguard, knurled silver Telecaster-style knobs, and a back route wide enough to take only three springs rather than the standard five. Otherwise, there has always been a lot of gray area between "late prototype" and "early production," and it's possible that several genuine prototypes were either lost, or intentionally destroyed, once the Stratocaster proper was actually released.

Regardless, by early 1954 Fender's new guitar had found its ultimate form and was ready to hit the market. The final ingredients were a nifty new jack plate design—and a name. The former took shape as a recessed jack plate mounted conveniently on the top of the guitar, alongside the switches, which both prevented the usual blind fumbling around trying to insert the 1/4-inch plug into the hole normally found on the lower edge of the body, and let the plug pull out cleanly if you accidentally stepped on your guitar cord, rather than bending the cord's plug end or, worse, ripping out a chunk of wood as you crowbarred the entire jack from the guitar.

The name, and what a good one it was, came courtesy of Don Randall, head of Fender Sales, who himself was a licensed pilot and was known to fly his own plane to important meetings and sales opportunities. His coinage of "Stratocaster" fit perfectly with the times: it pitched the guitar beyond the present, into a soaring future that the day's musicians—and Cold War citizenry in general—were only beginning to imagine. Regarding the team effort of putting together this new model, and the several apocryphal tales related to it, Randall told Tom Wheeler, "A lot of these guys who claim credit for the Stratocaster didn't have a damn thing to do with it. I don't mean to put any of them down, but the salesmen and I, we were the ones who knew the business, knew the competition, and we knew what we needed." What they needed was a guitar that both walked the walk and talked the talk, an electric that both looked and sounded unlike anything that had come before and could be boldly promoted as such. In the new Stratocaster, they received all that and more.

Early-production Stratocasters started rolling through the Fender factory by spring 1954, and Randall's sales team, now an independent entity after the creation of Fender Sales in summer 1953, was hot to crow about it. One notice to Fender dealers sent in early spring 1954, "Announcing the new Fender Stratocaster," declared "shipments are expected to begin May 15." The same notice claimed, of the new Synchronized Tremolo, "This sectional bridge is a patented feature which no other guitar on the market today can duplicate. . . ." In fact, the actual patent application wouldn't be filed for some three months, and the patent wouldn't be granted until two years later.

Regardless, Fender widely proclaimed this built-in tremolo to be a "first," and the feature would be one of its major selling points, along with its "Comfort Contoured" body, three pickups, new tone controls and switching, and surface-mounted "plug receptacle." The first print ad to promote the new guitar, published in the May issue of *International Musician* magazine (on the shelves in April), touted all of these features, along with an illustration of the new Stratocaster above a sketch of protons whirling through their orbits round a stylized atom. Whoever penned the ad, it certainly bore Don Randall's signature.

Despite this optimism over shipping dates, the Stratocaster didn't ramp up to full production until later that summer. The first hundred or so guitars were numbered 0100 to 0207 on the back of their spring-cavity covers (at a time when Telecasters' serial numbers were stamped into their bridge plates). From around late fall 1954, both the Telecaster and Stratocaster had their serial numbers stamped into the plates that reinforced the screws attaching neck to body. (In a further sharing of specs, in 1955 the Tele's bridge pickup would receive the staggered pole pieces originally developed for the Stratocaster pickups.) The guitar's initial retail price was set at $249.50 with Synchronized Tremolo (the Telecaster was $189.50 at the time), or $229.50 for the "hardtail" version without vibrato, plus $39.95 for the hardshell case covered in "grain hair seal simulated covering," according to early Fender Sales literature.

Some historians like to refer to Stratocasters produced prior to September or October as "pre-production models," although since Fender Sales had already announced the availability of a production model in May of that year, it seems sensible to think of the earliest guitars from spring 1954 onward simply as Stratocasters with rare early specs. Other than a handful of early guitars produced with anodized aluminum pickguards, the main differences were the somewhat smaller knobs made from slightly pearloid-looking white plastic found on the earliest Stratocasters, followed by a more brittle plastic, often referred to as Bakelite, that was used for knobs, pickup covers, and pickguard for a brief period. The wear that the pickup covers underwent in particular, it would seem, from constant abrasion from the player's pick or fingernails, led to the use of a more durable plastic for these components by early 1955.

Standard Early Appointments

Alongside these relatively superficial cosmetic details of the early run of Stratocasters, which nevertheless excite collectors to no end, the early specs and appointments of the model are probably even more significant, from the perspective of performance. Some of these details will be discussed at greater length in "Tone & Construction," but these basics essentially defined the original Fender Stratocaster of 1954 and the first few years that followed.

Swamp-Ash Body

The Stratocaster debuted with a body made from solid swamp ash, still the wood used for the Telecaster at the time, with forearm and ribcage contours—the latter in particular—that might seem extremely deep to those more familiar with later examples of the breed, making it an extremely comfortable guitar to play. In 1956 the wood of choice shifted to alder, although ash was still used beneath the blonde finish on most so-called "Mary Kaye" Stratocasters, and on some other custom-order examples.

All-Maple Neck

A solid maple neck with the truss rod inserted into a channel in the back (with tell-tale walnut "skunk stripe" and headstock "teardrop") was used from the guitar's debut until around mid-1959. While these appeared outwardly similar throughout the era, the profile (back shape) changed significantly over the years, giving quite a different playing feel to Stratocasters from different points within the decade. The early necks had a beefy, rounded shape, but by 1955 a chunky V-neck, or "boat-neck" shape arrived, which thinned out somewhat through the course of 1956 and 1957. During 1958, necks became more rounded and C shaped, though less chunky than the original 1954 necks, and began to slim out even more going into 1959 and 1960.

Six-In-Line Headstock

Fender had already used a six-in-line headstock for the Telecaster, but the shape introduced on the Stratocaster has become even more iconic and a universal symbol of the brand. It is frequently pointed out that the solidbody guitar built in the mid-1940s by Paul Bigsby, initially for artist Merle Travis and then others, had a similar headstock long before the Strat, and even before the Broadcaster and others; but Leo declared his own reasons for using the all-on-one-side design: "That's a very old idea that has been around for thousands of years. The Croatians, near Poland, have several instruments with tuning pegs located on one side of the guitar and they invented this years ago," he told *Guitar Player* magazine in 1971. And the reason to use such a design in 1954? Putting the tuners all on one side of the headstock allows a straight line from nut slot to tuner post, thus reducing hitching in the nut slots and resultant tuning instabilities.

Vibrato Bridge and Kluson Tuners

The most revolutionary element of the Stratocaster's hardware set, its Synchronized Tremolo, has already been covered in some detail. It was such a comprehensive component that the guitar didn't carry much else in the hardware department other than its Kluson tuners and a round string guide at the front of the headstock between the B and high-E strings that increased the tension of these in the nut slots on their long journeys to the tuner posts.

Single-Coil Pickups

The three narrow single-coil pickups that Leo and his team had developed for the prototype guitars at least a year before the Stratocaster's official production began, and which were intended as a major selling point of the new model, remained the standard at the guitar's release. Well known to players today as the ubiquitous "Stratocaster pickup," these had six individual pole pieces cut from Alnico V rod magnets to somewhat different lengths for staggered heights to balance out variances in string output. They were originally wound with an average of 8,500 or so turns of 42 AWG Formvar-coated wire.

Master Volume, Two Tones, Three-Way Switch

Although it has become another "standard" of sorts, the Stratocaster's complement of a single volume control, individual tone controls for the neck and middle pickups, and a three-way selector switch defined an impressive control setup when the guitar was released in 1954 and was another of its saleable features. Fender didn't change the main specifications of this configuration for a full *twenty-three years*—a five-way switch finally arriving as standard in 1977—although some players did modify it to suit their own particular playing needs. Quite early on, several guitarists would find use for the funky sounding in-between switch settings that blended the bridge-middle and middle-neck pickups by balancing the three-way switch between positions; others would find the second tone control more useful on the bright bridge pickup than on the warm neck pickup, and rewire accordingly.

Sunburst Finish

Although custom colors were more prevalent on the Strat than on the Tele, with a handful of notable examples early on, then several more later in the decade, the only truly "standard" finish available on the Stratocaster for twenty-five years was sunburst. This was a two-tone sunburst, running from dark edges to a golden-amber center, from the guitar's arrival in 1954 until mid-1958, when a three-tone sunburst included a red middle band between them. This red finish faded prematurely on many early examples, making many vintage Strats from 1958 to 1960 appear two-tone regardless, until a stronger, fade-resistant red tint came into use at Fender.

The Stratocaster: Launched into the Stratosphere

Added together, these simple—yet, then-revolutionary—ingredients paint the picture of the instrument that hit an unsuspecting music world in mid-1954 and ascended steadily toward its soon dizzying heights virtually from the day it left the Fullerton factory. It is impossible to comprehend today, with countless Strat-a-likes available in the form of everything from sub-$100 imports to $10,000 luthier-grade re-creations, just how new the Stratocaster must have appeared in 1954 and what its impact must have been, both in look and in tone. This was a world that needed the Fender Stratocaster, but until it actually came along, there was nothing remotely like it, either in the music world or in pop culture in general.

The economy and the culture were booming in the post–World War II, early–Cold War era of the early 1950s, yet by 1954 so many of the revolutionary cultural and commercial developments that would be commonplace by the end of the decade had yet to make their impact. Just imagine this world for a moment: The U.S. Navy commissions its first nuclear submarine. Hydrogen bomb tests are in full swing on Bikini Atoll in the Pacific Ocean. The first organ transplants are carried out in hospitals in Boston and Paris. *Brown* v. *Board of Education* makes segregation in US public schools illegal. British athlete Roger Bannister runs the first under-four-minute mile. NBC's *The Tonight Show* first airs, with host Steve Allen. Marlon Brando stars in two major hit movies, *On The Waterfront* and *The Wild Ones*. America's first jet airliner, the Boeing 707, takes its maiden flight. Swanson sells its first TV dinner.

(Continued on page 66)

1954 Stratocaster.
Chicago Music Exchange, www.chicagomusicexchange.com

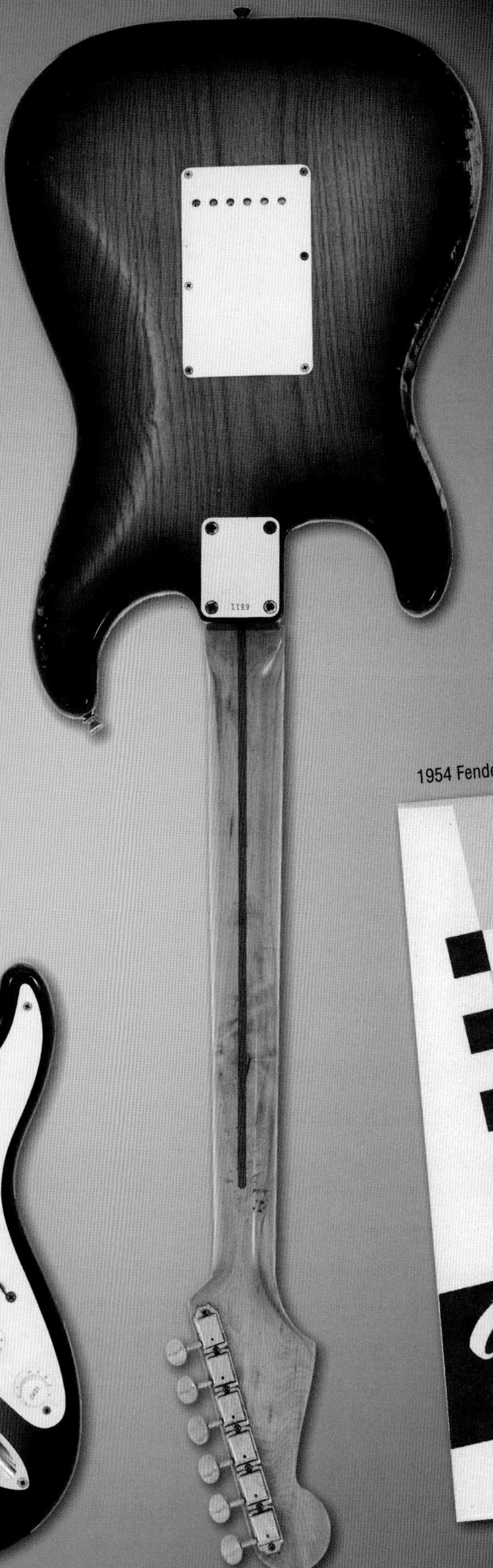

1954 Fender catalog.

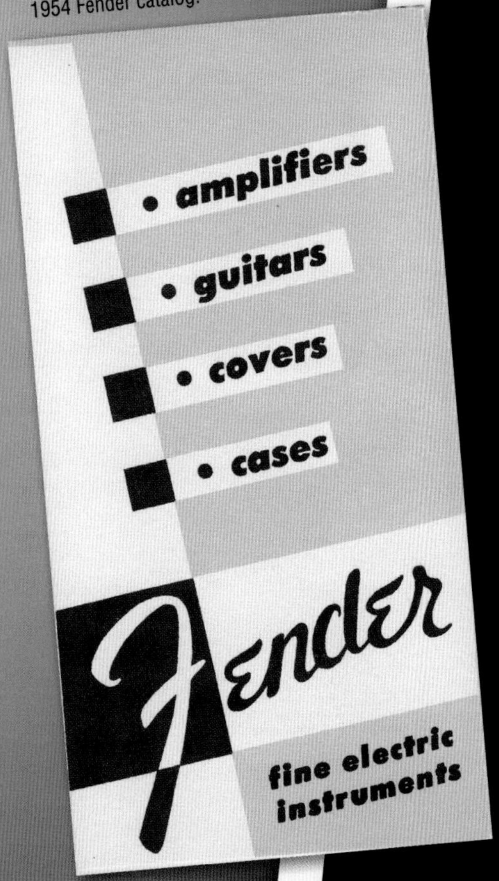

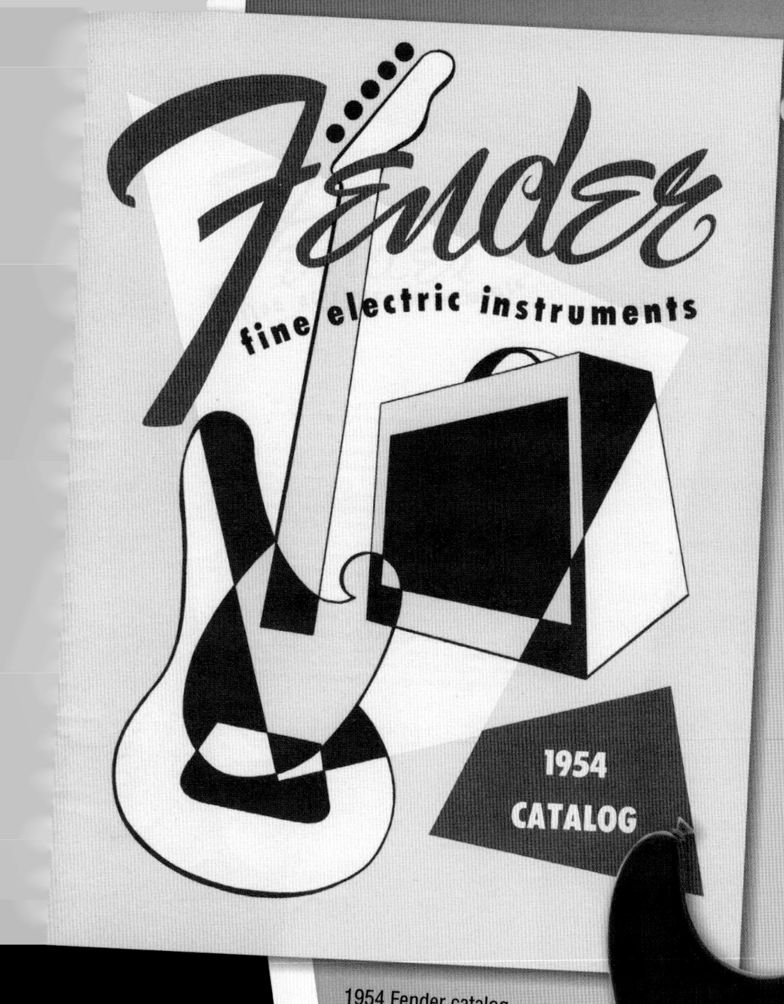

1954 Fender catalog.

1954 Stratocaster.
Chicago Music Exchange, www.chicagomusicexchange.com

Duane Allman's 1955 Stratocaster.
Will Ireland/Total Guitar Magazine/Getty Images

Billy F Gibbons's 1955 nontremelo Stratocaster. *David Perry*

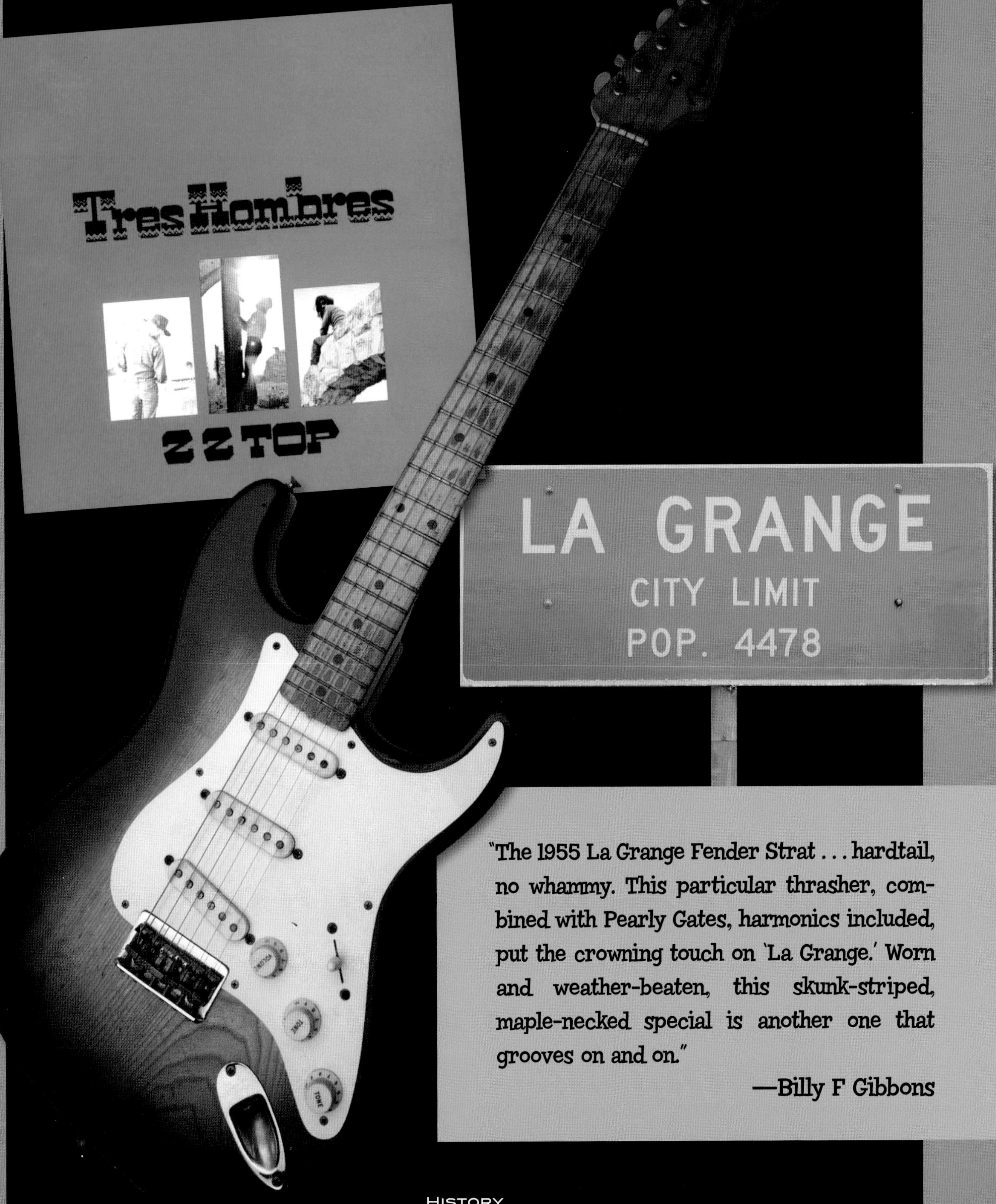

"The 1955 La Grange Fender Strat . . . hardtail, no whammy. This particular thrasher, combined with Pearly Gates, harmonics included, put the crowning touch on 'La Grange.' Worn and weather-beaten, this skunk-striped, maple-necked special is another one that grooves on and on."

—Billy F Gibbons

Bill Carson

Country guitarist Bill Carson was one of Leo Fender's favorite pickers and guitar testers. Here, Carson holds his 1954 red Stratocaster with gold anodized pickguard.

The name "Bill Carson" might be best known by Fender fans today for its frequent appearance in the written history of the development of the Stratocaster, but Carson was a true journeyman musician of the electric guitar and a significant name on the scene at the time. He undoubtedly played a significant role in bringing the Stratocaster into being, but he also deserves recognition for his musical career.

Carson was born in Meridian, Oklahoma, in 1926 and was raised in Amarillo, Texas, but eventually followed the road to California that had lured so many "Okies" and Midwesterners to the land of milk and honey—which was, in his case, the land of western swing. Shortly after his arrival in Los Angeles, Carson established himself as a reliable A-list sideman with a string of major acts

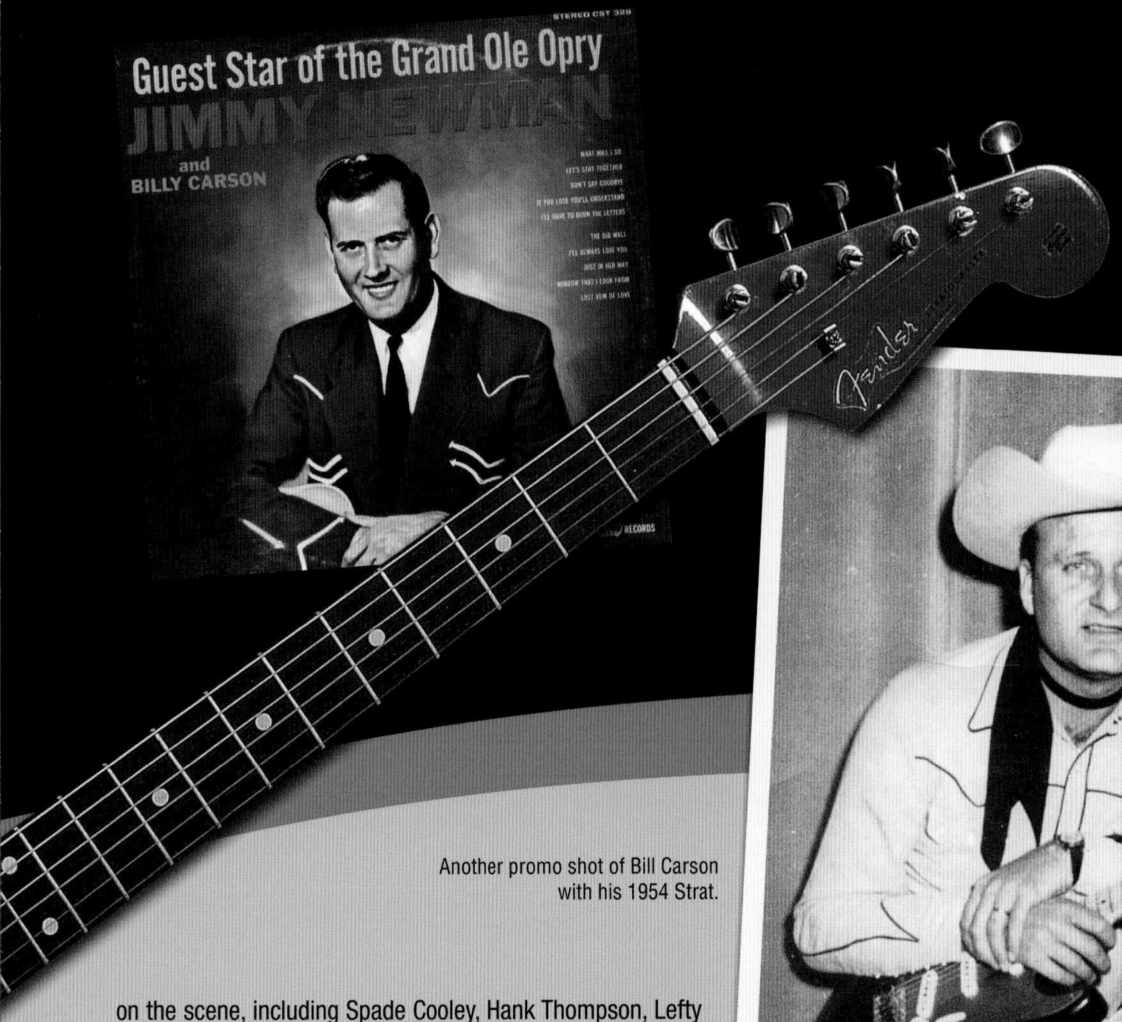

Bill Carson's 1959 Fender Stratocaster.
Christie's/Bridgeman

Another promo shot of Bill Carson with his 1954 Strat.

on the scene, including Spade Cooley, Hank Thompson, Lefty Frizzell, Wade Ray, and others. At the time, the lap steel player was often the star of the guitar world, since that instrument had been a success to amplify before the solidbody Spanish guitar came along. As such, Carson's playing style and sound were closely aligned to the clean, fluid, gliss-heavy approach of the steel players, and he often found work copping steel-style parts on guitar to double his session fees. Back in the day, though, even that kind of work was barely enough to keep a musician afloat, and Carson, like so many others, found need for a solid "day job" to help sustain his playing. He found it as a byproduct of his quest for a better instrument and forged a forty-year career as a result.

As legendary as the Fender of the early 1950s might seem to guitar fans today, it was part of what was then a pretty small world. Carson was fond of telling the story of how he visited the Fullerton factory in 1951 in search of a Telecaster and an amp to go with it and was greeted by Leo Fender himself. The relationship that ensued found Carson not only a Fender player, but soon a field-tester of guitars in development and an actual Fender employee. Carson first worked on the assembly line while maintaining his career as a gigging and recording guitarist, then dialed back his musical career in 1957 to move up the ladder at Fender, as a production supervisor, then head of artists relations, and eventually sales manager. Bill Carson's name had been established in Fender lore, however, largely for his contributions to the design and development of the Stratocaster in 1953 and 1954. Among the major new features that he is likely to have influenced—in part, at least, if not wholly—were the inclusion of a vibrato unit (Carson liked to use it, in conjunction with a volume pedal, to fake pedal-steel sounds) and the comfort-contoured body. The abiding image of this Strat pioneer might be from the oft-published publicity photo of the guitarist in cowboy garb, with a Cimarron Red Stratocaster in hand (rendered black by the monochrome image) and a two-toned boot perched upon a narrow-panel tweed Twin Amp, but Bill Carson worked at Fender well into his seventies, before passing away in 2006 at the age of 80.

Bob Wills and His Texas Playboys, circa 1950, with Eldon Shamblin cradling his grand Gibson ES-5 archtop in the days before he switched to his Stratocaster. *Michael Ochs Archives/Getty Images*

Eldon Shamblin's 1954 Gold Stratocaster, serial number 0569. *Ronny Proler (Anonymous Texas Collector); Photo by Dirk Bakker, Artbook.*

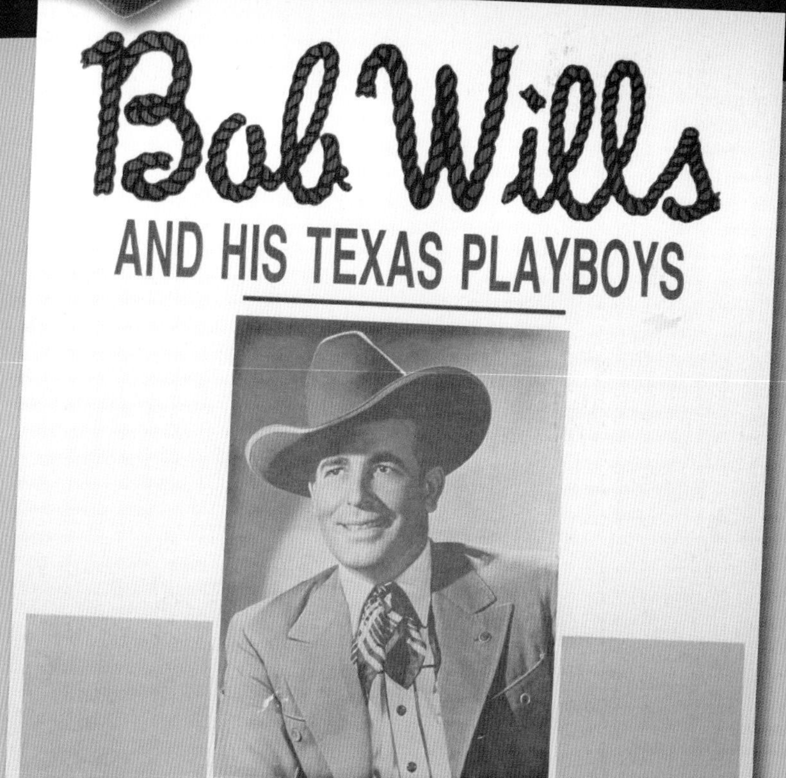

Leo Fender was a country music fan through and through, so it's little surprise that one of the first Stratocasters presented to an artist was given to a country picker. And considering that Bob Wills and His Texas Playboys were about the hottest country band going circa 1954, it's also no surprise that Leo gave the guitar to Wills's hot player, Eldon Shamblin.

Whether he was picking his original Gibson archtop or the futuristic Strat, Shamblin became hugely influential in western swing, country, and jazz. He helped create Wills's sound; arranged many of his most famous songs, such as the band's trademark tunes "San Antonio Rose" and "Faded Love"; and even managed the big band for a time. Fellow Texas Playboy Joe Ferguson crowned Shamblin "The Chord Wizard." Years later, *Rolling Stone* named him "the world's greatest rhythm guitar player." Merle Haggard, with whom Shamblin played in later years, wrote in his 1981 autobiography *Sing Me Back Home*, "Eldon's guitar work is so great that he can just stop everybody in their tracks."

Shamblin was born in Weatherford, Oklahoma, on April 24, 1916. He taught himself to play as a teenager and was soon picking guitar in the Depression-era beer bars of Oklahoma City's skid row. "I got my basic training in the joint days, in 1933 and 1934," he said in a 1985 interview. "Those [were] low-life places, the worst joints in the country. But I had such a yen for music that I played wherever I could."

Eldon Shamblin

Eldon Shamblin's 1954 Gold Stratocaster, serial number 0569.
Ronny Proler (Anonymous Texas Collector); Photo by Dirk Bakker, Artbook.

In 1934, he got a job picking on a regular thirty-minute program with an Oklahoma City radio station; his pay was two square meals per day. This exposure won him a seat with Dave Edwards's Alabama Boys, playing a lively, upbeat hybrid of country and jazz that became known as "western swing." Edwards's band with Shamblin picking his fluid, innovative guitar lines performed on KVOO radio station in Tulsa, where a cigar-chewing, hooting-and-hollering Texan fiddler named Bob Wills was also building his reputation. "I was the first one out of the Alabama Boys to join the Wills band," Shamblin remembered, "but they all gradually joined."

Wills's Texas Playboys was soon staffed by the best western swing players anywhere. The band began prolifically touring and recording, building Wills's reputation as the King of Western Swing. Shamblin co-wrote a number of the band's classics, including the bopping "Twin Guitar Special" with steel-guitar maestro Leon McAuliffe. Shamblin was a cornerstone of the band up until 1942, when he enlisted in the armed services during World War II. He re-upped with Wills in 1947 and played with him through 1957.

When Shamblin began with Wills, he was playing a radical Rickenbacker Electro B, the small semi-solidbody cousin to the firm's Frying Pan lap steel. As Shamblin told historian Rich Kienzle, Wills took him aside and said, "I like the sound of that thing, but hey, man, they don't know you're playin' a guitar." Shamblin soon bought a pair of massive Gibson Super 400 archtops that no one could mistake for anything but a guitar.

While Wills was antsy about Shamblin's first semi-solidbody, he didn't object to the newfangled Stratocaster. The 1954 Strat that Leo Fender presented to Shamblin was painted metallic gold, perhaps following the style of Gibson's Les Paul goldtop. Serial number 0569 wore a neck dated June 1954. But beyond the golden finish, the guitar was pretty much stock, not even having gold-plated hardware.

Shamblin remembered, "It was pretty beaten up when I got it; must have been some demonstrator." Or perhaps a test bed for Leo. Either way, Shamblin added many miles and many a show to its history, using the golden guitar the rest of his life.

—Michael Dregni

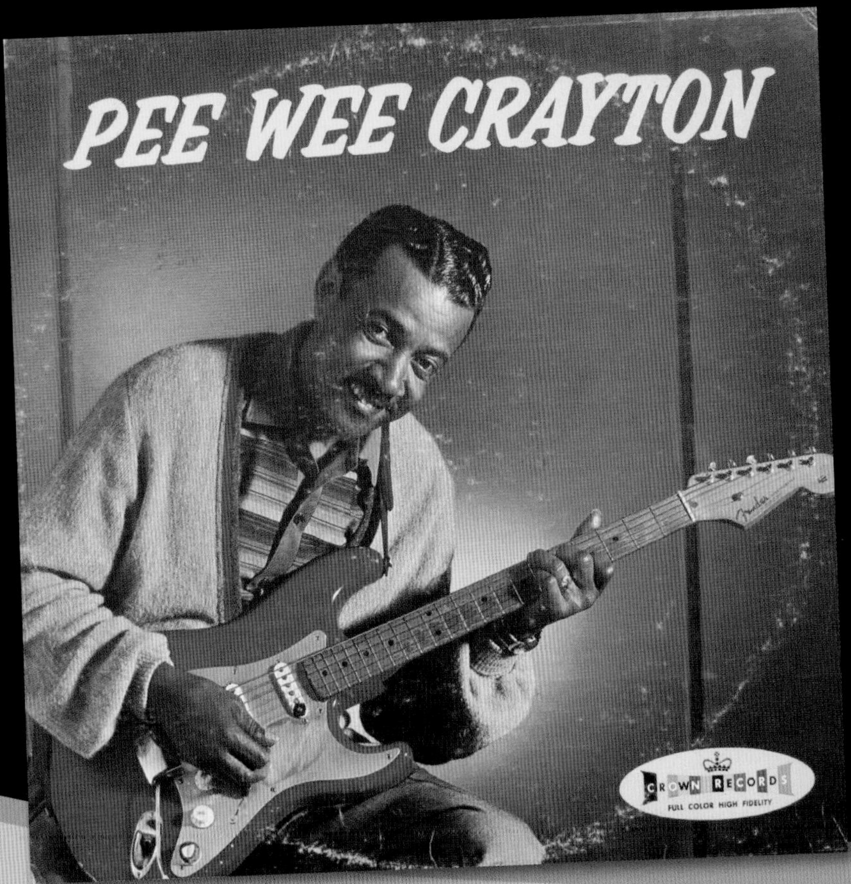

Crayton's 1960 Crown LP featured his custom-color Strat front and center.

2009 Custom Shop 1958 Candy Apple Red Stratocaster with gold-anodized pickguard, inspired by Pee Wee Crayton's guitar. *Fender Musical Instruments Corporation*

Swinging bluesman Pee Wee Crayton's 1955 recording of "The Telephone Is Ringing" on Vee-Jay 214 just may be the premiere recording of a Stratocaster. Whether it was indeed the first or not—we may never know—the song showcased a tone like no other record before. Crayton played his big bends and bluesy pentatonic riffs, punctuated by shimmering ninth chords, with a unique, biting sound. The tone was unlike that of T-Bone Walker's archtop Gibson ES-5 with its woody, out-of-phase-pickup voice or Clarence "Gatemouth" Brown's snarling Fender Esquire. It was a sound all its own.

Connie Curtis Crayton was Texas born and influenced primarily by Texan guitar slingers, such as Walker and jazzman Charlie Christian. He began by emulating T-Bone, playing his jazz-inflected blues licks on a big archtop Gibson before he was given a Stratocaster and a tweed Twin amp by the factory, likely in 1954. No one seems to remember the circumstances behind the present—how, where, or when Leo Fender or anyone else from the factory met Crayton. In fact, as Leo was a staunch country music fan, his giving such an early and special Strat to a bluesman seems odd in retrospect.

Nevertheless, Crayton's gift was one of the first Strats given to a musician by Fender, alongside the golden '54 given to Eldon Shamblin. And like Shamblin's guitar, Crayton's boasted a custom-color paint job and other special features.

Looking sharp in a sharkskin suit and toting his red Strat with gold-anodized pickguard, Pee Wee Crayton was ready to take on his archrival, T-Bone Walker, in a battle of the jump blues kings.

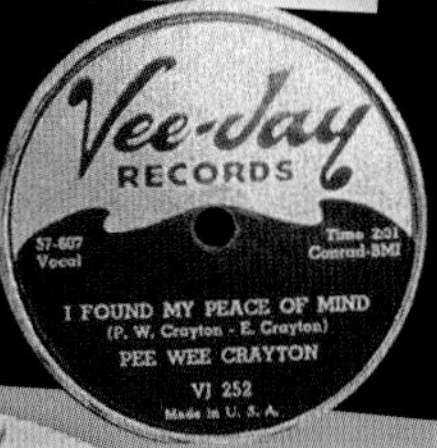

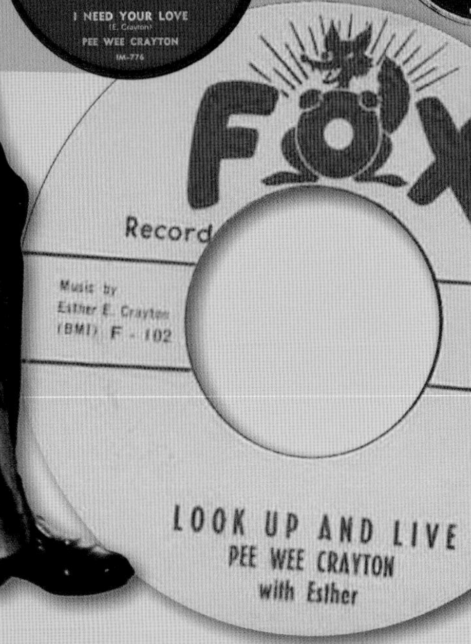

Crayton's "The Telephone Is Ringing" on VeeJay featured one of the first—if not *the* first—recorded Strat. The tone is unmistakable.

Crayton's Strat was painted a bright red hue, a color some have suggested was a Studebaker car color. Bill Carson had a similarly colored red Strat, which he termed "Cimarron Red," perhaps inspired by the band Leon McAuliffe and His Cimarron Boys, as McAuliffe played a red Fender Stringmaster. The color was also close to what would years later appear in Fender color charts as Dakota Red.

Crayton's Strat featured a gold-anodized metal pickguard in place of the typical Bakelite plastic pickguard. The rest of its features toed the line with production Strats, including the chrome-plated hardware, rather than the special gold plating.

Crayton had moved from Texas to California during the Depression years of the 1930s, and that's where he started seriously playing guitar. He was often known as T-Bone Walker Jr., a name that was somewhat derisive, but also of prime promotional benefit. In later years, he and the real T-Bone shared the bills in hard-fought fret wars.

Crayton signed on with Modern Records in 1948, playing T-Bone-inspired jump blues. One of his earliest sides was the instrumental, "Blues After Hours," which hit No. 1 on the *Billboard* R&B chart. In the 1950s, he cut sides for other labels, including T-Bone's home, Imperial, as well as Jamie and Vee-Jay.

Crayton was often pictured with the special Strat in hand, Crayton himself usually wearing a lean, shiny sharkskin suit, the consummate bluesman. He cradled it on the cover of his early eponymous Crown LP in 1960 and still held the guitar on the 1971 Vanguard album, *Things I Used to Do*. During the years in between, Crayton's Strat had obviously been well used, the red paint chipped away, the neck and headstock smoke- and time-darkened. —*Michael Dregni*

The photograph that launched a legend, appearing in Fender catalogs and ads in 1956–57.

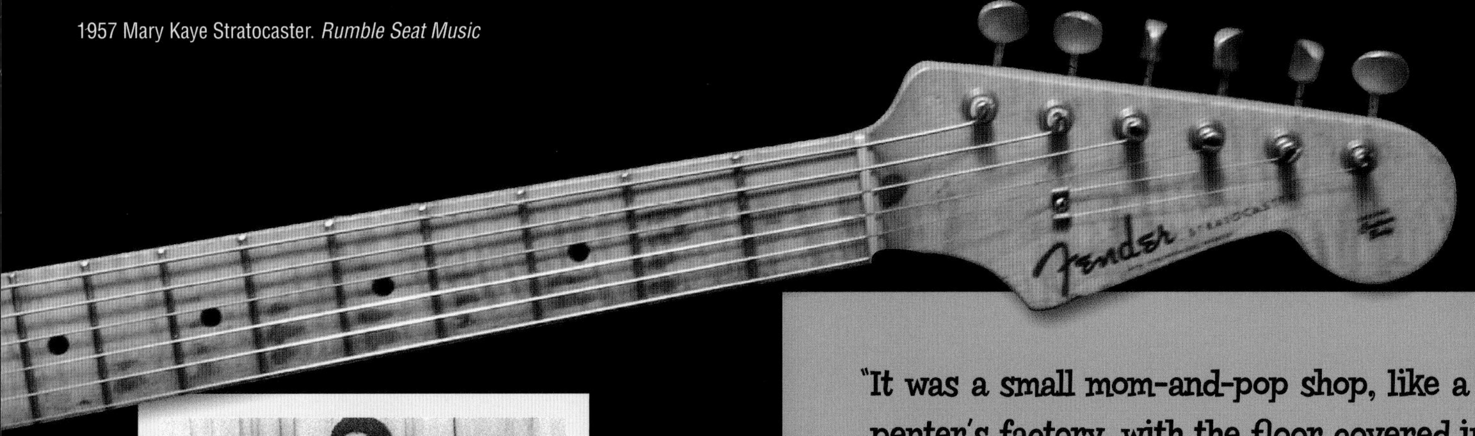

1957 Mary Kaye Stratocaster. *Rumble Seat Music*

"It was a small mom-and-pop shop, like a carpenter's factory, with the floor covered in the day's wood debris. It was what I had expected. I was greeted by Leo Fender himself; he was very nice."

—Mary Kaye on visiting the Fender factory, circa 1955

Mary Kaye holds *the* Mary Kaye—a Blonde Stratocaster with gold hardware that she was loaned by Fender for this photo shot. Then she had to give the guitar back.

Mary Kaye—the guitarist whose name became synonymous with the beautiful Blonde Stratocaster highlighted by golden hardware—never actually owned a Mary Kaye. Fender promised her the guitar she's holding in the catalog and promotional photos and played on another occasion in the 1956 film *Cha-Cha-Cha Boom!*, but the guitar remained in Fender's hands. This wrong was finally righted in 2002 when Fender presented Kaye with a one-and-only Custom Shop Stratocaster christened the White Beauty and bearing serial number MK001.

For much of her career, Kaye was actually a D'Angelico player, which is never a bad thing to be. Her full surname was Ka'aihue, which she also recorded and played under before switching to the stage name "Kaye." Her father was Hawai'ian royalty; her mother a Detroit socialite. From that background, Kaye became one of the first Las Vegas lounge acts.

Kaye began her professional career playing in her father's band, before starting the Mary Kaye Trio. As she told *Vintage Guitar* magazine in 2006, "While in Chicago, we hooked up with Billy Burton, who became our manager. He brought us to the Frontier Hotel in Vegas. . . . While playing our first gig in the main showroom of the Frontier, we were asked to stay over after our four-week engagement had ended. Without a room to go to, I suggested a stage be built in the bar area and it could be called a 'lounge.' Jack Kozloff, the owner, and Eddie Fox, the general manager, had it constructed immediately. During its first week of operation, Frank Sinatra and friends dropped $120,000 on the tables, during what became known as the 'dusk 'til dawn' hours. This impressed the other hotels to the point where they began to stay open 24 hours. . . . Hotels began hunting for entertainers to fill their newly constructed lounges. Not all entertainment worked, but smaller, tight-knit groups were working out better than the big bands of that time."

"Cha-Cha-Cha BOOM!"
A CLOVER PRODUCTION · A COLUMBIA PICTURE
Copyright 1956 Columbia Pictures Corp. Country of Origin U.S.A.

Mary Kaye played the original Mary Kaye Strat for a sequence in the 1956 film *Cha-Cha-Cha Boom!* but then had to hand it back to Fender, again.

In Vegas, Kaye was introduced to Fender sales maestro Don Randall: "Around 1954, Don brought me a Fender guitar—not the Strat—to play onstage. Though I refused to play it, Don started bringing me Fender amps to use with my D'Angelicos. In '55, Fender delivered the Blonde Strat to me, prior to the Trio going onstage at the Frontier Hotel for the famous publicity shot, taken backstage. [The guitar] was returned to Fender later that evening.

"Six months later, Billy, our manager, set up an arrangement with Fender to let me use the Blonde Stratocaster in a Columbia movie [*Cha-Cha-Cha Boom!*], and again it was returned to Fender."

Thanks to those publicity photos and movie appearance, the rare Blonde Stratocasters crowned by gold hardware have been referred to ever after as Mary Kayes. As Kaye herself said, "I remember Billy was upset that the guitar was returned to Fender after Leo Fender had promised it to me. We were too busy with the Trio's career to ever look back and correct the mistake." And Kaye was too busy picking her beloved D'Angelicos.

Although Kaye might not have gotten that original Mary Kaye Strat, Randall did keep her supplied with free Fender amps throughout her life.

—Michael Dregni

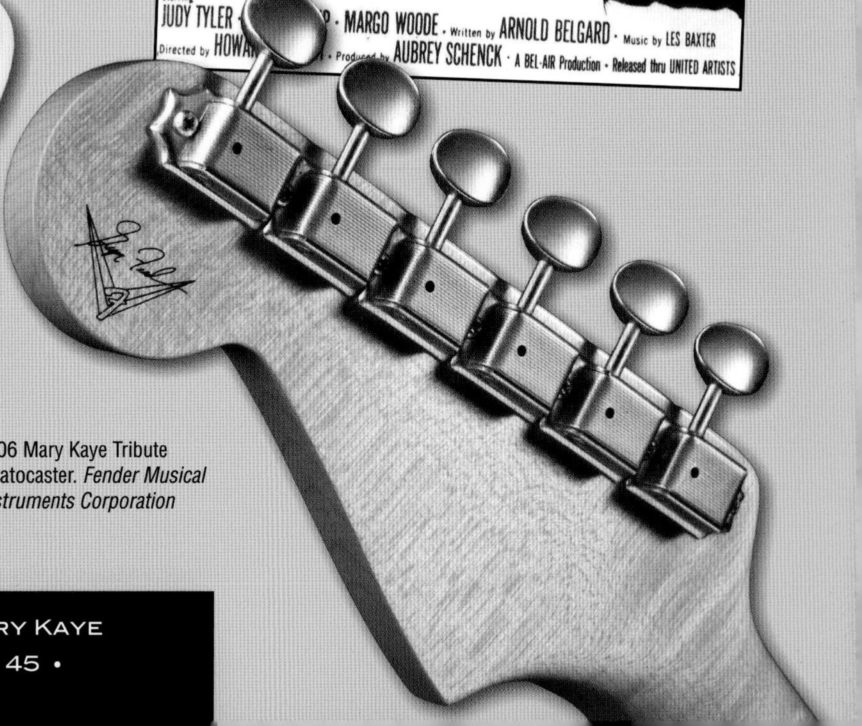

2006 Mary Kaye Tribute Stratocaster. *Fender Musical Instruments Corporation*

Ike Turner

Ike Turner plays his Strat with his Kings of Rhythm in 1956. In the back row from left, Jackie Brenston, Raymond Hill, Eddie Jones, Fred Sample, and Billy Gayles. Front row from left, Jesse Knight Jr., Turner, and Eugene Washington. *Gilles Petard Collection/Redferns/Getty Images*

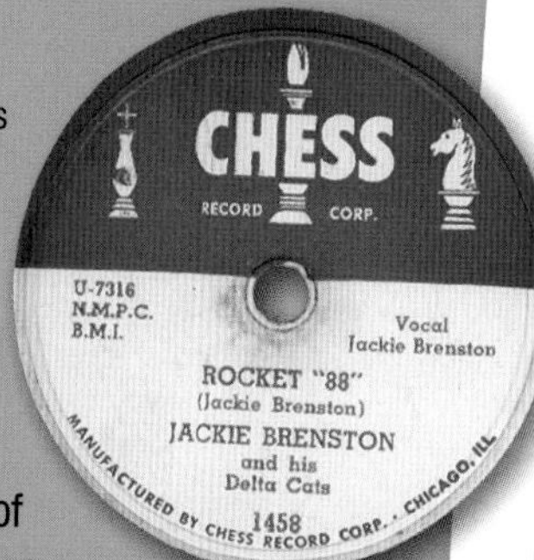

With saxman Jackie Brenston singing, Turner's Kings of Rhythm recorded one of the first—if not *the* first—rock 'n' roll songs of all time, "Rocket 88," at Memphis's Sun Studios. The song was licensed to Chicago's Chess Records for release in April 1951. *Poster: Michael Ochs Archives/Getty Images*

Ike Turner was not one of the Kings of Rhythm, as his longtime band was known. He *was* the king.

Rechristening the band "Jackie Brenston and His Delta Cats" for a session at the Memphis Sun Studios in 1951, he cut "Rocket 88," often tagged as one of the first rock 'n' roll songs. Ever. With Annie Mae Bullock—renamed for the stage as Tina Turner—he launched his Revue, shaking up the 1960s with a rafters-rattling blend of rock, R&B, and soul. Ike's career was often controversial, but throughout his life he made phenomenal music.

Ike was also one of the first—if not *the* first—bluesmen to take up the Strat. Photographs of the Kings of Rhythm dated circa 1955–56 show Ike armed with an early sunburst Stratocaster. The guitar looks brand spanking new too: it still has the ashtray bridge cover in place and a nice, polished sheen to the body.

With Tina Turner fronting the Kings of Rhythm and Ike Turner playing what became his trademark Sonic Blue Strat, R&B would never be the same again. Here, they perform in Dallas, Texas, in 1962. *Michael Ochs Archives/Getty Images*

From the early days of the Ike and Tina Turner Revue, Ike was toting the Strat that he made famous: a Sonic Blue guitar with rosewood fret board that was believed to date from 1961. He played that guitar and other Strats for the rest of his career.

Ike was born in 1931 in the heart of the Mississippi Delta in the county-seat town of Clarksdale. He was hardened early in life when he witnessed his Baptist minister father beaten and left for dead by a mob of white men. His mother remarried a violent alcoholic, who beat the young boy until Ike knocked him out with a piece of wood and ran away to Memphis. Ike began playing piano and guitar, forming the Kings of Rhythm in high school; he kept the name of the band throughout his career.

Along with playing across the South, Ike became a music scout. He brought B. B. King and Howlin' Wolf to the attention of Sam Phillips at Sun Records, who first recorded them and leased the sides to Bihari brothers' Modern Records in Los Angeles. Ike himself recorded in the 1950s and 1960s for Modern, Chess, Flair, and Mississippi's local label, Trumpet. With the Revue, he graduated to larger labels, including Sue, Blue Thumb, and eventually, United Artists. Together, he and Tina won two Grammys and were nominated for three others.

Ike's personality came through in his guitar sound: a biting tone and a driving sense of rhythm that propelled his band. Like James Brown, he was domineering and demanding of his Kings of Rhythm, not settling for less than music perfection and thrilling showmanship.

Interviewed by writer Dave Rubin in 2006, Ike explained that he started out on piano, learning boogie-woogie rhythms from his early idol, Pinetop Perkins, and always considered himself first and foremost a piano player: "B. B. King says I'm not a guitar player, and he's right. I just do tricks. I started playing because I couldn't get my guitar players to do what I wanted. Also, I can lead the band better when I'm not confined to the piano. I don't want to holler across the stage if somebody is out of tune. . . . I always had trouble with drummers, so I mostly

played rhythm the way a drummer plays a high hat. That way I could hold the tempo down or pick it up."

POMPEII
VOCAL
PP-14393-MO
CSG Processed
Mono Master
45-66700
Pub., Vapac, BMI
Time: 2:15
SHAKE A TAIL FEATHER
(O. M. Hayes - A. Williams - V. Rice)
IKE & TINA TURNER
Produced by Ike Turner
From Pompeii LP-6000
DIST. BY ATCO, DIV. OF ATLANTIC RECORDING CORP., 1841 B'WAY, N.Y., N.Y.

Playing that Sonic Blue Strat, Ike would intermix chords, riffs, and bass lines, much like a piano player. As Ike's then-guitarist in the Kings of Rhythm, Seth Blumberg, detailed, "His life is the rhythm—that's why his band is called the Kings of Rhythm. He plays with his left-hand thumb hooked over the neck laying down the rhythm, and he rarely plays upstrokes. A lot of the time, he doesn't even play chords; he's just shucking the rhythm on the muted strings. He has a great knack for what he calls 'marrying the rhythm,' where he'll decide how to accent the beat while the drummer is really driving. . . . Ike's all about energy, and he says, 'I don't wanna hear that mama-papa two and four. It makes me tired. You got to lay it down, man. Don't step around it—you got to step *in* it.'"

—*Michael Dregni*

Sue
2003
IKE & TINA TURNER'S
Kings of Rhythm
DANCE
TWISTAROO
IT'S GONNA WORK OUT FINE
THE GULLEY
TRACKDOWN TWIST
SQUARE DANCE
LET'S PONY AGAIN
POTATO MASH

ULTRA HIGH FIDELITY
KENT
K 418x45
LOIS MUSIC PUBL. CO. BMI
HI-FI
TIME 2.05
PROMOTIONAL COPY
HE'S THE ONE
(Ballard)
IKE AND TINA TURNER
(K 418-1)

KST 519 STEREO
KENT records
THE SOUL OF
IKE & TINA
HURT IS ALL YOU GAVE ME • IT'S CRAZY BABY • I DON'T NEED • HARD TIMES • IF I CAN'T BE FIRST
I WISH MY DREAM WOULD COME TRUE • DON'T YOU BLAME IT ON ME • CHICKEN SHACK
GONNA HAVE FUN • GOOD BYE SO LONG • AM I A FOOL IN LOVE • SOMETHING CAME OVER YOU

Artistic
Armel Music
BMI 3:05
C 1063
Vocal by
TOMMY HODGE
Record No.
1504
DOWN & OUT
(I. Turner)
Ike Turner's Kings of Rhythm

Otis Rush was one of the first bluesmen to adopt the Strat, and he owned an early left-handed model. *Gilles Petard Collection/ Redferns/Getty Images*

1956 Blonde Stratocaster. *Rumble Seat Music*

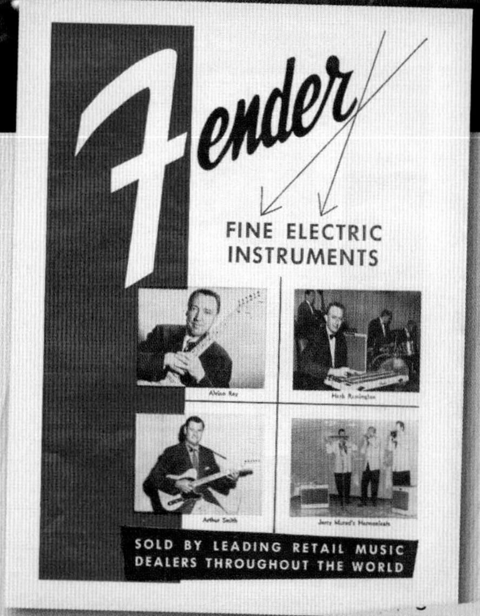

SOLD BY LEADING RETAIL MUSIC DEALERS THROUGHOUT THE WORLD

1956 Fender catalog.

SPANISH GUITAR — BASS

*Stratocaster Guitar (no tremolo) (Three Pickups)	14	249.50
*Stratocaster Guitar (with tremolo) (Three Pickups)	14	274.50
Stratocaster (with tremolo) in Blonde with 14 Carat Gold-Plated Hardware	14	330.00
*Telecaster Spanish Guitar (Dual Pickup)	14	199.50
*Esquire Spanish Guitar (Single Pickup)	14	164.50
Duo-Sonic Three-quarter Spanish Guitar (Dual Pickups)	12	149.50
Musicmaster Three-quarter Spanish Guitar (Single Pickup)	10	119.50
*Precision Bass	17	219.50
150 Student Spanish Guitars (packed 6 to packing ctn.)	29	each 17.95

* Available in custom DuPont Ducco finishes — 5% additional cost.

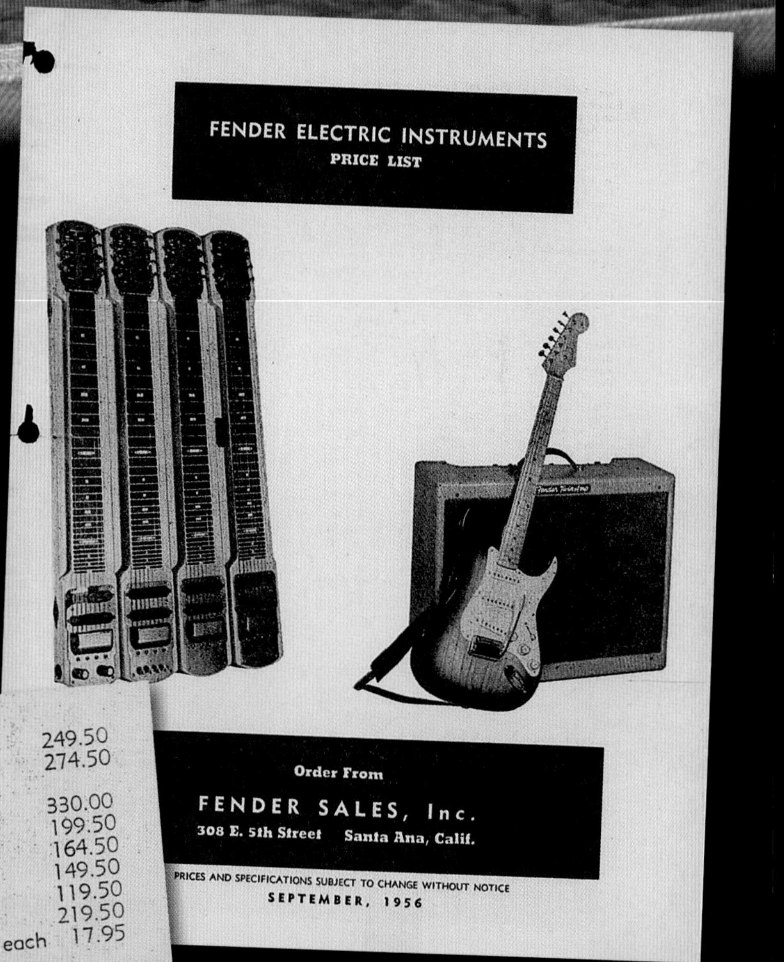
FENDER ELECTRIC INSTRUMENTS
PRICE LIST
Order From
FENDER SALES, Inc.
308 E. 5th Street Santa Ana, Calif.
PRICES AND SPECIFICATIONS SUBJECT TO CHANGE WITHOUT NOTICE
SEPTEMBER, 1956

1956 Fender price list shows the Blonde Stratocaster with 14-karat gold hardware listed for $330—almost 20 percent more than a regular Strat. The footnote stated that the Strat, Tele, Esquire, and Precision Bass were all available in "custom DuPont Ducco finishes" for 5 percent extra.

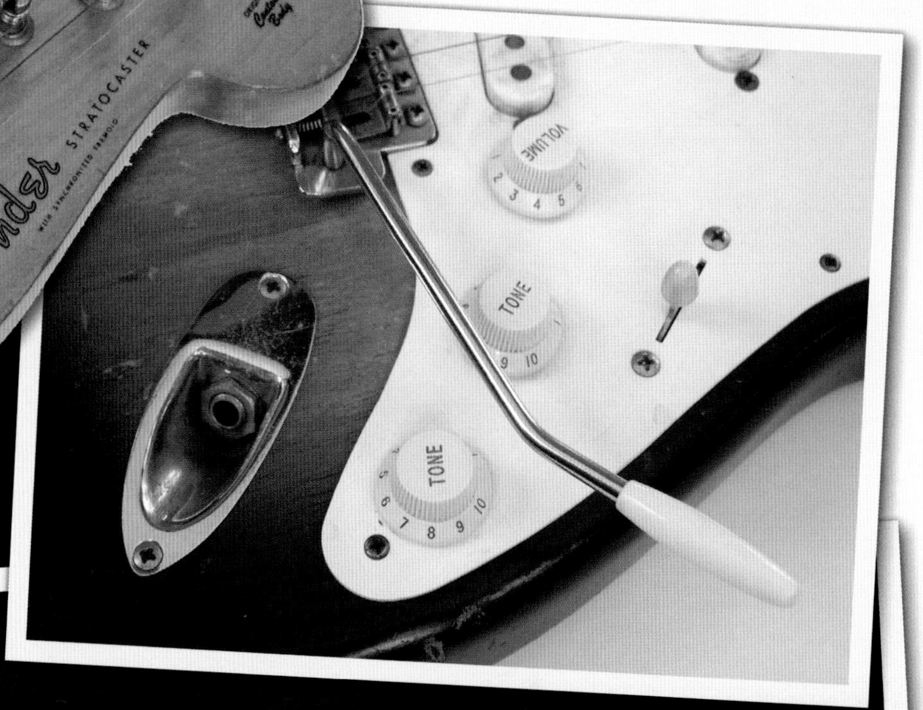

1956 Stratocaster. *Michael Dregni*

VOLUME
TONE
TONE

Fender
STRATOCASTER

1956 Stratocaster. *Jean Versaveau*

Koylon

1956 Fender advertisement.

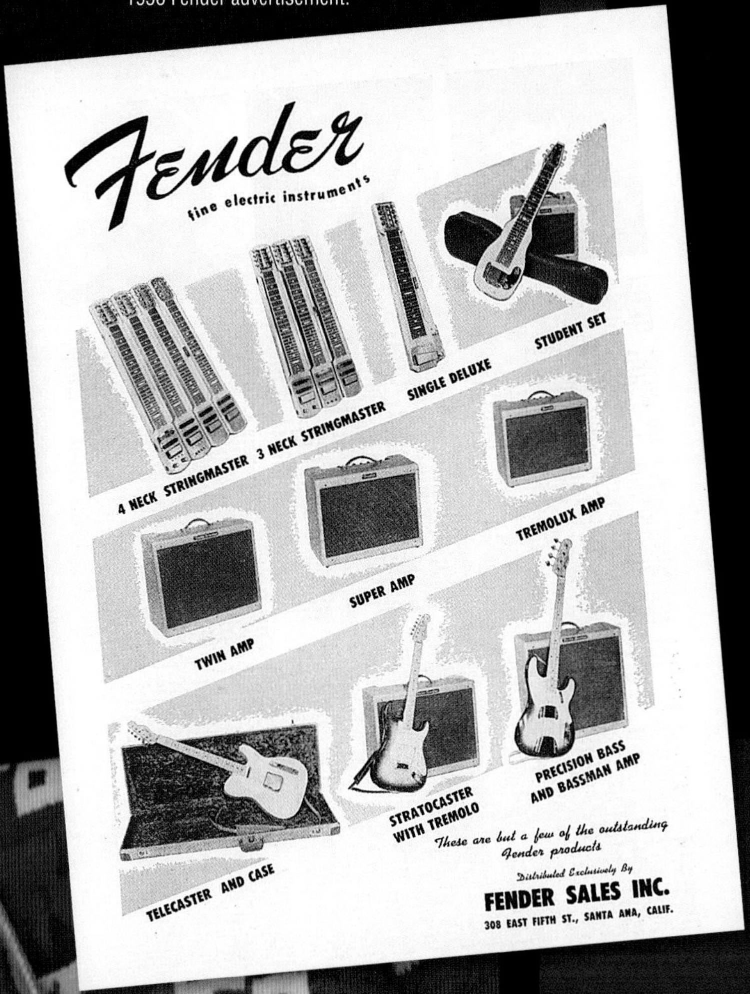

1956 Shoreline Gold Stratocaster with gold hardware.
Rumble Seat Music

Gene Vincent and his Blue Caps, including guitarman Johnny Meeks, ham for the camera with their sharp new blonde Stratocasters, Precision Bass, and a grand tweed Twin-Amp. *Michael Ochs Archives/Getty Images*

1956 Blonde Stratocaster. *Skinner Auctioneers*

1956 Black Stratocaster. *Heritage Auctions*

Buddy Guy

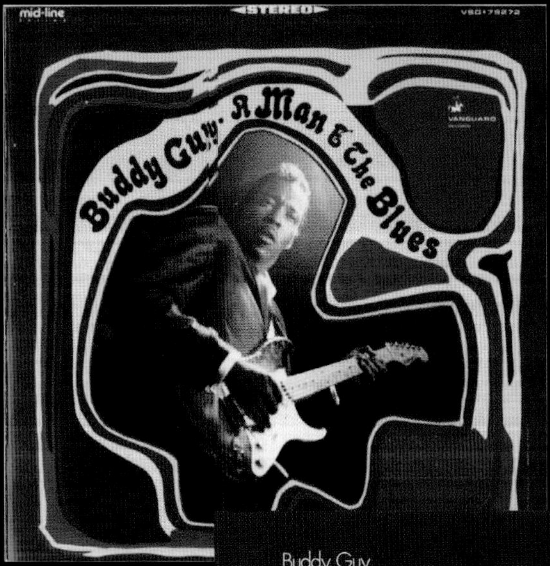

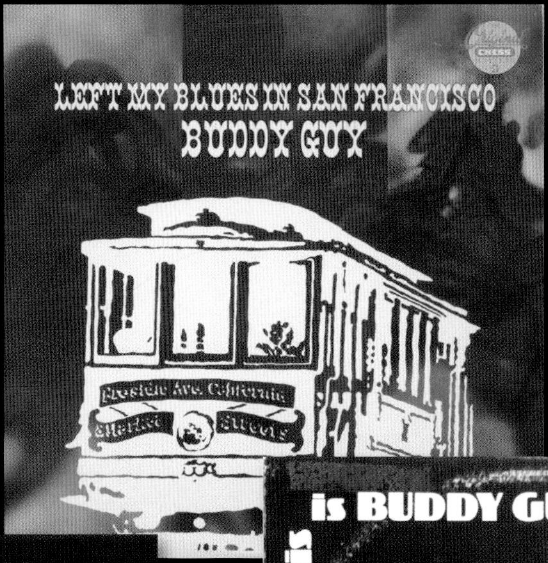

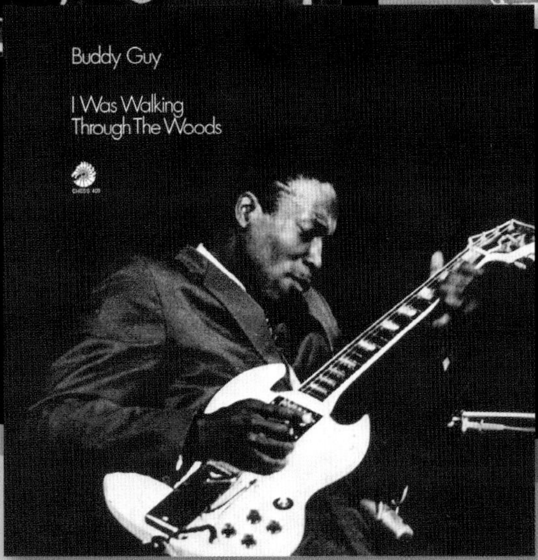

There's no better example of supercharged, hard-blowing, electric Chicago blues than Buddy Guy. His guitars of choice—and the amps he plays them through, for that matter—are staples of the bluesman's toolbox. As simple as these ingredients may be, they are capable of producing no end of firepower when used with attitude. Listen to any of Guy's early recordings for examples of his legendary stinging pick attack and extreme bends, then sample 2001's raw, stripped-down outing, *Sweet Tea*, for evidence that the artist has retained that incendiary style five decades later. Although Guy has occasionally strutted his stuff with a Guild Starfire semi-acoustics, he is far and away best known for his use of Fender Stratocasters and has played plenty of examples of this legendary model throughout his career. For many years, Guy wielded vintage 1950s Strats with maple fingerboards, but in recent years has been the subject of not one but two Fender signature models and has lately been most associated with the Buddy Guy Standard Polka Dot Stratocaster, which expresses his desires in a modified Strat, as well as his flare for fashion and performance.

The Polka Dot Stratocaster follows classic Strat lines, with an alder body and all-maple neck, vintage-style vibrato, five-way switch, and single-volume and dual-tone controls (for neck and middle pickup only), but its pickups gain a little extra poke courtesy of their ceramic magnets. The second of Guy's Fender signature models, the high-end Artist Series Buddy Guy Stratocaster, changes the alder body for ash, the ceramic-magnet pickups for three Lace Sensor Golds, and adds a midboost to the guitar's electrics. Both aim to offer classic Strat playability and versatility, but to hit the amp harder than many bluesmen might seek to do.

Guy's amps deserve some consideration in their own right, as does the way in which he uses them. Throughout his early career, Guy preferred a model that can lay claim to the tag "ultimate blues amp of all time": a late 1950s Fender Tweed 5F6-A Bassman. Purportedly, he played these 4x10-inch combos with all knobs wound up toward max, save the bass tone control, which he kept down low. Like most artists with his sort of longevity in the business, Guy has diversified his arsenal over the years. In the late 1990s and early 2000s, Guy often played a Victoria 45410 (a hand-wired reproduction of a Bassman) and has lately endorsed the Buddy Guy Signature Series Amp from Chicago Blues Box, which is modeled specifically on Guy's own favorite '59 Bassman. Between guitar and amp, Guy has often favored a Crybaby wah pedal, a duty now performed by the Jim Dunlop Crybaby Buddy Guy Signature Wah—in black with white polka dots, naturally.

As with most guitar stars, though, it's not so much the ingredients as the way the artist attacks them that accounts for the hot, stinging tone. And now into his seventies and counting, Buddy Guy is still hitting those strings hard.

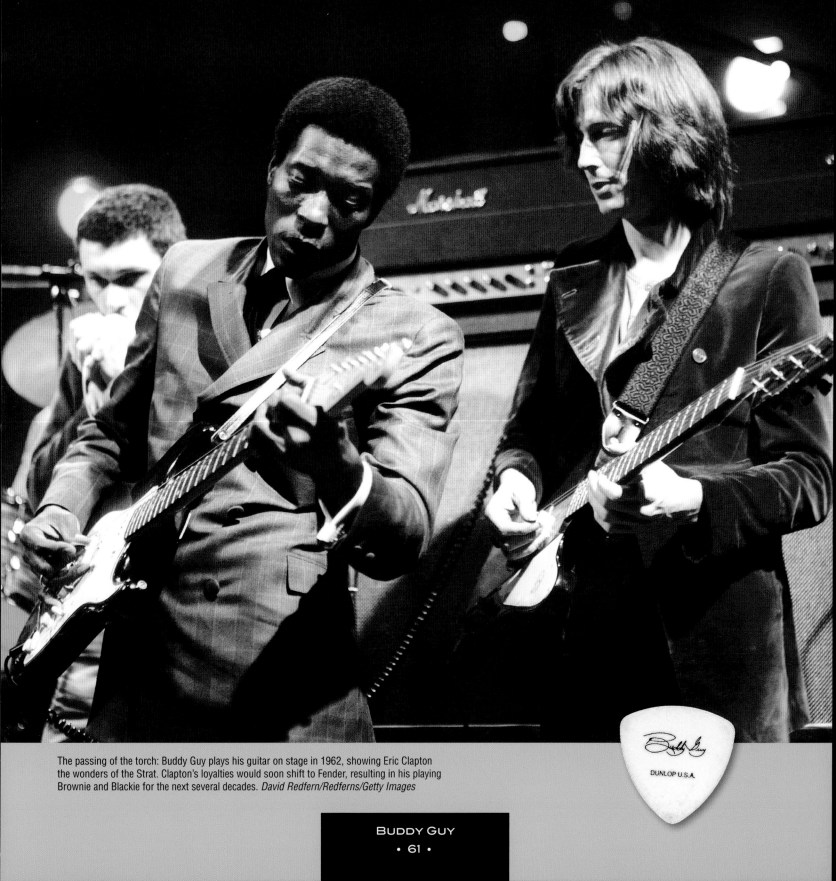

The passing of the torch: Buddy Guy plays his guitar on stage in 1962, showing Eric Clapton the wonders of the Strat. Clapton's loyalties would soon shift to Fender, resulting in his playing Brownie and Blackie for the next several decades. *David Redfern/Redferns/Getty Images*

Buddy Guy's 1958 Stratocaster.
Rick Gould

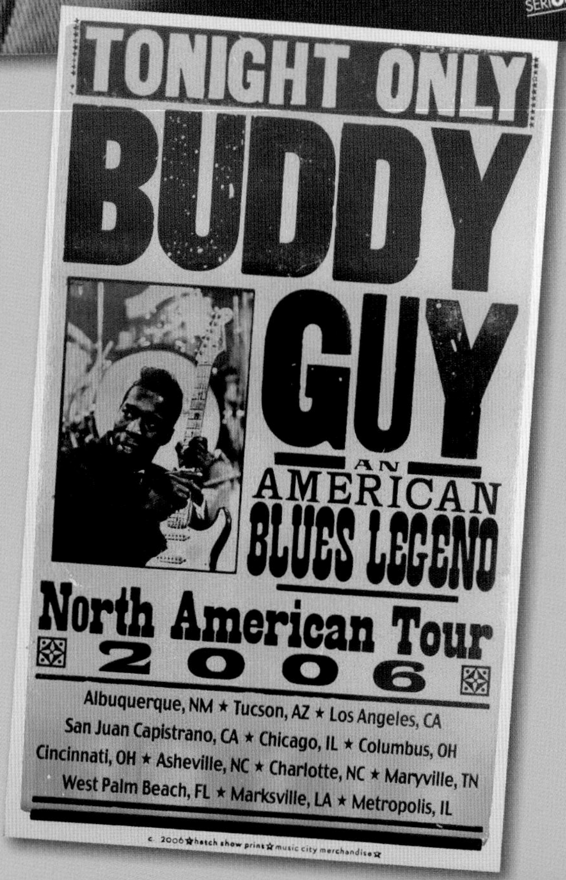

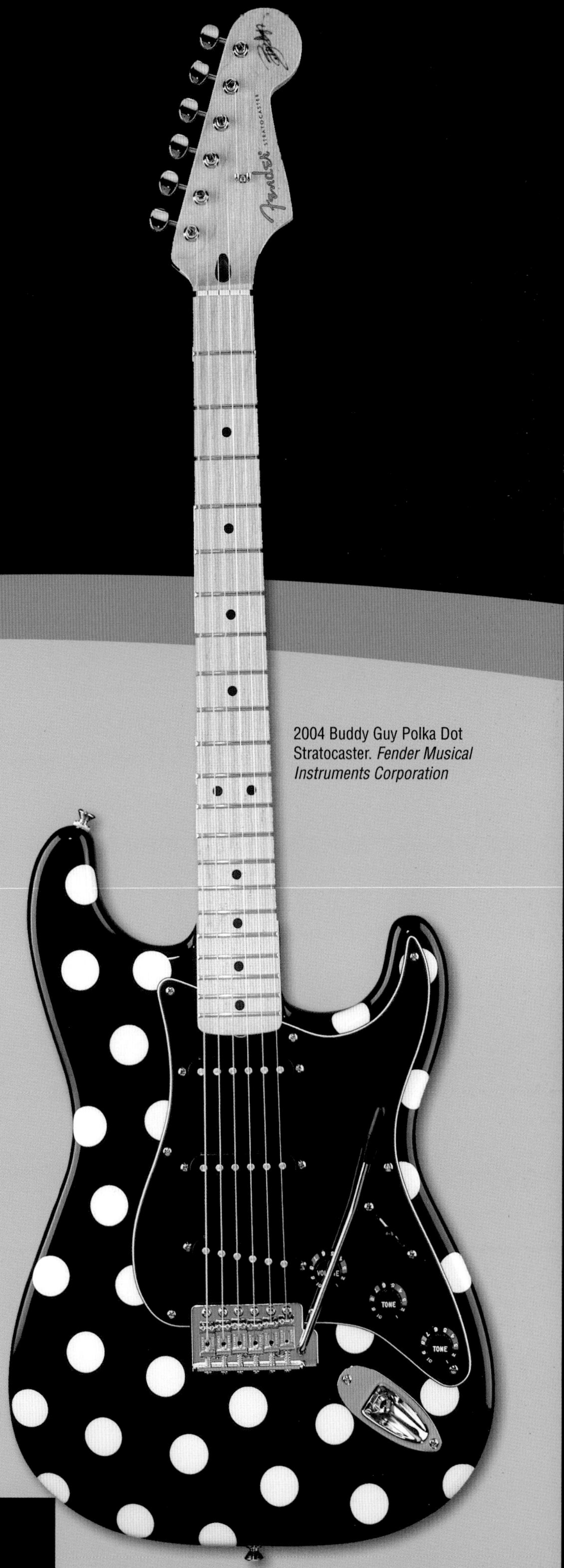

2004 Buddy Guy Polka Dot Stratocaster. *Fender Musical Instruments Corporation*

1956 Blonde Stratocaster.
Rumble Seat Music

1956 Dakota Red Stratocaster.
Rumble Seat Music

"A nice maple-neck three-tone from 1956 compete with fully sprung whammy bar. This one's behind the bluesy sound tracked on 'Apologies to Pearly' from *Rio Grande Mud.* Original electronics, Bakelite parts, and the deep V-neck shape make this instrument way desirable. This one was injected into the set to add to the range of sounds additional to Pearly Gates."

—Billy F Gibbons

1957 Stratocaster.

Billy F Gibbons's 1956 Stratocaster.
David Perry

(Continued from page 29)

The term "rock 'n' roll" is only beginning to enter the lexicon, thanks in part to the release of the movie *Blackboard Jungle*, featuring "Rock Around the Clock" by Bill Haley and the Comets and the start of Elvis Presley's recording career. Amid it all, here comes the Fender Stratocaster: startling, radical, stylish, and entirely awe-inspiring, even in this fast-paced, future-now context.

For all its potential and invention, however, the Stratocaster didn't set the guitar world ablaze overnight. After all, this was a conservative crowd (for that matter, guitarists' tastes, en masse, still run to the conservative today), and Fender was still struggling uphill for acceptance amid the traditional names of the industry. Keep in mind, too, that even large, traditional makers often had their more adventurous efforts shot down by a wary buying public. Not only did Gibson's radical Flying V and Explorer guitars fail to find any significant market, even in the rock 'n' roll hotbed of the late 1950s, but another of the three undeniable solidbody classics, the Les Paul—often considered the single most valuable standard-production electric guitar on the vintage market today—sold so poorly in its final years, 1958–60, that it was dropped from the catalog thereafter.

With that in mind, even if the Stratocaster wasn't launched to universal gasps of wonder and amazement, it's impressive to think how steadily its acceptance gained momentum. For that matter, what an achievement it was that Fender's Telecaster and Stratocaster would be the only true solidbodies from a major maker to survive through the 1950s and 1960s, and even beyond, without being majorly redesigned or dropped from the catalog all together. That statement in itself goes a long way toward summing up the impact of those designs, and their long-haul success in the guitar market. Gibson's Les Paul changed throughout the 1950s and was dropped after 1960, essentially gone for eight full years and never really back in quite the same form until the "re-issue" days (the ES-335 had a steadier run, but was a semi-hollow electric design). Gretsch's rockabilly standards, the Duo Jet and 6120, went from single-coil DeArmond pickups to Gretsch Filter'Tron humbuckers and from single-cutaway to double-cutaway body designs, with other changes to boot. They were very different guitars by the early 1960s than they were in the mid-1950s. The Strat and Tele, on the other hand, abided, and barring a change of fingerboard wood here or a different type of pickguard there, remained essentially "themselves" throughout their days, into the early CBS years at least.

Still, it didn't happen overnight, and there was work to be done in establishing this new sensation's place in the guitarists' lexicon. Several of Leo's western swing test-bed buddies and many of their pals took up the cause with some gusto, and the Stratocaster, in its infancy, gained acceptance rather more steadily than had the Telecaster before it. Often, too, the early adopters seemed to have been won over by the glamor of a custom finish—always a badge of honor on the country scene, to some extent—even when no custom-colored Strats were yet officially available.

Bill Carson was clearly delighted with the release of the new model he had helped to midwife and was one of the first artists seen in print ads for the new product, proudly cradling his own early custom-color Cimarron Red Stratocaster (which often looked merely black in the monochrome photos). Eldon Shamblin, guitarist for Bob Wills and His Texas Playboys, had virtually denied the entire premise of the Telecaster when it was first presented to him, but was an enthusiastic recipient of a gold-finished Stratocaster, a guitar that seems to have been either a late prototype or a very early production model, and probably something from that gray area in between.

Soon after, the Stratocaster sidestepped successfully into rock 'n' roll. Two of Gene Vincent's guitarists (we might call them "Cliff Gallup stand-ins"), Howard Reed and Johnny Meeks, both played Stratocasters and more custom-color examples at that, Black and Blonde models, respectively. But the Strat really landed in the hands of its first pop-idol front-man when Buddy Holly took up a late 1954 or early 1955 model at the start of his career, and continued to play one until his death in 1959. He went through four or five guitars in his short career. His first was stolen from a tour bus in Michigan in 1955, and his second, a new '57 Stratocaster, was stolen from the band's station wagon during a restaurant stop in St. Louis in April 1958; but the ubiquitous look of these, all in standard sunburst finish, helped to establish the model nationwide through his many TV and concert appearances. By the late 1950s, call it just half a decade since its introduction, the Stratocaster was going strong and getting stronger in virtually all genres of popular music. Even so, it provides some perspective on the times to consider that few people today can name more than half a dozen prominent artists who were regularly using a Stratocaster by the end of the decade—and to consider, in that light, what a classic it already was and what a legend it was on its way to becoming.

Fender Promotions Get Stylish

With two major solidbody electric guitars to promote (three if you count the Esquire as a separate model), a range of steel guitars, and an evolving amplifier lineup that was fast becoming the most respected in the business, Don Randall and his team of executives at Fender Sales knew Fender needed more than the usual in-house or small-time add man promos to get the word out in style. And the ad campaign that he would eventually instruct to do so—the long-running "You won't part with yours either" series—has become one of the most famous and successful in the business. Perusing the series of hip, stylish ads that ran from 1957 to 1969 we can't help but imagine, from a contemporary perspective, *Mad Men*'s Don Draper and a young team of Madison Avenue creatives riffing and wheeling to pitch their visions

(Continued on page 76)

Texas bluesman extraordinaire Anson Funderburgh and his well-traveled 1957 Stratocaster. *Bill Crump*

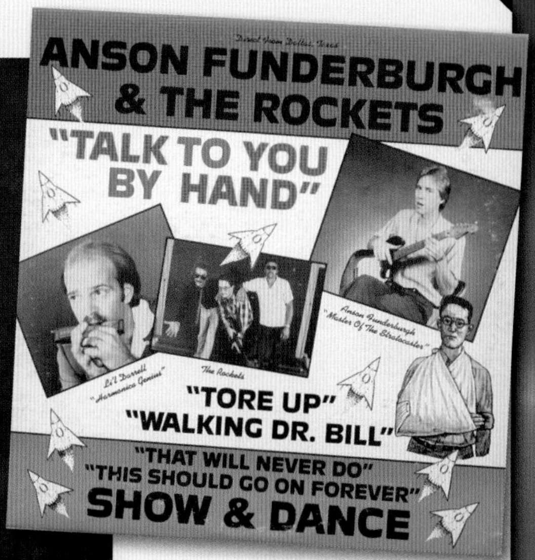

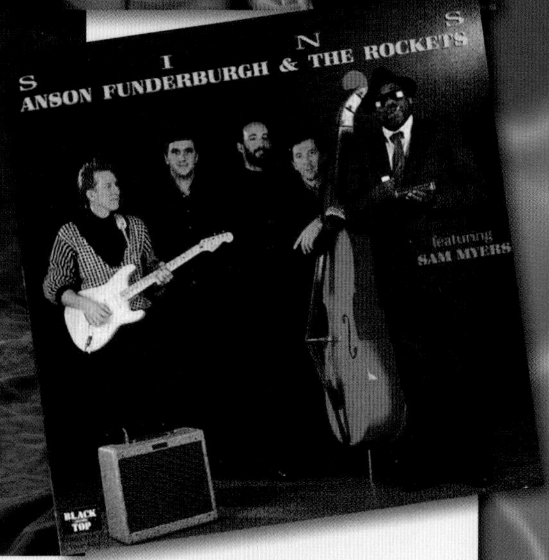

Fender Twin-Am

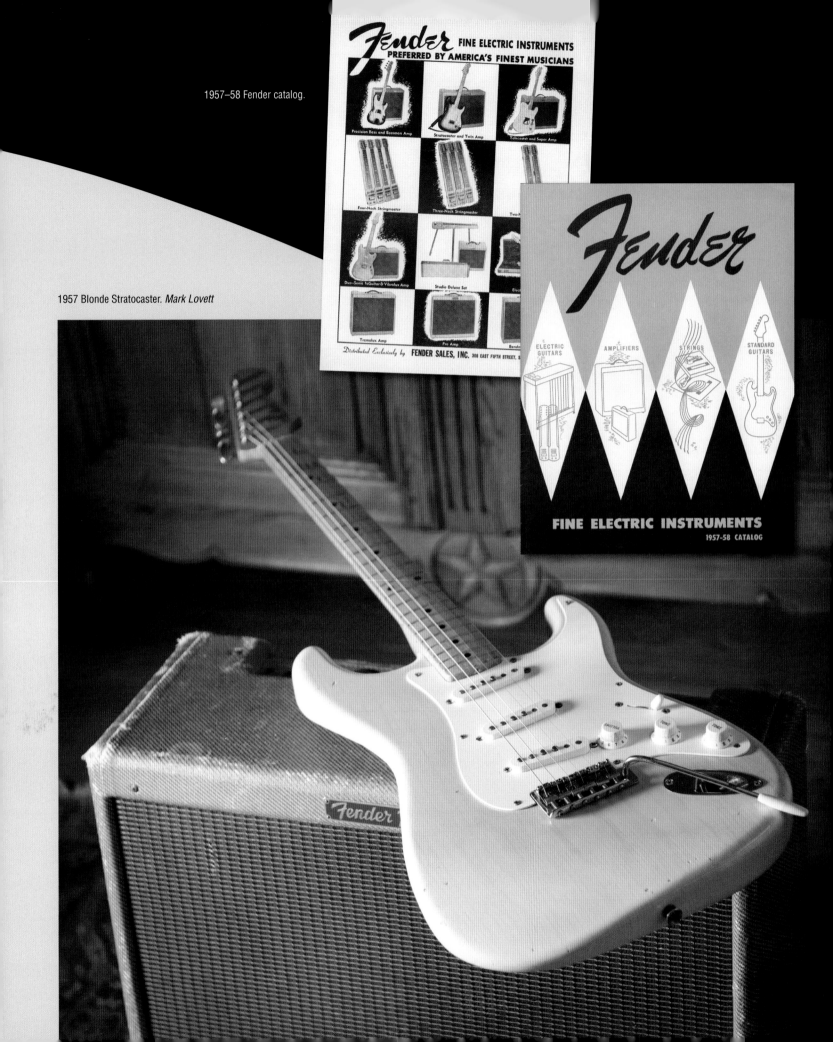

1957–58 Fender catalog.

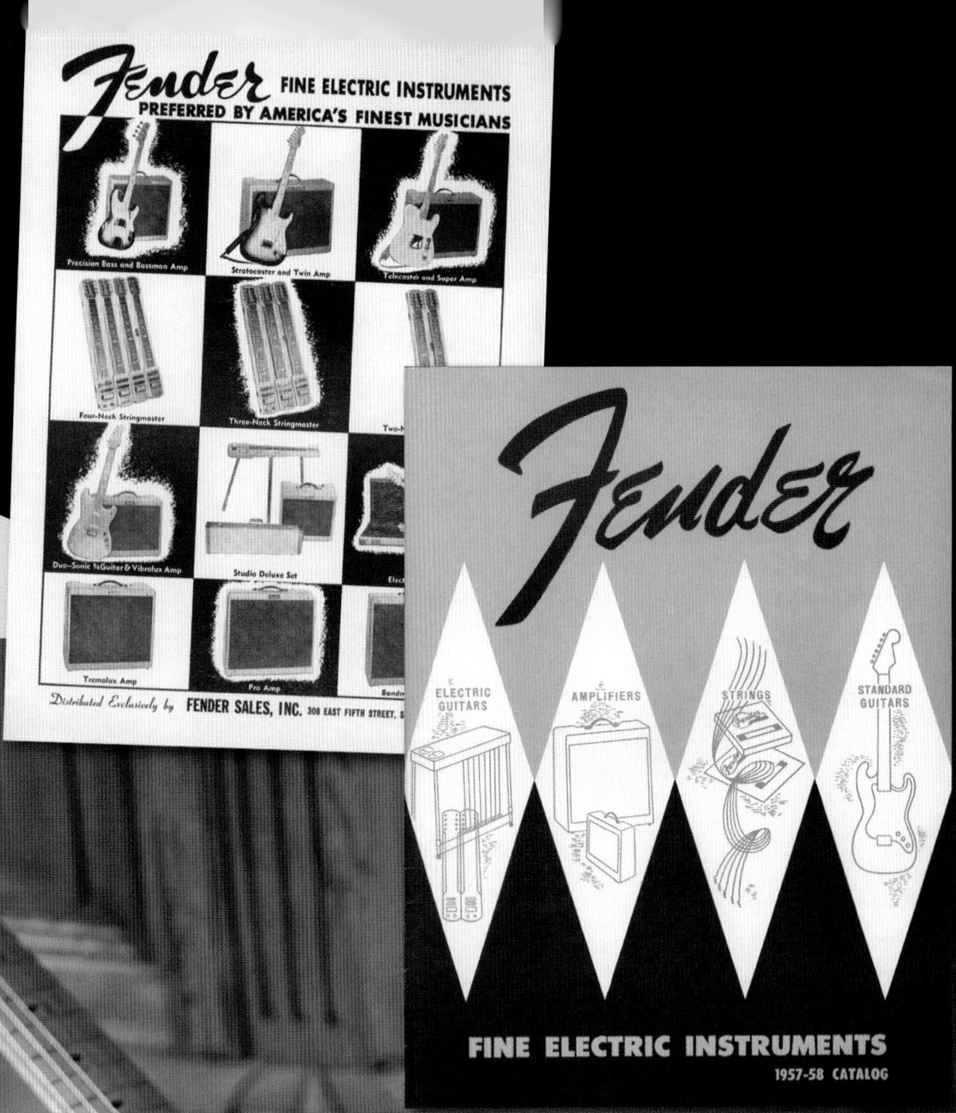

1957 Blonde Stratocaster. *Mark Lovett*

1957 Fender catalog.

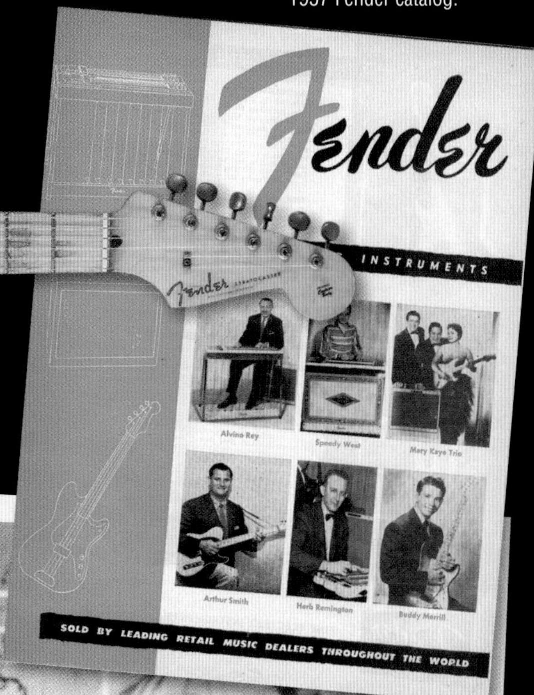

1958 Stratocaster. *Skinner Auctioneers*

The doo-wopping Moonglows harmonize in the 1957 flick *Mister Rock and Roll* with Billy Johnson strumming his Stratocaster. From left, Pete Graves, Bobby Lester, Prentiss Barnes, and Harvey Fuqua join in. *Michael Ochs Archives/Getty Images*

1958 Fender catalog.

1958 Stratocaster, along with Fender Champ amp, polishing cloth, hang tags, and original Fender matches. *Willie's American Guitars/photo by Doug Youland*

VOLUME
TONE
STRINGS

1958 Blonde Stratocaster. *Rumble Seat Music*

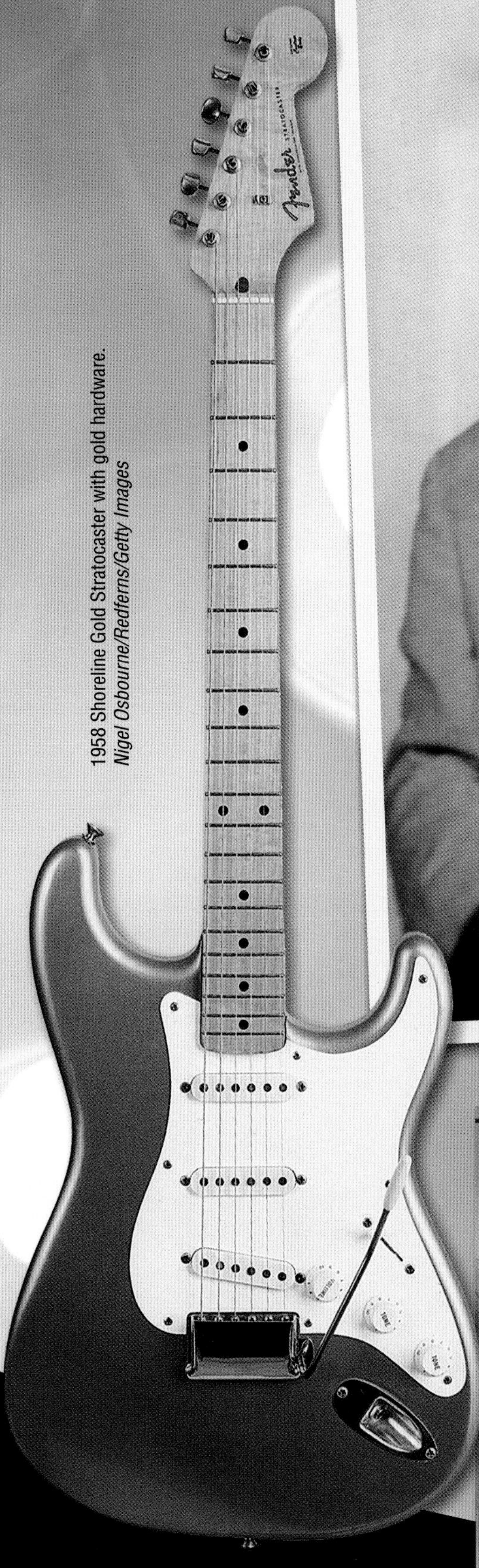

1958 Shoreline Gold Stratocaster with gold hardware.
Nigel Osbourne/Redferns/Getty Images

Curtis Mayfield picks his Stratocaster.

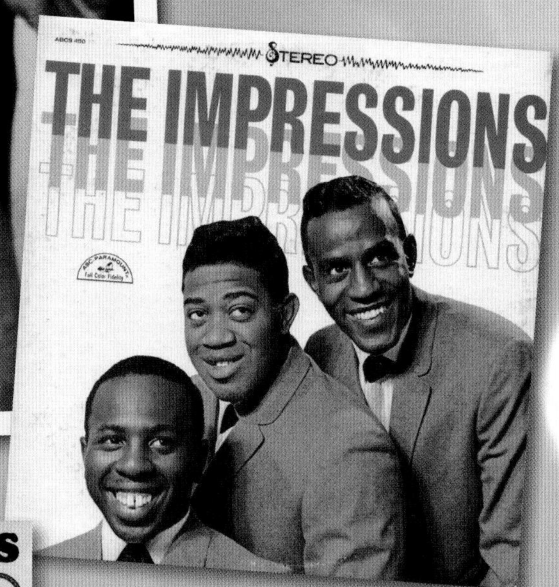

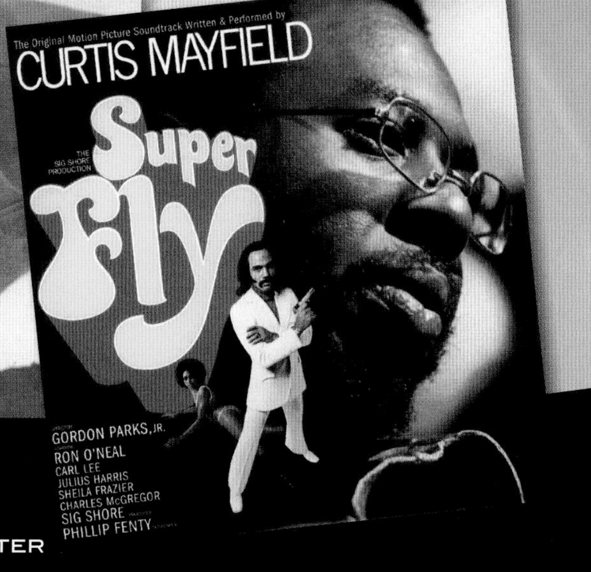

The Original Motion Picture Soundtrack Written & Performed by
CURTIS MAYFIELD
Super Fly
GORDON PARKS, JR.
RON O'NEAL
CARL LEE
JULIUS HARRIS
SHEILA FRAZIER
CHARLES McGREGOR
SIG SHORE
PHILLIP FENTY

1958 Fiesta Red Stratocaster.
Nigel Osbourne/Redferns/Getty Images

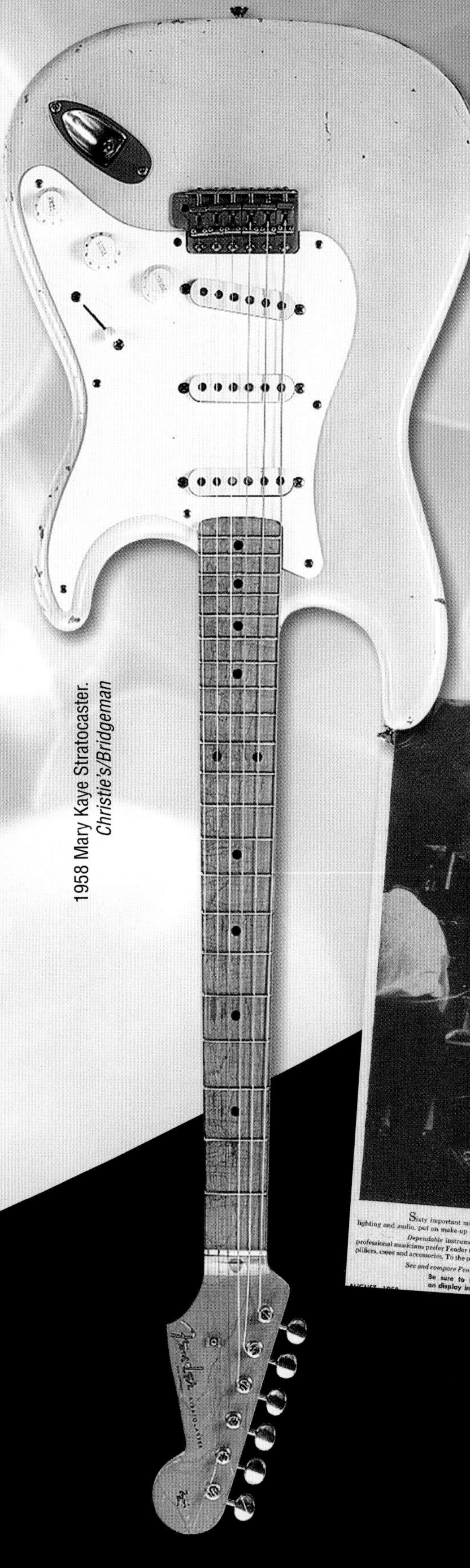

1958 Mary Kaye Stratocaster.
Christie's/Bridgeman

1958 Fender advertisement.

(Continued from page 66)

for promoting this brand that was fast embodying the essence of rock 'n' roll. In truth, however, the inspiration came from a slightly less glamorous source, and one far closer to home.

The firm hired by Fender to undertake more than a decade of intensive promotion, through the company's true "golden age," was the Perine/Jacoby Agency of Newport Beach, California, a small firm headed by Robert Perine and Ned Jacoby, who had set up shop only a year before. Perine, who had learned to play the guitar a little while serving in the navy in World War II, told of his first encounter with the young guitar company in a piece he wrote for *Vintage Guitar* magazine in May 2003:

"After a Rickenbacker ad I designed for F. C. Hall appeared in *Music Trades Magazine*, I received a call from Stan Compton at Fender Sales, asking me if I would be willing to do something similar for Fender. Like your average citizen in those days, I hadn't heard of Rickenbacker or Fender guitars, yet I jumped at the chance to lend my graphic design skills to a product I had learned a little about in the service."

Of his inspiration for the legendary ad series, Perine wrote, "I conceived the idea of doing a series of ads that would photographically show this relationship of guitar to player. Wouldn't it be interesting, I thought, to depict musicians of all ages unwilling to leave their wonderful, precious Fender guitars unattended. Why not play with this idea of attachment run amok, the needle hitting the peg on the possessiveness meter?" Over the years, following this theme, the Perine/Jacoby print ads showed Fender guitars strapped to the backs of jet pilots, scuba divers, downhill skiers, tank commanders, football players, motorcyclists, and parachutists; in the hands of skateboarders, mid-curl surfers, subway passengers, and country pickers on foot amid city traffic (the latter two apparently gig-bound, each with a tweed amp also in hand); and perched on their own in a wide assortment of unlikely settings—though invariably with a youthful slant, or an exciting or romantic activity going on as backdrop. On occasion, later in the 1960s, Perine even featured his own daughter in some of the catalog shots, noting a particular favorite in 1968 that showed her climbing into his own red Thunderbird with a red Fender Coronado in hand.

As the "You won't part with yours either" series has, in essence, become part of the universal consciousness of guitar fans today, any real appreciation of its success, in terms of style and creativity, is aided by a revisit of the promotional efforts of other major guitar manufacturers of the day. Up until the Beatles appeared in its ads of the mid-1960s, Gretsch was mainly pitching its wares with jazz players like Jimmy Webster and Al Caiola, and of course pop-country-jazz star Chet Atkins, all respectable players but not quite rock 'n' roll. Gibson ads boasted a lot of Les Paul and Mary Ford, of course, as well as other artists with signature models, such as Herb Ellis, Barney Kessel, and Trini Lopez, but even into the early 1960s the emphasis remained extremely staid and traditional, artists frequently attired in jackets and ties, often politely perched on stools to play their guitars. Even Fender's own ads immediately pre-Perine/Jacoby now appear a world away in style and attitude: the politely dressed young Lawrence Welk guitarist, Buddy Merrill, for example, gently fondling a Stratocaster in a prominent full-page print ad from December 1956.

By setting Fender products among the youth of the day—and amid some exciting activities too—Perine/Jacoby thrust the image of the electric guitar manufacturer firmly forward and helped to establish Fender as a new breed, a brand that was ready for whatever the rapidly changing music scene would throw at it next. The new Fender Stratocaster was perfectly cut out to wear the mantle of "guitar of the future," certainly, but Don Randall's deft promotional guidance, and the creative work of the Perine/Jacoby Agency in particular, really secured its long-standing place in the market, and right at the peak of the guitar boom too.

Woods Evolve: Ash to Alder, Maple to Rosewood

The Stratocaster's specs didn't change as much over its first few years of production as did those of the Telecaster. We have already mentioned the change in plastics that occurred over the course of the early production models of 1954. The next significant change of spec came with the uptake of alder as a primary body wood in 1956, with ash remaining in use mainly in Blonde custom-colored Strats. Leo Fender was always clearly concerned with consistency and basic quality, and alder clearly appeared a suitable substitute for the more highly figured swamp ash, which was getting more difficult to obtain in adequate supplies. While ash's broad grain was still readily apparent under the Telecaster's standard blonde finish, and that of the few Strats sprayed in the same color, alder looked perfectly good under a sunburst or opaque finish and was also easier to obtain in adequate supplies of suitably light timber. The change did alter the Stratocaster's core tone somewhat, but this was a sonic shift rather than a decline, as alder itself has many desirable sonic properties (as discussed in more detail in the "Tone & Construction" chapter).

Although it's less obvious at a glance, the Stratocaster's neck profile evolved rather steadily throughout the 1950s, too, parallel to that of the Telecaster. The chunky, rounded C shape of the early necks segued into a beefy V profile in 1955, which slimmed down through 1956 and 1957, then flattened into a slim, then slimmer, C shape as 1958 rolled into 1959 and 1960. From around mid-1959 to mid-1961 or so the Stratocaster's neck shape reflected a contemporary predilection for extremely thin necks, which were clearly considered "fast" at the time. Interestingly, many Gibson electrics, notably the Les Paul and SG, were given similarly thin necks over roughly the same period of time.

Alongside the change in neck profiles, the shape and depth of the Stratocaster body's ribcage and forearm contours evolved

(Continued on page 96)

1959 Stratocaster. *Brunk Auctions*

1959 Fender catalog.

1959 Blonde Stratocaster. *Rumble Seat Music*

1959 Blonde Stratocaster with black-anodized pickguard.
Rumble Seat Music

1959 Mary Kaye Stratocaster. *Rumble Seat Music*

1959 Burgundy Mist Stratocaster.
Nigel Osbourne/Redferns/Getty Images

1959 Sonic Blue Stratocaster.
Nigel Osbourne/Redferns/Getty Images

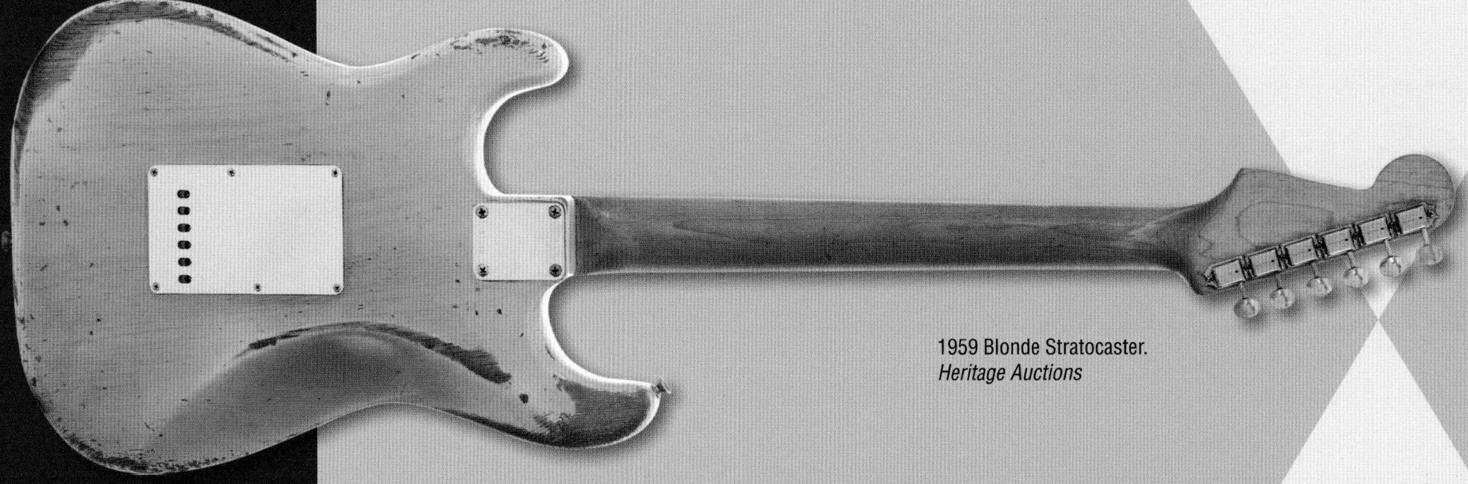

1959 Blonde Stratocaster.
Heritage Auctions

1959 Blonde Stratocaster.
Heritage Auctions

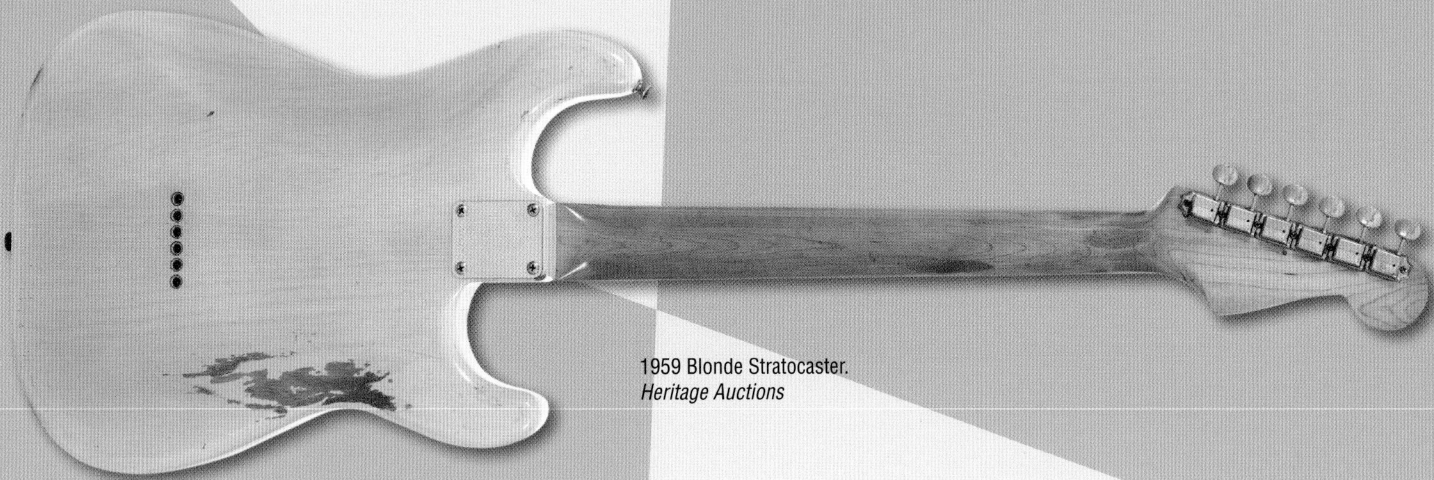

1959 Blonde Stratocaster.
Heritage Auctions

1959 left-handed Blonde Stratocaster.
Heritage Auctions

1960 Stratocaster. *Mark Lovett*

Tex-Mex singer-songwriter Freddy Fender gets happy with his Stratocaster and Fender piggy-back amp, circa 1960.
Michael Ochs Archives/Getty Images

1961 left-handed Stratocaster.
Rumble Seat Music

VOLUME
TONE

Buddy Holly

Buddy Holly picks his Strat on stage in March 1958. *Harry Hammond/V&A Images/Getty Images*

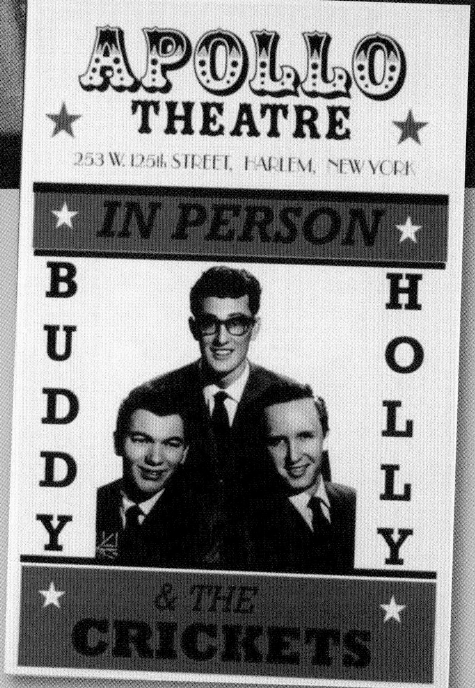

Beaming out from photos with his thick-rimmed glasses and the bright smile of a schoolboy on picture day, Buddy Holly might not appear like much of a rebel. But Holly was nothing less than a rock 'n' roll revolutionary with a knack for innovation in just about everything he did. In an age when recording artists were still largely packaged by record company execs and backed by studio house bands and Tin Pan Alley songwriters, Buddy Holly and the Crickets established a template that would define the genuine rock artist: they wrote their own songs, played their own recording dates, and—with the aid of an occasional sideman—took it all out on the road too.

Holly's playing was likewise innovative, blending chunky rhythm and high-string lead work in a style that owed an equal tip of the hat to country, R&B, and rockabilly (and to his predecessor, Bo Diddley, among others). Amid all this avant garde behavior, his guitar choice was radical too: while other heroes on the burgeoning rock 'n' roll scene were playing Gretsches or big-bodied Gibson archtops, Holly—with a loan from his brother Larry—purchased a new Fender Stratocaster, a guitar that had been designed for country players and released onto the market just a year before. In doing so, Holly (born Charles Hardin Holley) also became the first household name in popular music to perform regularly on a Stratocaster.

Holly played his first Stratocaster, a late-1954 or early-1955 model, for about two years and used it to record his first hits, including "That'll Be the Day" and "Peggy Sue," before it was stolen from a tour bus in Michigan in the fall of 1957 during DJ Alan Freed's "Biggest Show of Stars" package tour. The 1957 Stratocaster that he acquired to replace it, however, purchased hurriedly in Detroit in time to make the show that evening, is possibly the most recognizable of all of the four or five Strats Holly owned. Another two-tone sunburst model with maple fingerboard, it appears in several popular photos of Holly performing in 1957 and 1958 and is notable for the wear that soon developed in the covers of the middle and neck pickups just below the high E string, which eventually revealed the black-fiber coil formers beneath.

This iconic 1957 Stratocaster accompanied Holly on many of his most prominent performances of the time and certainly helped to establish Fender's modernistic new model as a standard of solidbody design. It was played on TV appearances on *The Ed Sullivan Show* and *The Arthur Murray Dance Party* (with a tweed Fender Bassman amp visible in the background, finally earning a little spotlight time for the backline), and traveled to the UK with Holly for his historic British tour. In April 1958, Holly lost yet another Stratocaster when the 1957 instrument was stolen from the band's station wagon during a stop at a restaurant in St. Louis, Missouri. The star acquired at least two or three more Strats before his death in 1959, one of the last of which is on display at the Buddy Holly Center in his hometown of Lubbock, Texas.

★ TEEN-AGE SPECIAL ★
SUNDAY, JAN. 25, 7:30 to 11:00
$1.50 a person. Parents invited, no charge. Dress right to feel right.
This 5 Great Attractions - - In Person.
WINTER DANCE PARTY
BUDDY HOLLY AND THE CRICKETS
"PEGGY SUE"
BIG BOPPER
"CHANTILLY LACE"
THESE TOP RECORDING STARS IN PERSON
RITCHIE VALENS
"DONNA"
"COME ON, LET'S GO"
DION AND The BELMONTS
"I WONDER WHY"
Extra Attraction
FRANKIE SARDO
New Hit "TAKE-OUT"
AP665 Printed in UK

James J. Kriegsmann N.Y.
CLEAR LAKE IOWA
THE FINEST BANDS
Surf
THE FINEST PEOPLE
Fri., Jan. 30th MIDWEST CARAVAN
Sat., Jan. 31st RAY LEWIS And His Orchestra
MONDAY, FEBRUARY 2nd — DANCING 8 TO 12 P. M.
WINTER DANCE PARTY
BUDDY HOLLY AND THE CRICKETS
"PEGGY SUE"
BIG BOPPER
"CHANTILLY LACE"
RITCHIE VALENS
"DONNA"
"COME ON, LET'S GO"
DION AND The BELMONTS
"I WONDER WHY"
Extra Attraction
FRANKIE SARDO
New Hit "TAKE OUT"
For Ages 12 to 21. This All-Star Cast
Bob Hale to M.C. & Spin Records. Adm. $1.25; Checking 10c
KISS

Dick Dale and His Del-Tones played music by surfers for surfers—and they wanted it loud. Armed with a piggyback Fender Showman and his trademark Fender Stratocaster, a.k.a. "the Beast," Dale and his band rocked coastal California ballrooms and school gymnasiums. Here, they play at the Rendezvous Ballroom in Balboa, California.

2004 Dick Dale Signature Chartreuse Sparkle Stratocaster. *Fender Musical Instruments Corporation*

Arguments about who originated surf guitar continue to rage, but for pure kinetic energy few would argue with crowning Dick Dale the "King of the Surf Guitar." Dale enjoyed a career resurgence after his signature tune, the eastern-inflected "Misirlou," was featured prominently in the 1994 film *Pulp Fiction*, but from late 1959 to early 1961 Dale (born Richard Monsour) and his Del-Tones packed the Rendezvous Ballroom in Balboa, California, and for a time after that, the Pasadena Civic Auditorium with upward of 3,000 to 4,000 young patrons nearly every weekend night of the year. To satisfy their lust for action, he generated furious levels of energy—and copious amounts of sheer volume—to translate surfing's extreme physical experience into a representative musical performance. Naturally, Dale's guitar choice was an important part of the process, but the need to satisfy such vast crowds with the volume and power that the music demanded meant that he also became one of the first proponents of the entire rig, and arguably the first artist to front a truly arena-worthy backline.

Fender's Jazzmaster and Jaguar have come to be known as classic surf guitars, alongside the Mosrites that other artists, most notably the Ventures, also gravitated toward; but Dick Dale played a Stratocaster from the outset of his professional career and has stuck with it for fifty-plus years. Having started out as an aspiring country singer and guitarist, Dale was drawn to the Strat shortly before solidifying his stance as a surf guitarist. As a left-hander, he played the guitar strung "upside down," the way many lefties would approach the instrument upon flipping over a

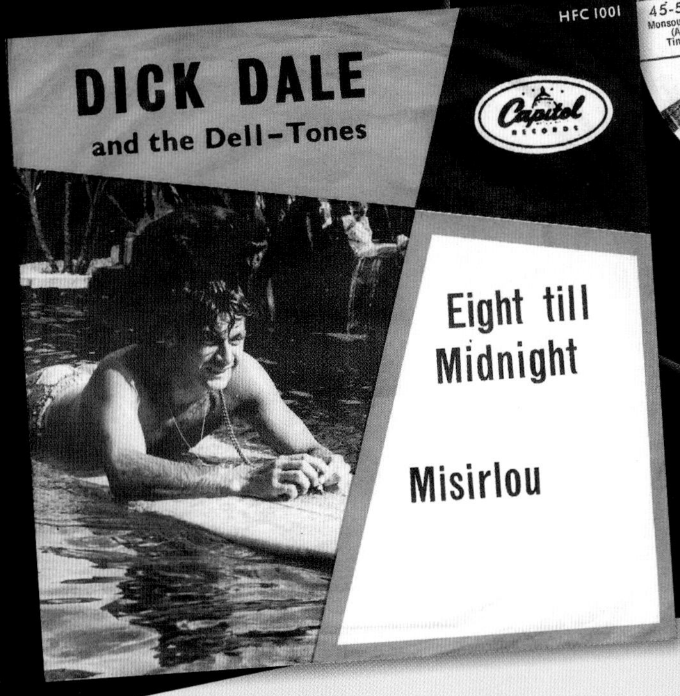

right-handed guitar. After initially being given a right-handed Stratocaster by Leo Fender in the late 1950s and told to "beat it to death," as Dale recalls on his website, DickDale.com, he moved over to left-handed Strats (most notably a chartreuse metalflake example known as "The Beast"), but continued to string the guitar with the low E on the bottom.

Other than this quirk, Dale's use of a Strat for the bright, cutting tones of surf guitar really isn't all that unusual. The model is designed to excel in these tones just as much as the Jaguar and Jazzmaster. The bigger part of Dale's sonic revolution came in his amp of choice and his promotion of that super-wet, reverb-laden sound, although it was not always thus. In order to broadcast his big sound to the big crowds he was drawing, Dale used his budding relationship with Leo Fender to acquire a suitable amp. Fender had always turned directly to musicians for feedback about his developments, and Dale's pleas for more punching power made an impression. Accounts of how much input the guitarist himself had on the development of the Showman amp vary greatly (with Dale's own recollections often putting him right there at the drawing board, while those of other Fender employees occasionally minimize his role), but the powerful new Fender model, introduced in the new Blonde Tolex covering in 1960, was undoubtedly designed specifically to belt the young surfing guitarist's music to the masses.

As wet as the surf sound eventually became, however, Dale's first hit single, "Let's Go Trippin'"; his entire first album, *Surfer's Choice*; and his legendary early Rendezvous Ballroom shows were all performed *sans* reverb. Once the Fender Reverb Unit hit the streets in early 1962, though, with prototypes having been road-tested by Dale, there was no turning back from the big splash.

The Ventures

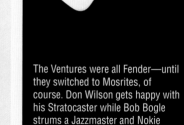

The Ventures were all Fender—until they switched to Mosrites, of course. Don Wilson gets happy with his Stratocaster while Bob Bogle strums a Jazzmaster and Nokie Edwards holds his bass. *Michael Ochs Archives/Getty Images*

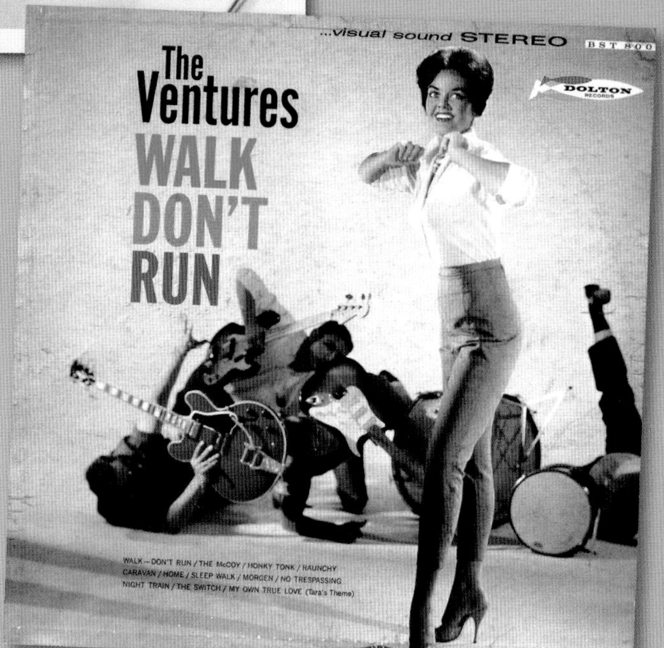

Don Wilson and Bob Bogle were Seattle masonry workers who played some guitar after hours just for fun. In 1958, they decided to put together a band, which they humbly named the Versatones before changing their moniker to the Ventures. Their guitar-driven instrumental tunes were almost instant radio-friendly hits, and even though neither Wilson nor Bogle surfed, their songs soon became a soundtrack to the surfer world, along with cuts by Dick Dale, the Surfaris, and others. Whichever way you looked at it, the Ventures made a splash.

In 1960, they recorded a hopped-up version of "Walk Don't Run." The song had been penned by guitarist Johnny Smith and recorded by Chet Atkins, but it was the Ventures' version that became a mammoth hit. Still, the group didn't really hit their stride until bassist Nokie Edwards moved over to guitar duties in 1962, with Bogle taking up the bass. They went on to sell more than 110 million albums and log a whopping 37 albums on the *Billboard* charts. In a short time, they had become the world's biggest-selling guitar instrumental act.

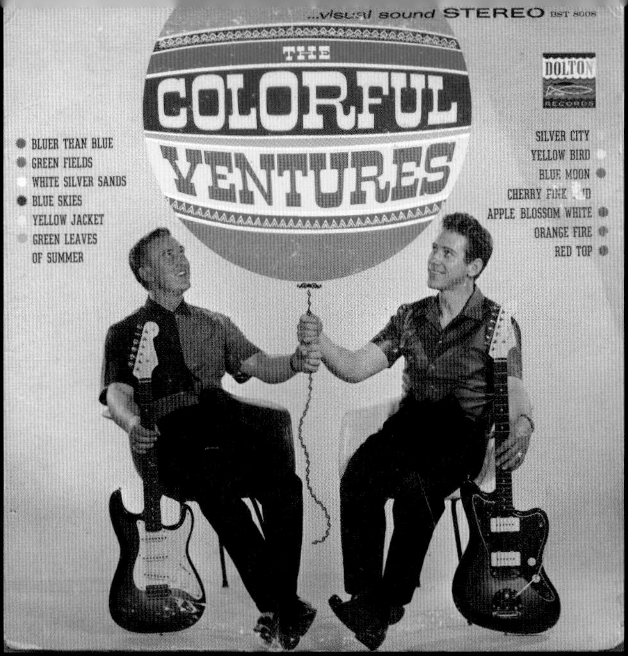

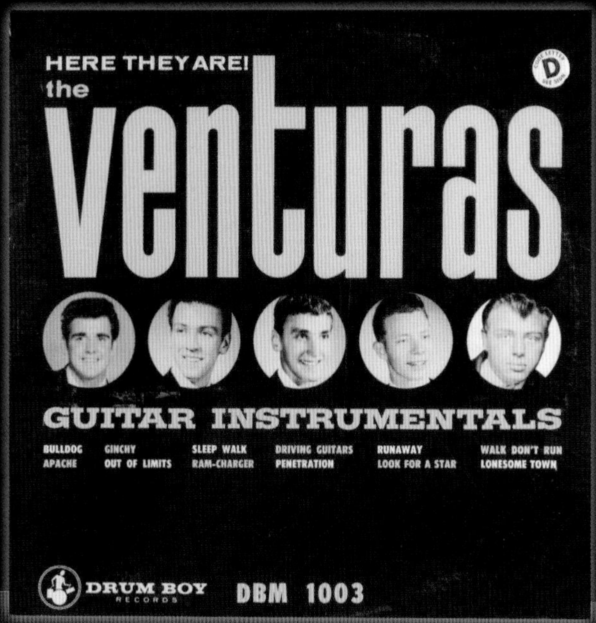

Early on, the Ventures played Fender guitars, crafting their trebly, twangy sound with Stratocasters, Jazzmasters, and Precision Basses. On many of their album covers and singles picture sleeves, they were pictured proudly toting those Fender products, such as on *The Ventures, Bobby Vee Meets the Ventures* and *The Colorful Ventures*. Their sound and their songs provided inspiration for many a youth yearning to learn guitar to save his paper-route money for a Strat.

Ironically, Fender never quite realized what a good thing it had in the Ventures. The company let a huge promotional opportunity slip through its corporate fingers and into the grasp of the miniscule guitar-making firm of Mosrite. Shortly after his move to guitar, Edwards borrowed an early Joe Maphis model from Mosrite founder Semie Moseley to test out in the studio, and he was hooked. Before the end of 1962, Edwards, Bogle, and Wilson began using prototypes of the Ventures model Mosrite guitars and basses, and the line was officially released in 1963. The band's name and popularity helped put Mosrite on the map, even if it wasn't the Ventures model.

Still, the earliest Ventures classics all boasted that Fender sound. The Ventures were often credited as "The Band That Launched a Thousand Bands," and their use of Strats and Jazzmasters launched many thousands of fans. —*Michael Dregni*

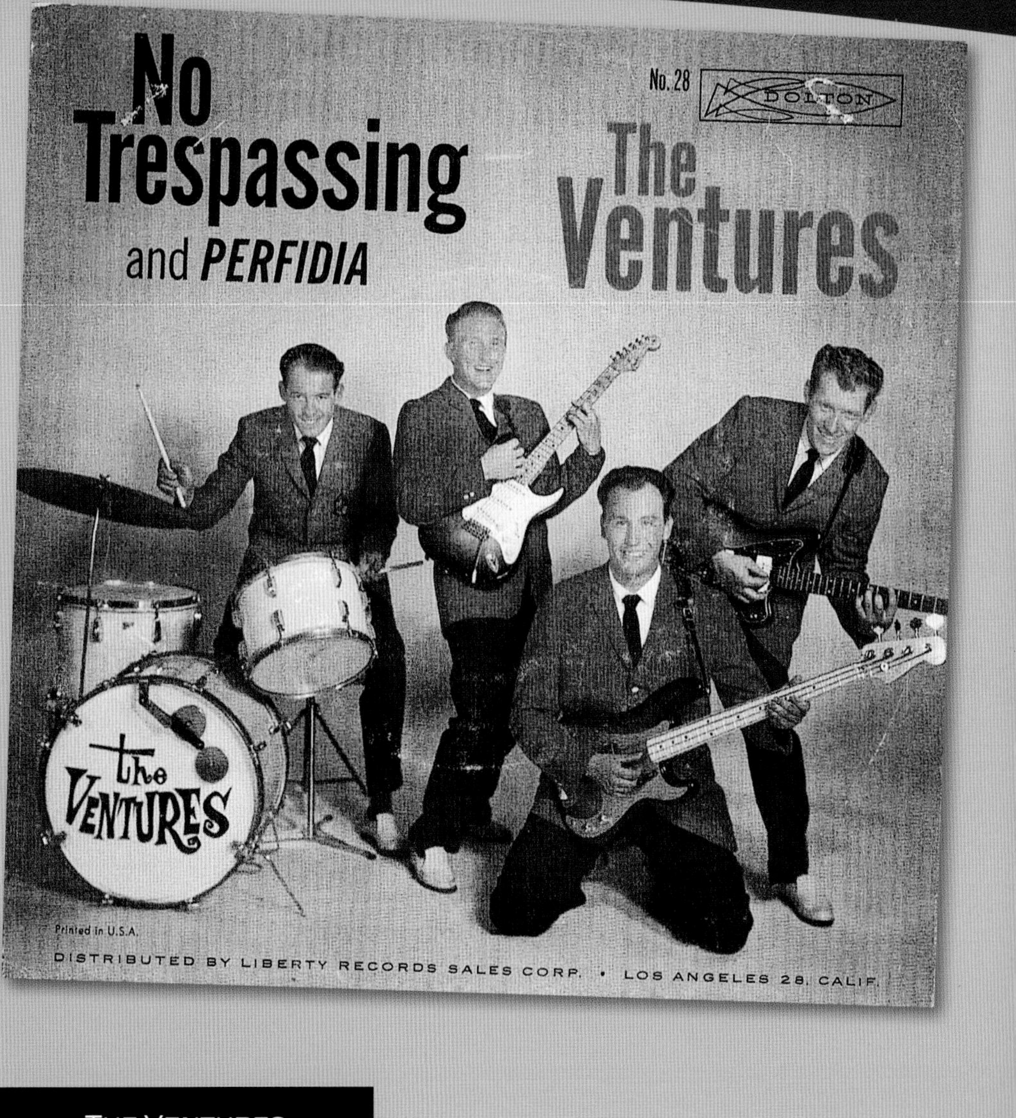

1962–63 Fender catalog.

1962 Sea Foam Green Stratocaster. *Rumble Seat Music*

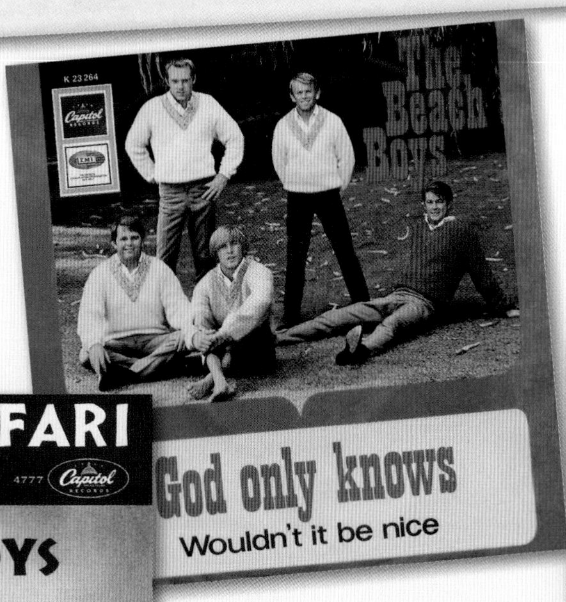

The Beach Boys rehearse at home in Los Angeles in 1962, with Al Jardine toting his Olympic White Strat. From left, Mike Love, Dennis Wilson, Brian Wilson, Jardine, and Carl Wilson. *Michael Ochs Archives/Getty Images*

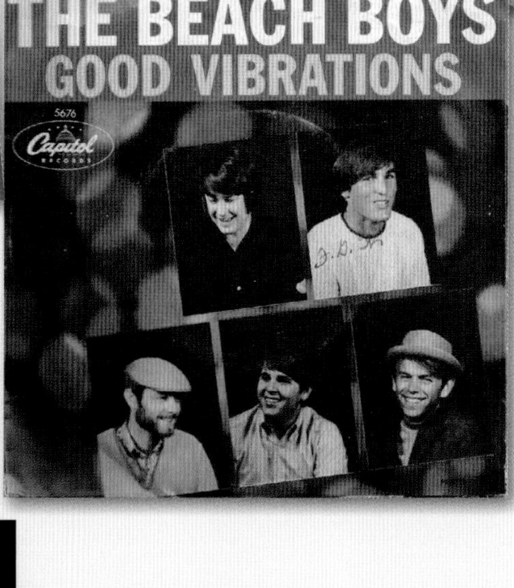

(Continued from page 76)

slightly. Earlier guitars tended to have a greater depth and a more prominent overall curve to these areas, whereas the contours flattened out slightly through the early 1960s and into the middle of the decade. Since these contours were both rough-cut and finished by hand—cut first on the bandsaw following a line of a prescribed angle, then sanded smooth—they always varied somewhat anyway, but their depth over time tended to follow a trajectory toward the more shallow.

As the end of the decade approached, a more noticeable change was visited on the neck of the Stratocaster. A new Fender model, the Jazzmaster, brought a rosewood fingerboard to the Fender stable when it was introduced at the 1958 summer NAMM show, proving a successful test bed for a change that would hit the Stratocaster and Telecaster midway through 1959. Several reasons might have been behind the change of fingerboard woods, and indeed the true motivation might have been a combination of several or all of them. It's likely that Fender felt the more traditional looking and feeling neck was a necessity on any guitar with pretensions toward jazz—the Jazzmaster's original target market—and with any hopes of appealing to the more traditional musicians who played it. It seems that many Fender dealers, however, and hence the reps at Fender Sales, had been inquiring about the availability of a rosewood 'board on the Tele and Strat for some time, and for reasons of their own. The darker neck would ally Fender guitars with more traditional instruments, and therefore make for easier acceptance in corners that were still reticent to embrace the "plank." Simultaneously, it would do away with the detrimental image of the smudged, poorly wearing maple fingerboards that were being seen everywhere by this time, nearly ten years into the life of the Telecasters and five years after the Stratocaster's arrival.

One story, possibly apocryphal, goes that Leo Fender saw a Telecaster in the hands of a performer on TV with dark, worn patches on its maple fingerboard and was swayed to take up the rosewood option out of dismay at this grimy look. Although maple is virtually as hard as rosewood, it is certainly much lighter; maple 'boards were finished with a clear-coat of nitrocellulose lacquer to seal the light wood and prevent it from absorbing dirt, but nitro's resistance to finger wear only goes so far. The grimy patches on these fingerboards gradually appeared as the finish was worn away beneath the strings and the players' fingertips, and once that coat of finish was gone, dirt, sweat, and grease took hold and began to discolor the exposed wood. Whatever the impetus, the rosewood fingerboards brought a new look to the Stratocaster, as well as other Fenders, and would serve as a demarcation point between the guitars of the 1950s and those of the early 1960s.

For about the first two and a half years, these separate fingerboards were sawn with a flat underside and glued to a flat-neck face, a style that has since been dubbed the "slab board" for its thick, flat-bottomed appearance. Partway through 1962 Fender introduced the practice of radiusing the face of the maple neck as well as both sides of the fingerboard, which enabled the use of a thinner piece of rosewood and created what is now often referred to as a "laminated" or "round-lam" fingerboard. (By request from the mid-1960s, and as an official option from 1967, maple fingerboards would again be available, but until 1969 such necks were made much like the rosewood fingerboards, with a separately milled piece of maple glued to the face of the neck, a construction now known as a "maple cap" neck.)

Many players have expressed a preference for the earlier "slabboard" necks, usually in the belief that the thicker piece of rosewood is somehow superior. In a recent discussion about all things vintage-Fender, however, Fender Custom Shop master builder Chris Fleming expressed his predilection for round-lam rosewood 'boards. "Somebody asked me why I thought Leo decided to do round lams," Fleming explained, "and although I can't know for sure, I think it was for a couple of reasons. One is that he liked the idea of the maple being more of a majority of the wood, and he liked the idea that it was kind of a custom way to do it; it was proprietary. And I'd also like to think that he liked the sound of it. I feel like the slab 'board was the way that they did it because they had to figure out how to do it quickly. Then they had to tool up to make the rounded 'board and never turned back."

Considered in this light, it's clear that the thinner, rounded rosewood 'board used after mid-1962 took more work to produce, and the earlier flat-bottomed 'board never encompassed so thick a piece of rosewood that it would have been significantly costlier, from a lumber-supply perspective, than the thinner board. In any case, Fleming, for one, declares the tonal difference between the two to be negligible, if detectible at all.

Along with the rosewood fingerboard came off-white "clay" position-marker dots, which have come to represent another of the hallmarks of the pre-CBS Stratocaster. These were first inlaid in the same size and pattern as the black plastic dots that preceded them on maple fingerboards, namely with a wider spacing between the two twelfth-fret dots. In the latter half of 1963, the two twelfth-fret dots were moved slightly closer together. Another appointment change that accompanied the rosewood fingerboard was the new three-ply pickguard mounted with eleven screws, replacing the single-ply white plastic guard mounted with eight screws. Ostensibly white with a black center layer, the new guard was made from celluloid (aka nitrate) and had a slight greenish tint.

Add them together and these minor alterations in the formula—the rosewood fingerboard, clay dots, and "green guard"—are the obvious signs of guitars from the final era of the pre-CBS Stratocaster, which ran from around mid-1959 to mid-1964. (Although the clay dots and celluloid pickguard weren't replaced until early 1965, with pearloid and plastic respectively, a change of headstock decal to the new-styled "Fender" logo in late summer 1964 tends to mark the end of the pre-CBS era for many collectors.)

(Continued on page 107)

1962 Fiesta Red Stratocaster. *Heritage Auctions*

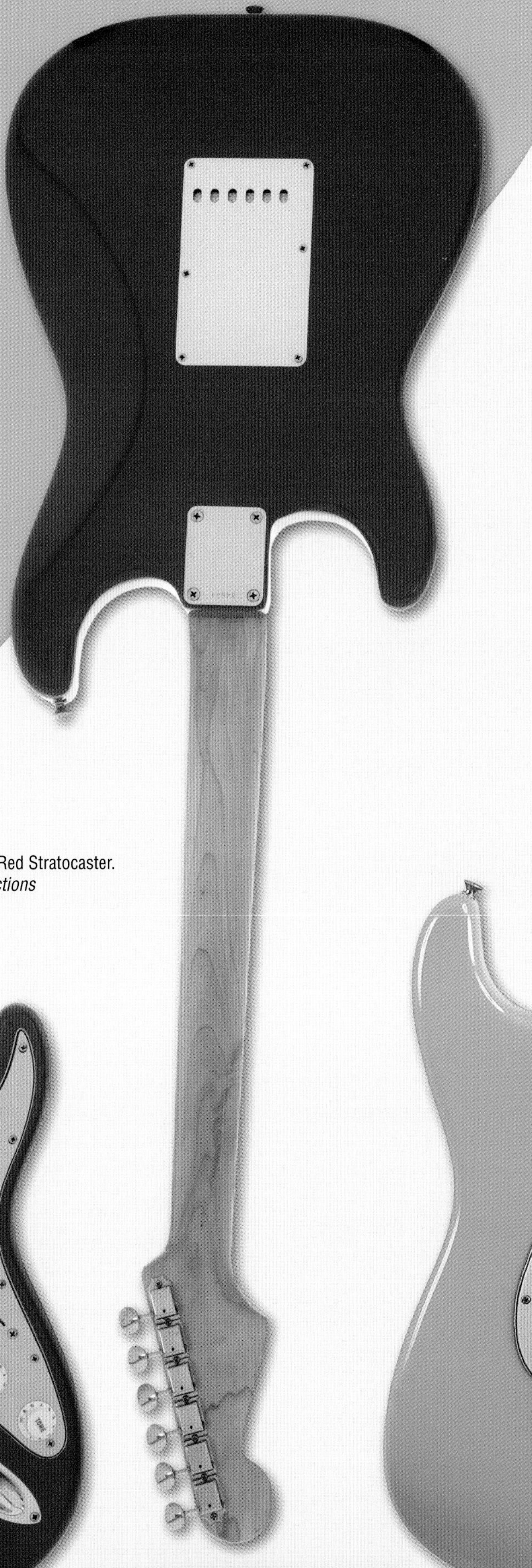

A 1962 Sea Foam Green Stratocaster with gold hardware. *Nigel Osbourne/ Redferns/Getty Images*

Hank Marvin

Hank Marvin and the Shadows with one of Marvin's famous red Strats in the foreground.

Hank Marvin's 1959 Stratocaster with gold hardware, the first Strat imported directly into England. The guitar has since been restored. *Nigel Osbourne/ Redferns/Getty Images*

Most of the early stars of the electric guitar were American musicians, an understandable phenomenon given rock 'n' roll's birth on the left side of the Atlantic *and* a ban on U.S. imports to the United Kingdom through much of the 1950s that deprived British musicians of American-made guitars. Shortly before this embargo was lifted in 1960, though, Hank Marvin received a guitar that would become famous as the first Stratocaster owned by an English guitarist. It was brought into the country by singer Cliff Richard, whom Marvin backed in the Shadows.

Marvin was already on his way to stardom by this time, thanks to the early instrumental hits the Shadows had logged, in addition to the band's hits with Richard, but with red Strat in hand the lanky, bespectacled guitarist forged a more recognizable identity on both sides of the pond and went on to become one of the most influential early British rock 'n' rollers. With hits split nearly fifty-fifty between Shadows instrumental releases and vocal numbers recorded as Cliff Richard and the Shadows, Marvin was at the forefront of sixty-nine British Top 40 chart singles, a number that includes a whopping twelve No. 1 hits. The most seminal of these, the classic "Apache" among them, were laid down with his '59 Stratocaster.

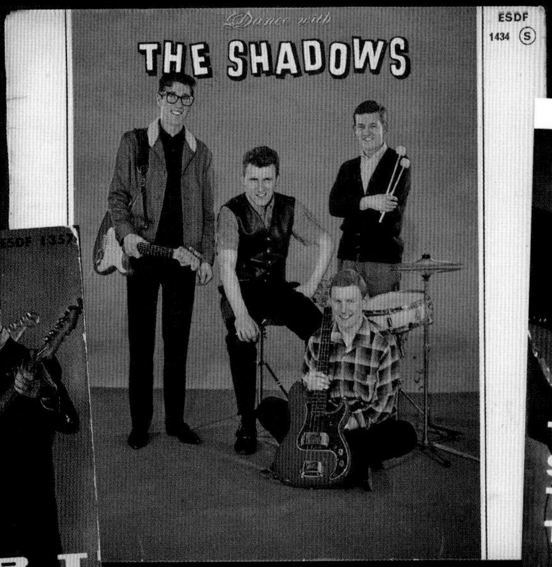

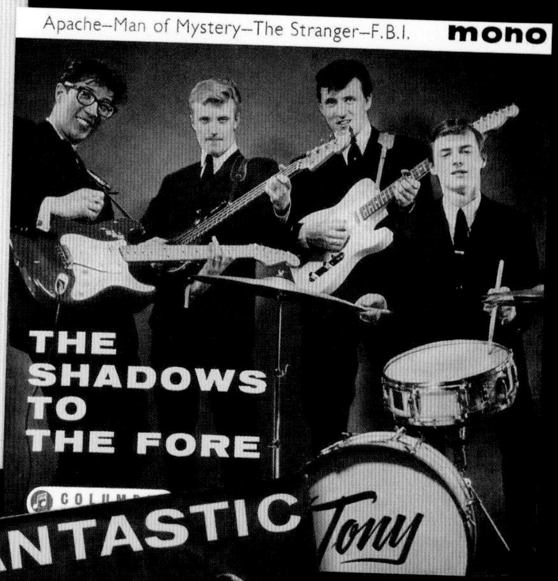

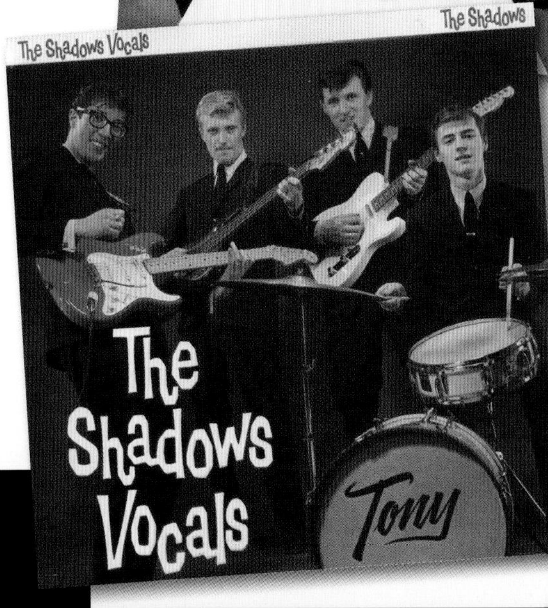

Marvin's acquisition of said Strat involves a now-famous case of mistaken identity. Ironically, Buddy Holly was an early influence, and Marvin says that hearing one of Holly's songs on the radio inspired him to drop the banjo in favor of the guitar, but American rock 'n' rollers were near-mythical creatures at the time, and Marvin had no idea what guitar Holly played. A fan of James Burton's work with Ricky Nelson, Marvin discovered that Burton played a Fender but didn't know precisely what model. While perusing a catalog in 1959 with his front man Richards, Marvin spotted a red Stratocaster with gold-plated hardware. "I decided that had to be the model he played," Marvin told this writer in a 1994 interview for Teletext, "because it was the most expensive one, and I figured James Burton must play the top model." An upcoming trip that Richards was making to the United States afforded Marvin the chance to acquire a guitar just like the one in the catalog image with which he had become besotted. Weeks later the singer returned with red Strat in hand. Marvin didn't discover until a short while later that James Burton in fact played a Telecaster, but by this time it didn't matter—the Strat was the guitar for him.

And what a fortuitous error it was. The Stratocaster's bright, well-defined sound, and its versatile vibrato system in particular, became a major part of Marvin's playing style. He used the vibrato bar on just about everything he played, applying it to subtle tremulous wiggles and deeper, emotive bends that evoked a rich, atmospheric tone through the tape echo unit he used between guitar and Vox AC15 amplifier (later an AC30). All told, this setup established a sound that Pete Townshend, Mark Knopfler, and even Frank Zappa have acknowledged as a major influence.

Marvin's original '59 Stratocaster is now in the possession of Shadows bandmate Bruce Welch, although Hank has continued to play Strats—alongside the occasional Burns guitar—throughout his career.

1963 Candy Apple Red Stratocaster.
Mark Lovett

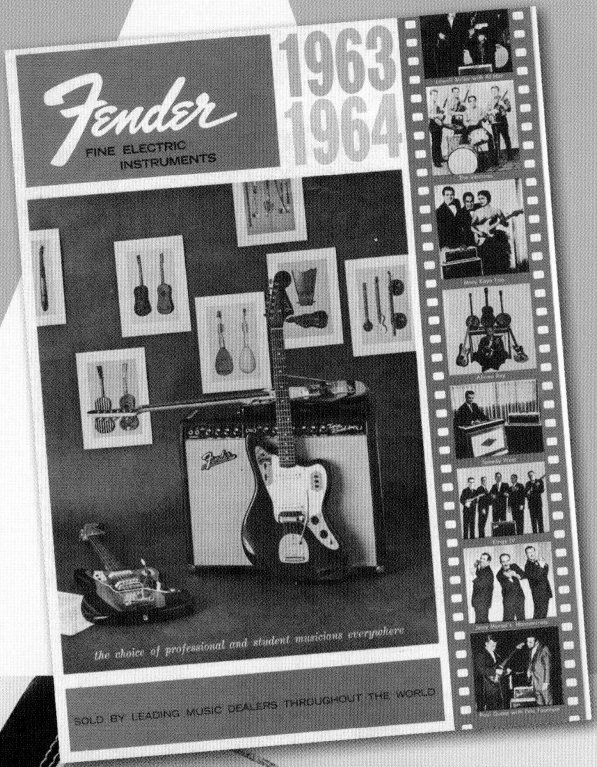

1963–64 Fender catalog.

1962 Fiesta Red Stratocaster.
Rumble Seat Music

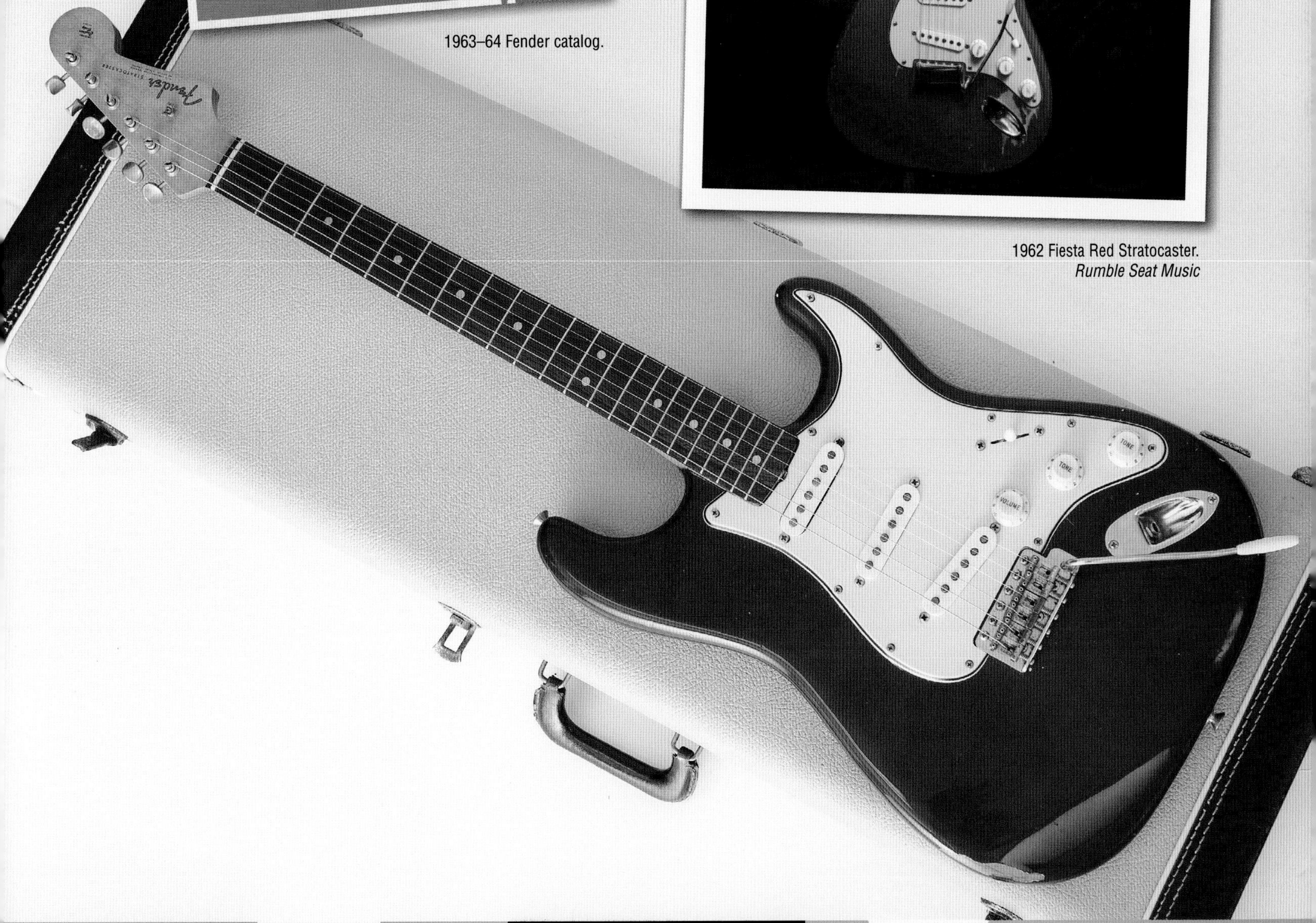

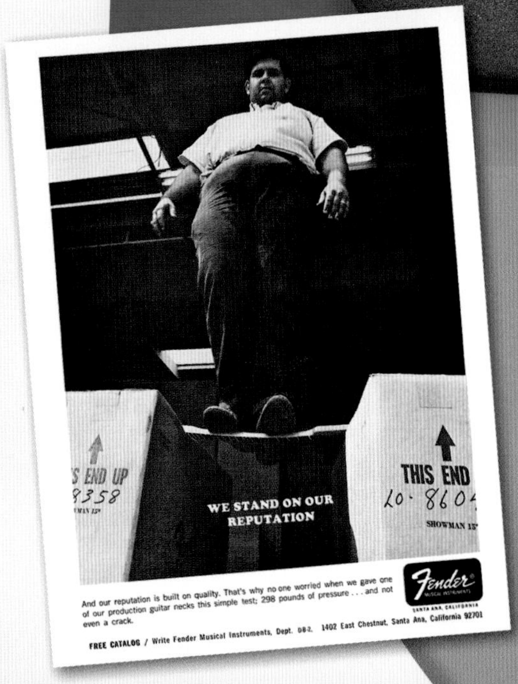

S END UP
8358
THIS END
LO-8604
SHOWMAN 15"
WE STAND ON OUR REPUTATION
And our reputation is built on quality. That's why no one worried when we gave one of our production guitar necks this simple test; 298 pounds of pressure . . . and not even a crack.
Fender
MUSICAL INSTRUMENTS
SANTA ANA, CALIFORNIA
FREE CATALOG / Write Fender Musical Instruments, Dept. DB-2. 1402 East Chestnut, Santa Ana, California 92701

1963 Gold Sparkle Stratocaster.
Christie's/Bridgeman

1960s advertisement
for Fender's truss-rod
reinforced necks.

1963 Blonde Stratocaster.
Rumble Seat Music

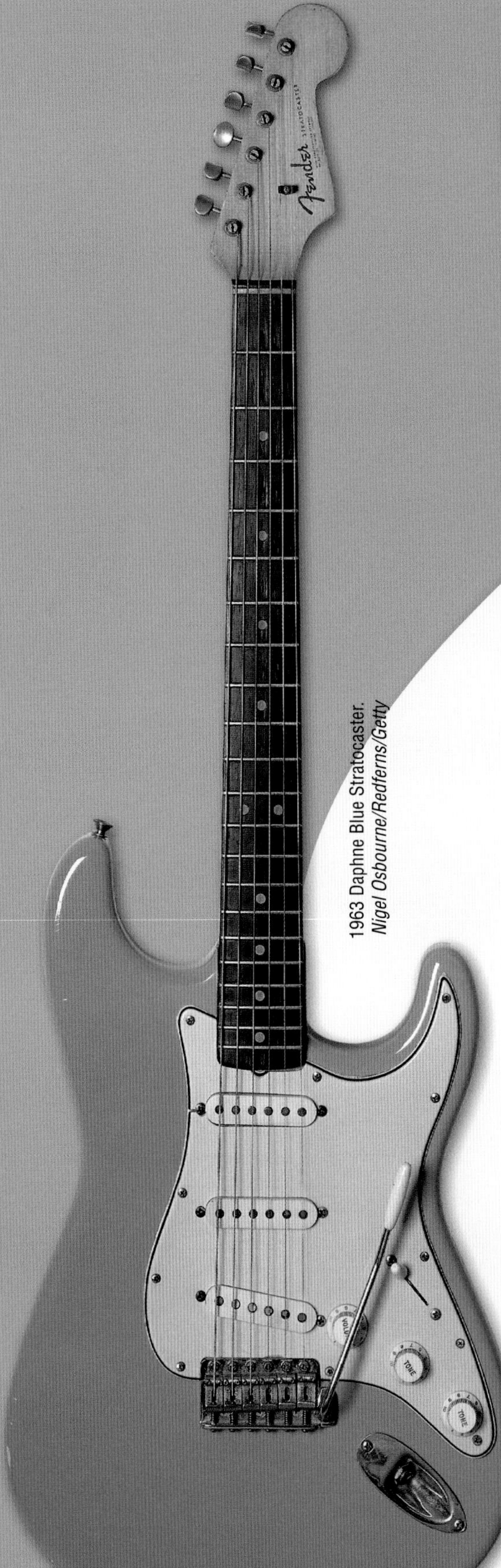

1963 Daphne Blue Stratocaster.
Nigel Osbourne/Redferns/Getty

1963 Sparkle Blue Stratocaster.
Garrett Tung/Boingosaurus Music

1963 Blonde Stratocaster owned by Philip Sayce.
Rob Monk/Guitarist Magazine/Getty Images

1963 Sonic Blue Stratocaster. *Rumble Seat Music*

1963 Shoreline Gold Stratocaster.
Heritage Auctions

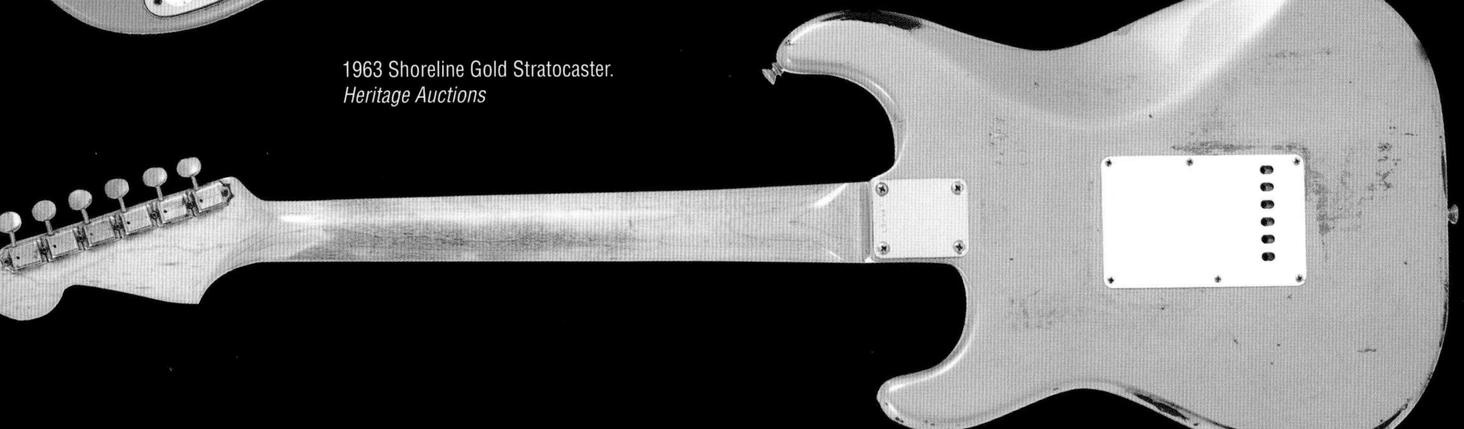

1963 Sonic Blue Stratocaster.
Heritage Auctions

1964 Stratocaster and Band-Master amp with original shipping cartons. *Rumble Seat Music*

(Continued from page 96)

Detroit-Style Flash Comes to Fullerton

Something that gets collectors even more hot and bothered than these several alterations of the late 1950s is the increased uptake of the custom color program at Fender. Custom colors were officially available from 1957, and as we have seen, several notable players had requested truly custom paint jobs right from the start of the Stratocaster's availability, but the changing musical and social styles of the late 1950s seemed to bring with them a greater demand for less-traditional guitar finishes, and the production of Stats in a range of custom colors increased considerably from the end of that decade and into the early and middle parts of the one that followed. Relatively few custom colors other than Blonde, Fiesta Red, and Shoreline Gold were seen before the turn of the decade, and even those are extremely rare (and therefore highly collectible).

The first actual chart of custom colors was produced in 1960 and included fourteen official paint options plus Blonde, each of which could be ordered through a Fender dealer at a 5 percent premium on the guitar's list price. It was money well spent, if, that is, you hung onto the guitar for several decades: a custom color on a pre-CBS Stratocaster can today add as much as 50 percent to the value of the guitar, as compared to another Stratocaster in sunburst, from the same year and in similar condition. Included on the official 1960 Custom Finishes chart were those listed below:

- Lake Placid Blue Metallic
- Daphne Blue
- Sonic Blue
- Shoreline Gold Metallic
- Olympic White
- Burgundy Mist Metallic
- Black
- Sherwood Green Metallic
- Foam Green
- Surf Green
- Inca Silver Metallic
- Fiesta Red
- Dakota Red
- Shell Pink

An additional option, not listed on the chart but mentioned in its caption, was the Tele-like blonde finish, which was almost invariably applied over an ash body. In 1963, Shell Pink was dropped and Candy Apple Red Metallic added. Two years later, in 1965, Daphne Blue, Shoreline Gold Metallic, Burgundy Mist Metallic, Sherwood Green Metallic, Surf Green, and Inca Silver Metallic were also dropped, replaced by Blue Ice Metallic, Firemist Gold Metallic, Charcoal Frost Metallic, Ocean Turquoise Metallic, Teal Green Metallic, and Firemist Silver Metallic. In what seemed quite a natural rock 'n' roll tie-in, most of these colors equated with paints used by one or another Detroit automaker from the late 1950s to the mid-1960s, and Fender's custom-colored guitars could see their twins in cars made by Pontiac, Chevrolet, Ford, Cadillac, Lincoln, Buick, Mercury, Oldsmobile, and Desoto.

Most custom colors were ordered by customers via local dealers, so guitars weren't always built from the ground up with that particular option in mind. As a result, many were finished in the standard sunburst before being shot with a custom-color coat and sent on their way, unbeknownst to their new owners. Over time, playing wear imposed on some custom-color Strats occasionally reveals a fresh undercoat of vibrant sunburst, even if the guitar is officially and entirely originally a "custom-color Stratocaster."

Meanwhile, the color of the standard sunburst finish was livened up mid-1959, along with so many other changes. The standard procedure had, roughly from the start, been to spray the sanded body in a clear primer coat to seal and fill the grain (using a product called Fullerplast from 1963 onward), then dip it in a vat of yellow stain, then spray the edges in black lacquer to create the original two-tone sunburst look before hitting it with a lacquer clear-coat. In 1959 Fender added a red band between the black and the yellow stain visible toward the center of the guitar, but on many early examples this pigment faded severely over time and exposure to light, leaving guitars that looked much like they had only received two-tone finishes. From the early 1960s, though, Fender found a red that would better withstand exposure and survive the rigors of time, creating a more prominent three-tone sunburst (and one that, when sprayed a little too boldly toward the mid-1960s, rendered some gaudy "bull's-eye burst" guitars that were a little less appealing to collectors as a result).

A Proliferation of Players

The Stratocaster's early acceptance among some of the more adventurous country players on the West Coast is fairly well documented, and we have already seen how it segued from there into the rock 'n' roll and rockabilly scenes. The Strat had yet to rock heavily, though—or as heavily as it would eventually be known for—nearly a full decade into its existence, although several blues players were perhaps giving it a serious workout. B. B. King did plenty of memorable work on a sunburst 1956 Stratocaster, and Buddy Guy laid down some even more aggressive licks on his own late-1950s model (performances that a sheepish Chess records generally failed to capture in the day, feeling Guy's aggressive live style needed to be tamed for the studio).

Perhaps unexpectedly, though, the most creative early use of the Stratocaster's versatile vibrato unit in a pop-music context arguably occurred on the other side of the pond. In 1959, Hank

(Continued on page 194)

1964 Fiesta Red Stratocaster. *Chicago Music Exchange, www.chicagomusicexchange.com*

1964 Stratocaster. *Skinner Auctioneers*

1964 Olympic White Stratocaster. *Chicago Music Exchange, www.chicagomusicexchange.com*

1964 Dakota Red Stratocaster. *Chicago Music Exchange, www.chicagomusicexchange.com*

1965 Lake Placid Blue Stratocaster. *Rick Falkiner Guitar Centre, Sydney, Australia*

1965 Stratocasters in Ice Blue Metallic, Dakota Red, Shoreline Gold, and Charcoal Frost Metallic. *Rumble Seat Music*

1965 Candy Apple Red Stratocaster.
L. Finklea Tomlinson, photo by Steve Armato

"Jimi Hendrix Plays Fender Stratocaster":
What more did this late 1960s ad need to say?

1965 Olympic White Stratocaster.
Skinner Auctioneers

1965 Candy Apple Red L Series Stratocaster with maple-cap fretboard. *Rick Falkiner Guitar Centre, Sydney, Australia*

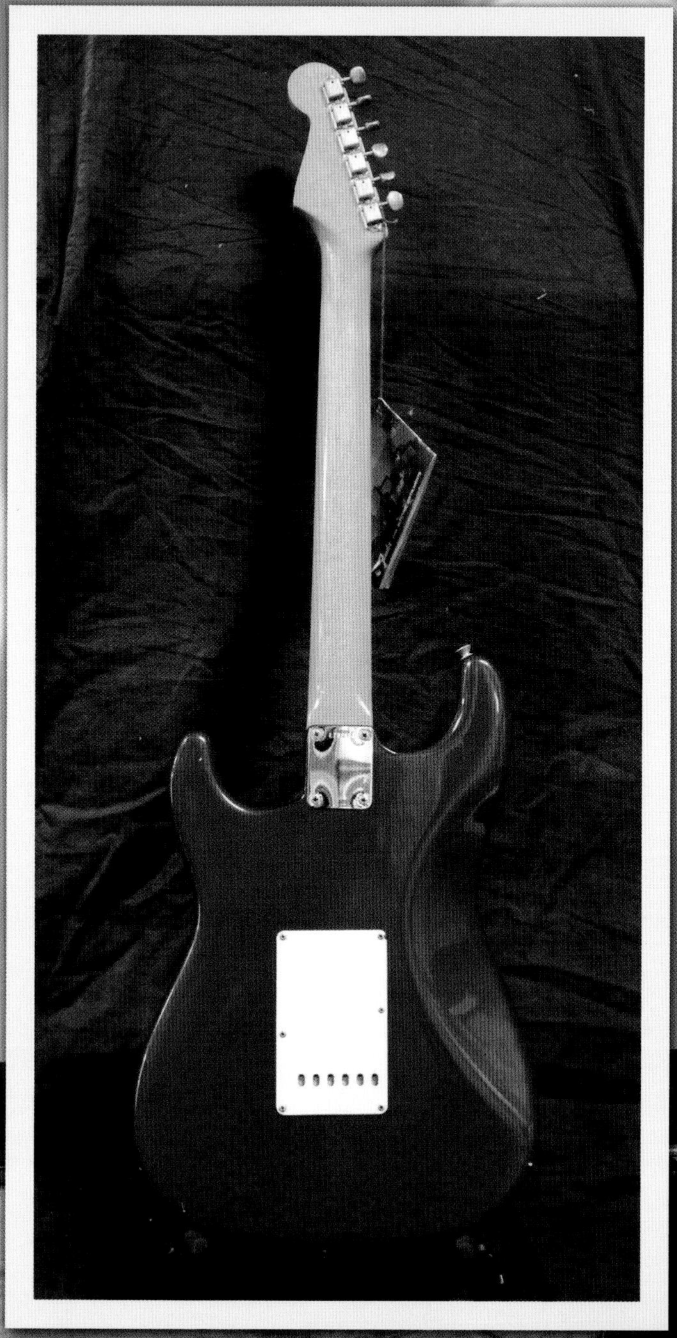

The Surfaris and many other surf bands quickly adopted the Stratocaster and fell in love with its trebly tone. *GAB Archive/Redferns/Getty Images*

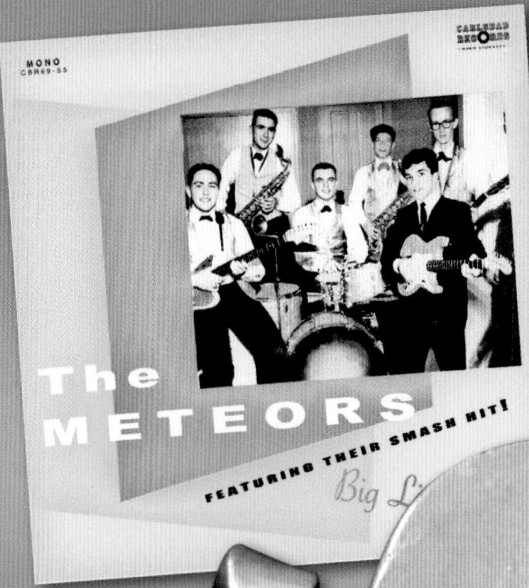

1965 Shoreline Gold Stratocaster. *Rumble Seat Music*

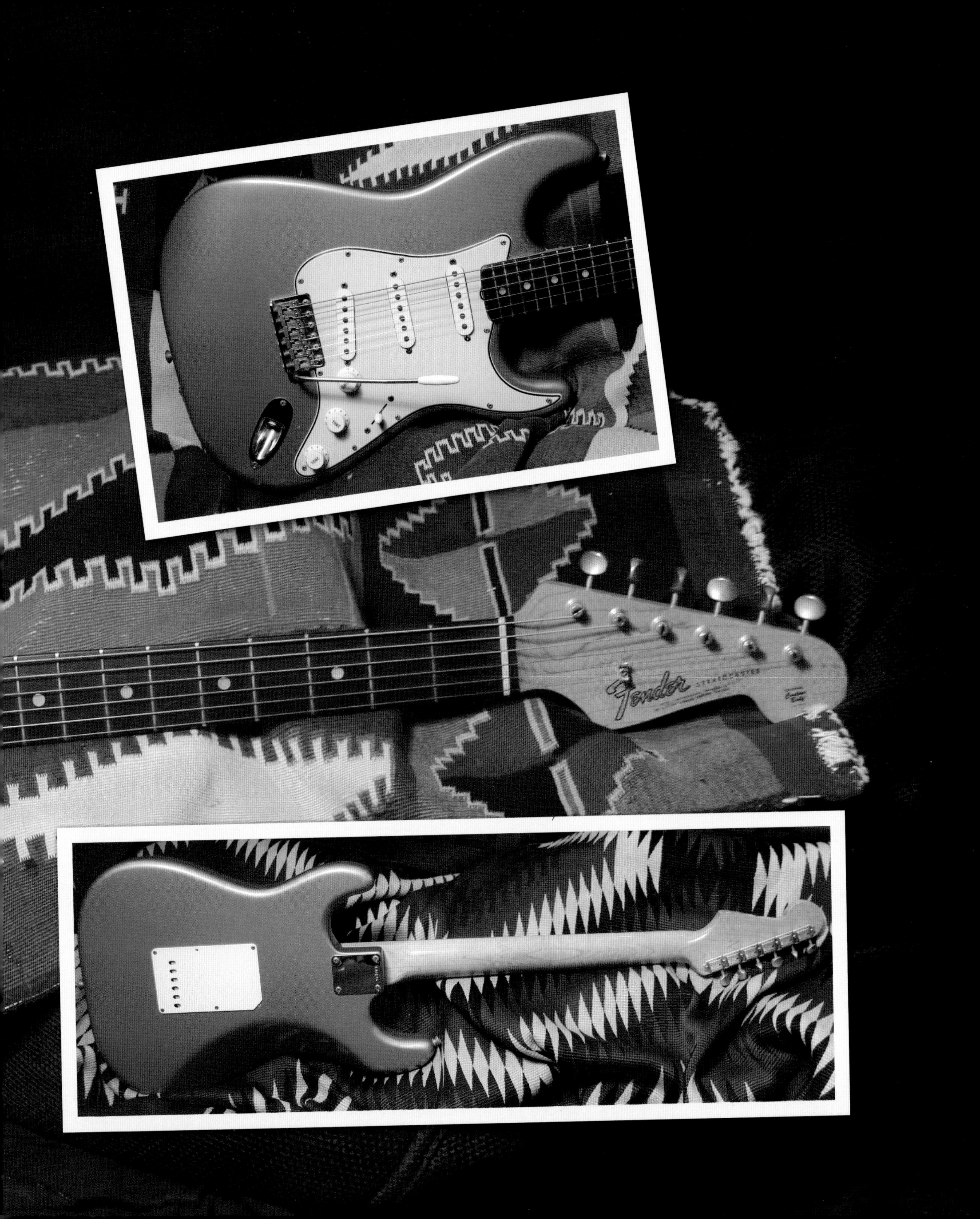
Fender STRATOCASTER

1965 Charcoal Frost Metallic Stratocaster.
Rumble Seat Music

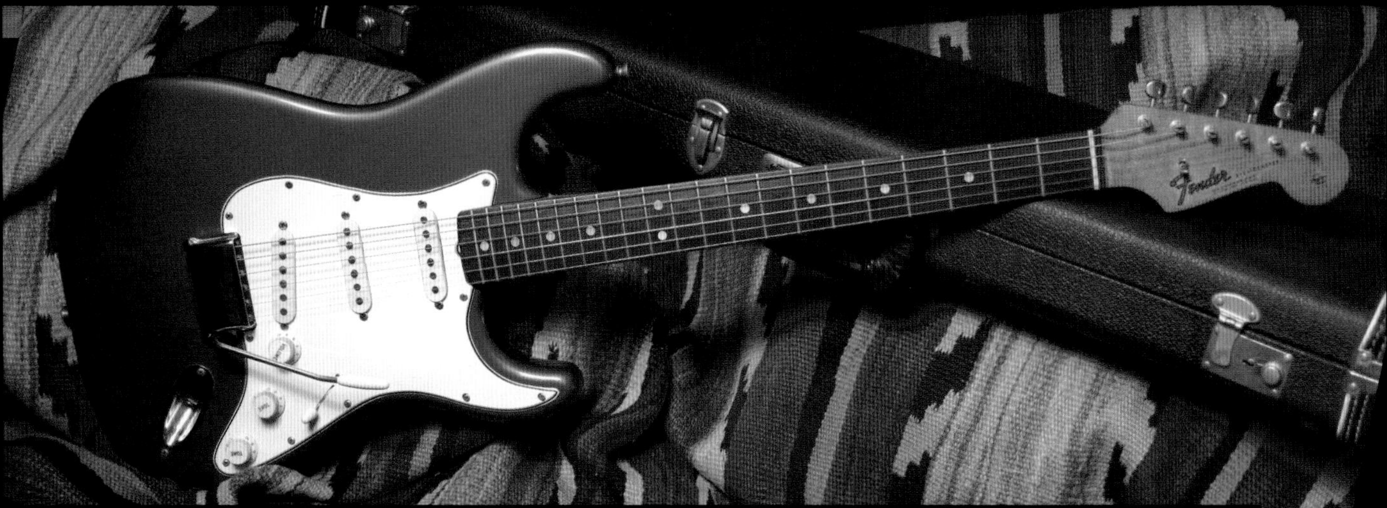

1965 Ice Blue Metallic Stratocaster.
Rumble Seat Music

1965 Black Stratocaster.
Nigel Osbourne/Redferns/Getty Images

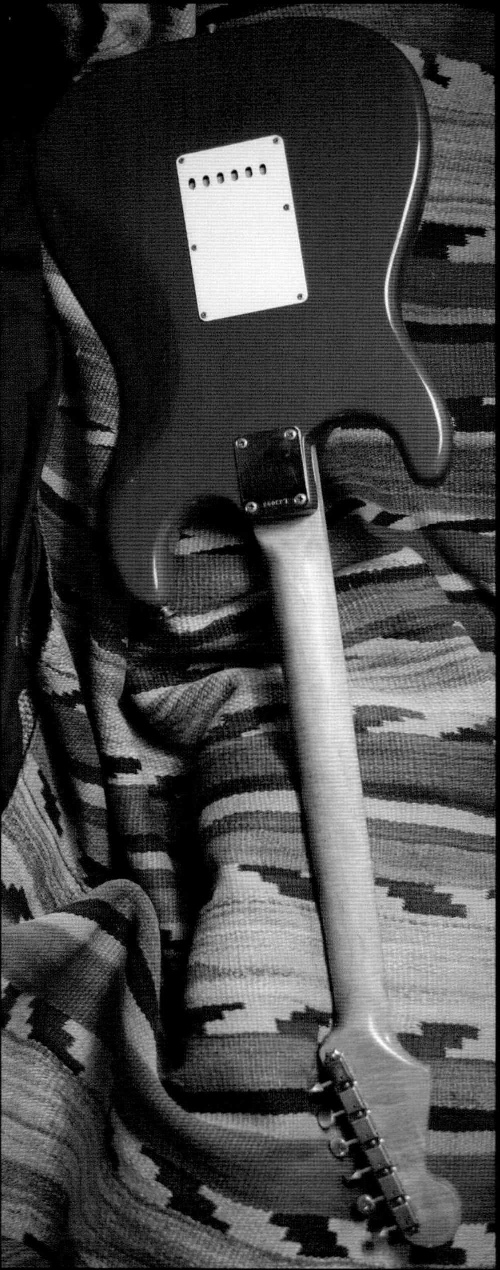

1965 Lake Placid Blue Stratocaster.
Rumble Seat Music

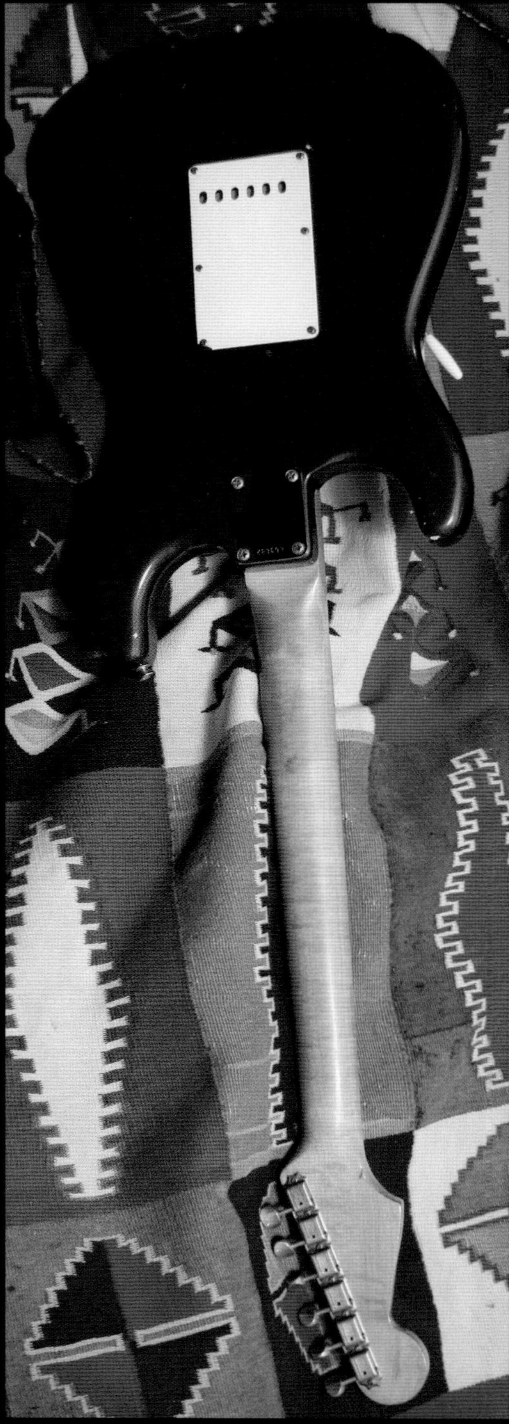

1965 Firemist Gold Stratocaster.
Nigel Osbourne/Redferns/Getty Images

1965 Lake Placid Blue Stratocaster with gold hardware.
Nigel Osbourne/Redferns/Getty Images

1965 Black Stratocaster.
Nigel Osbourne/Redferns/Getty Images

1966 Shoreline Gold Stratocaster.
Rumble Seat Music

Steve Winwood (in white shirt) and his Olympic White Strat pose with Traffic in 1965. *King Collection/Photoshot/Getty Images*

Bob Dylan plays his Stratocaster, performing at the Island Garden in Hempstead, New York, on February 26, 1966. *Alice Ochs/Michael Ochs Archives/Getty Images*

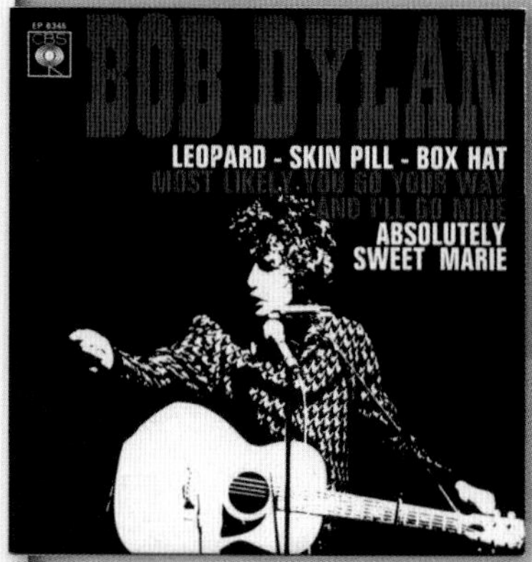

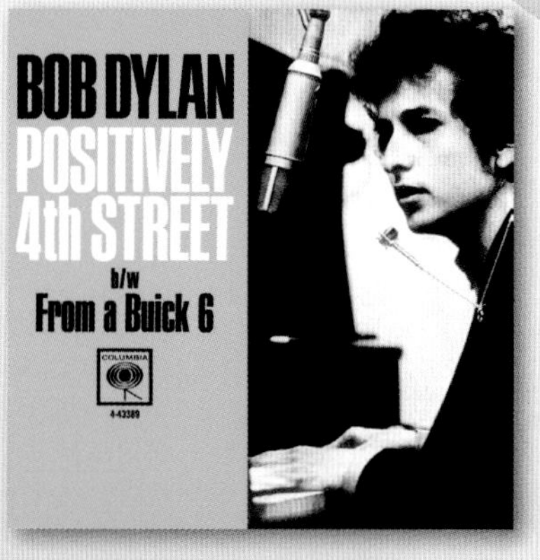

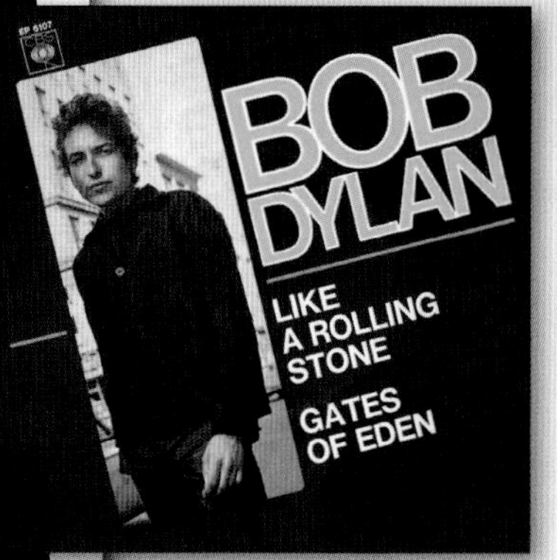

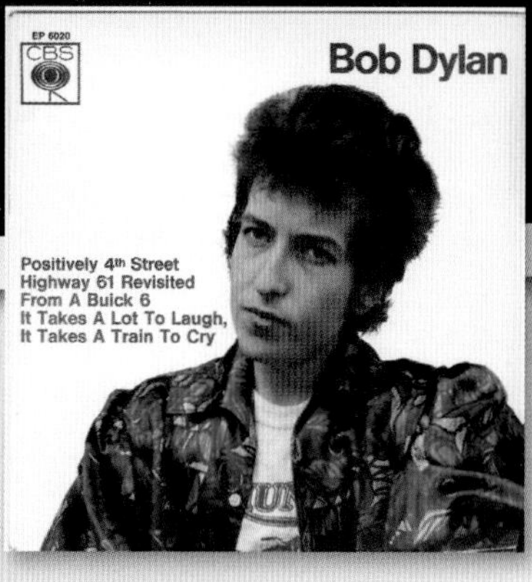

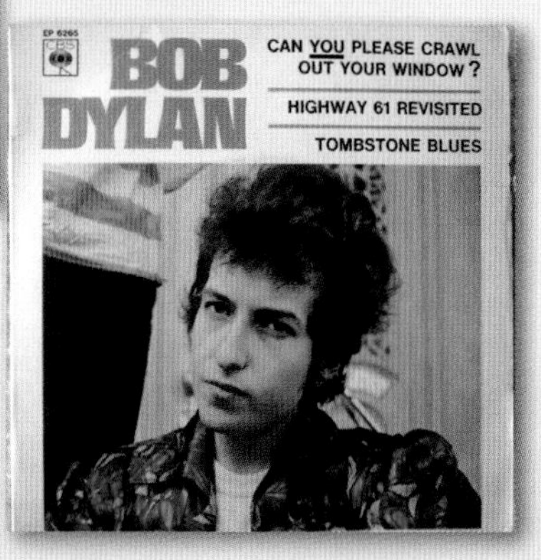

1966–67 Fender catalog.

1969 Black Stratocaster. *Jean Versaveau*

1968 Fender catalog.

1969 Candy Apple Red Stratocaster.
Fretted Americana, www.frettedamericana.com

1969 Lake Placid Blue Stratocaster.
Chicago Music Exchange,
www.chicagomusicexchange.com

A young guitar fan questions Jimi Hendrix about his new Stratocaster during a soundcheck for his performance at the Hollywood Bowl on August 18, 1967, in Los Angeles, California. *Michael Ochs Archives/Getty Images*

The gear of all major guitar heroes attracts some attention, but the equipment used by Jimi Hendrix, and his Fender Stratocasters in particular, has drawn more intense analysis than most. Hendrix played several Strats during his short time at the top, and famously also used a Gibson Flying V and SG. His supposed preference for later-1960s CBS-spec Strats over early- to mid-1960s Strats with pre-CBS (i.e., pre-1965) specs remains a hotly debated issue. Certainly the last Stratocasters the world saw him playing were CBS-era models with large headstocks, modern logos, and maple fingerboards. Among these, the white Strat played at Woodstock in 1969 and the black Strat played at the Isle of Wight in 1970 are the instruments he was most photographed with.

In the early days, however, around the time of *Are You Experienced* and his inflammatory performance at the Monterey Pop Festival in 1967, Hendrix was usually seen playing one of a handful of pre-CBS or transition-era Stratocasters with small headstocks and "spaghetti" or transition logos. Hendrix played two Strats at Monterey: a black mid-1960s model with characteristic rosewood fingerboard and small headstock and a guitar at the center of what is possibly the most legendary "Hendrix moment" of all—the Stratocaster that Hendrix doused in lighter fluid and lit on fire at the end of his performance of "Wild Thing," a transition-era '65 Strat, also with the

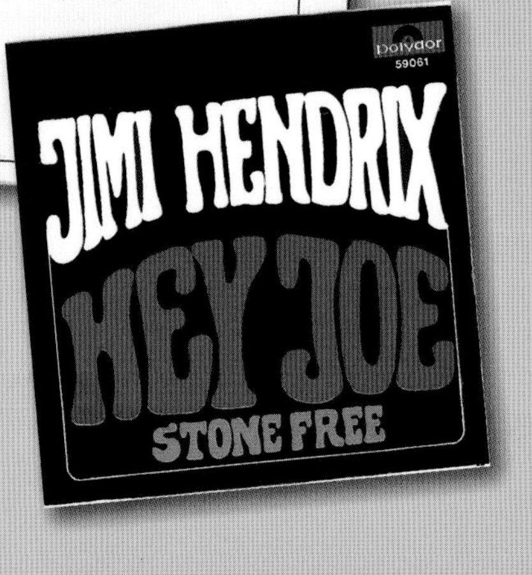

The first Strat that Hendrix burned on stage. He set the 1965 Strat alight in March 1967 at Finsbury Astoria in London. *Andrew Cowie/Photoshot/Getty Images*

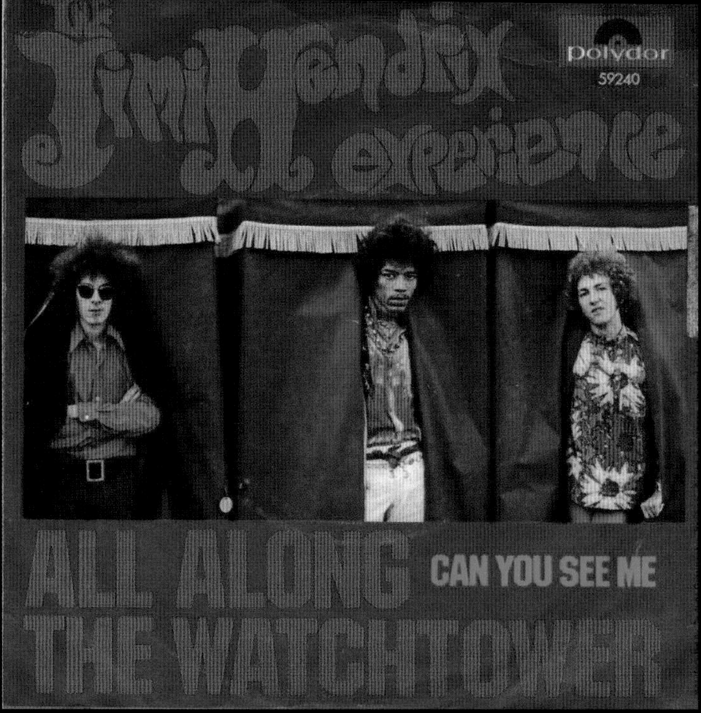

early-style small headstock. This incalculably famous Hendrix Strat was photographed far less than his later instruments for the simple fact that he wasn't yet as big a star at Monterey as he would be from that moment forward—and also because by the end of this climactic moment the guitar was charred and smashed to pieces. Seen little before the Monterey appearance, it had recently been customized by Hendrix, who painted approximately half of the Fiesta Red body white and adorned it with floral graphics. Otherwise, the standard late-'65 Stratocaster carried a short-lived combination of features, including a fatter new-style gold logo with black outline on a small headstock and rosewood fingerboard with pearloid inlays. Another '65 Stratocaster, a sunburst model, was also played, burned, and smashed by Hendrix at the London Astoria and later given to Frank Zappa, who left it to his son, Dweezil, upon his death.

While pre-CBS Stratocasters have attained far greater status as collector items, many Hendrix-philes believe Jimi preferred post-'65 guitars for tone-based reasons. One theory is that he found the extra wood in the larger post-CBS headstocks to increase sustain. Another holds that the slightly weaker single-coil pickups of the late-1960s Stratocasters added up to a bigger sound when injected through his 100-watt Marshall stacks. (This might sound contrary to reason, but the theory itself is sound: weaker pickups prevent the signal from breaking up too early in the signal chain, so a little more fidelity is maintained through to the output stage of a large amp.) Also frequently discussed is his preference for right-handed Strats played upside down, when left-handed Strats did exist. Among other observations, much is made of the fact that restringing the right-handed guitar with the low-E back on top, and thus wound around the tuner post that was now farthest from the nut, created a change in the vibrational characteristics of that string.

Perhaps the best authority on these theories is the tech who worked with Hendrix live and in the studio and had hands-on experience with Jimi's guitars. British effects guru Roger Mayer not only built and modified many of the pedals that Hendrix used, but he also worked as an all-round right-hand man and even helped select and set up many of the star's guitars. What does he have to say about the wide headstock/greater sustain theory? "No, Jimi wouldn't have considered that," Mayer told this writer. "All the guitars that we used were bought out of necessity; there weren't that many Stratocasters around [in London] in those days, and they were very expensive. Also, in the 1960s nobody paid much attention to whether pre-CBS Fenders were any better than CBS Fenders. They were all about the same. I can't see a slightly bigger headstock making any difference anyway."

Of course, the final word in all of this is that the Strats Hendrix played are iconic simply because he played them—and whatever Strat Jimi wailed on, it was sure to make a heavenly sound.

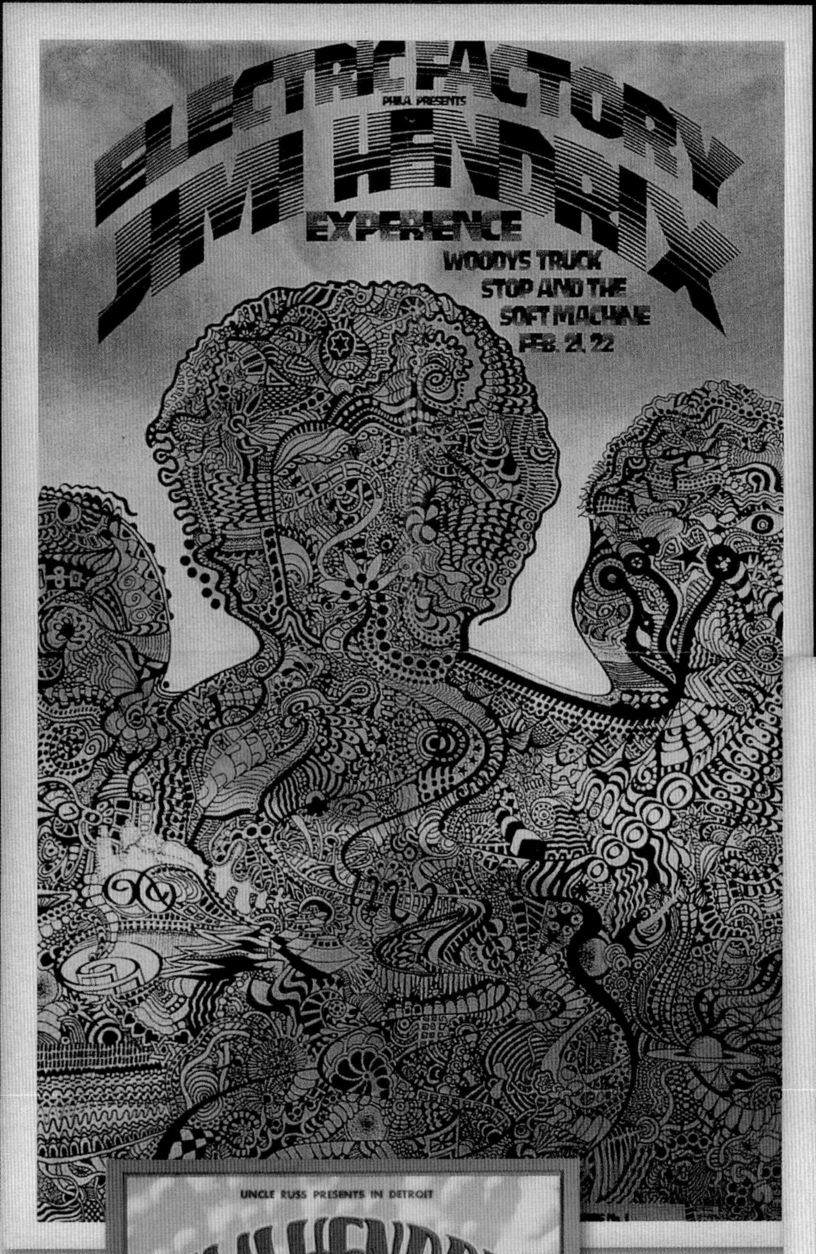
ELECTRIC FACTORY
PHILA PRESENTS
JIMI HENDRIX
EXPERIENCE
WOODYS TRUCK
STOP AND THE
SOFT MACHINE
FEB. 21, 22

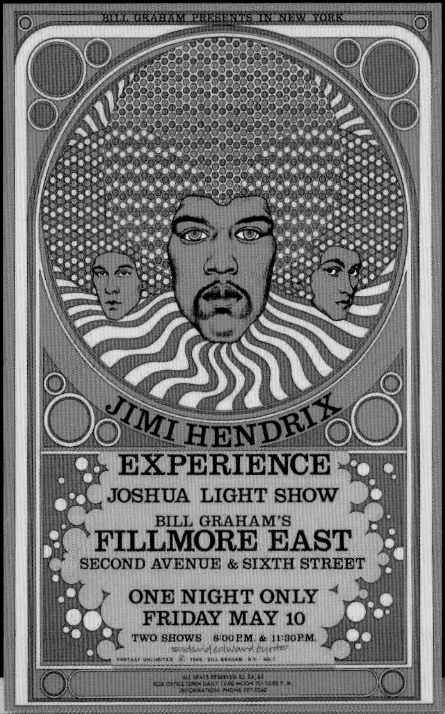
BILL GRAHAM PRESENTS IN NEW YORK
JIMI HENDRIX
EXPERIENCE
JOSHUA LIGHT SHOW
BILL GRAHAM'S
FILLMORE EAST
SECOND AVENUE & SIXTH STREET
ONE NIGHT ONLY
FRIDAY MAY 10
TWO SHOWS 8:00 P.M. & 11:30 P.M.

UNCLE RUSS PRESENTS IN DETROIT
JIMI HENDRIX
EXPERIENCE
SOFT MACHINE MC5
RATIONALS
FRI FEB 23
MASONIC
TEMPLE

AUG. 19
HENDRIX
EXPERIENCE
TIM BUCKLEY

Jimi Hendrix

Jimi Hendrix's 1968 Olympic White Stratocaster.
Nigel Osbourne/Redferns/Getty Images

Hendrix plays his Strat at Royal Albert Hall in London on February 24, 1969. *avid Redfern/Redferns/ Getty Images*

Jim Hendrix's 1968 Stratocaster.
Christie's/Bridgeman

Eric Clapton

Eric Clapton plays Brownie with Derek and the Dominos in 1971.
Elliot Landy/Redferns/Getty Images

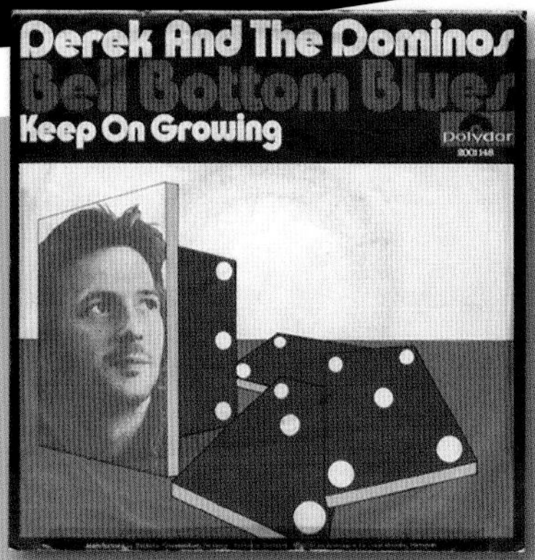

Throughout his career, Eric Clapton has been an arbiter of tone, and while he has moved through several makes and models of guitar over the past forty-five years, he has been extremely devoted to each at certain periods and has inspired major guitar lust in the hearts of many at every stop along the road.

Clapton's boyhood love was the Stratocaster, however. He remembers first being struck by the Strat when he saw Buddy Holly with one, but he became obsessed when he saw Buddy Guy play one live. "The Strat had that initial appeal to me when I was a kid," he told *Rolling Stone* in 2013. "But then somewhere down the road I heard Buddy Guy on an album called *Folk Festival of the Blues* where he was the new kid on the block playing

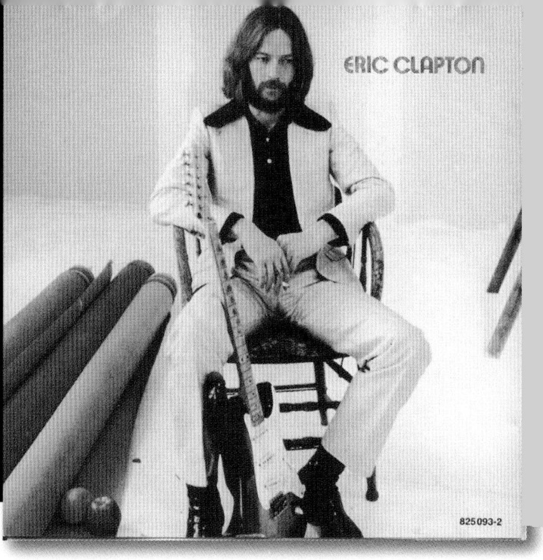

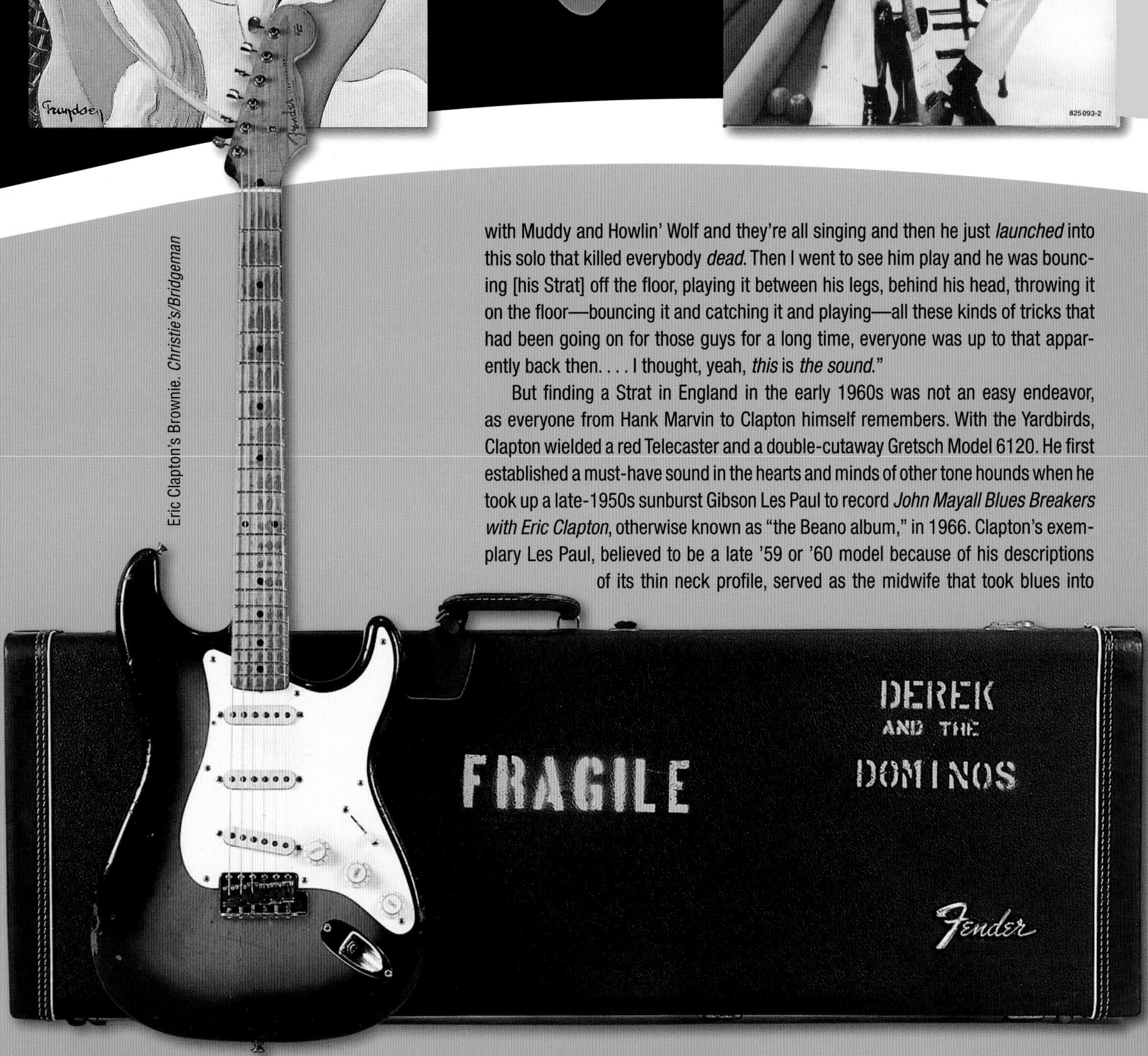

Eric Clapton's Brownie. *Christie's/Bridgeman*

with Muddy and Howlin' Wolf and they're all singing and then he just *launched* into this solo that killed everybody *dead*. Then I went to see him play and he was bouncing [his Strat] off the floor, playing it between his legs, behind his head, throwing it on the floor—bouncing it and catching it and playing—all these kinds of tricks that had been going on for those guys for a long time, everyone was up to that apparently back then. . . . I thought, yeah, *this* is *the sound*."

But finding a Strat in England in the early 1960s was not an easy endeavor, as everyone from Hank Marvin to Clapton himself remembers. With the Yardbirds, Clapton wielded a red Telecaster and a double-cutaway Gretsch Model 6120. He first established a must-have sound in the hearts and minds of other tone hounds when he took up a late-1950s sunburst Gibson Les Paul to record *John Mayall Blues Breakers with Eric Clapton*, otherwise known as "the Beano album," in 1966. Clapton's exemplary Les Paul, believed to be a late '59 or '60 model because of his descriptions of its thin neck profile, served as the midwife that took blues into

Clapton plays Blackie on stage in 1978.
Richard E. Aaron/Redferns/Getty Images

Eric Clapton's Blackie. *Getty Images*

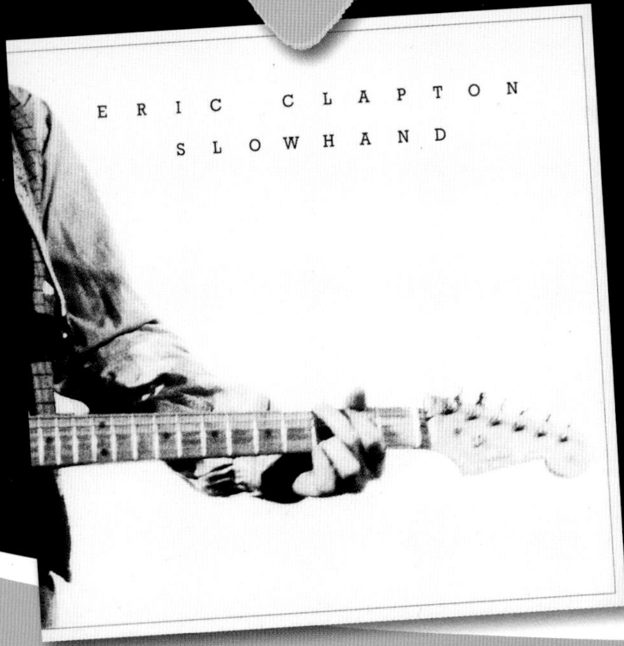

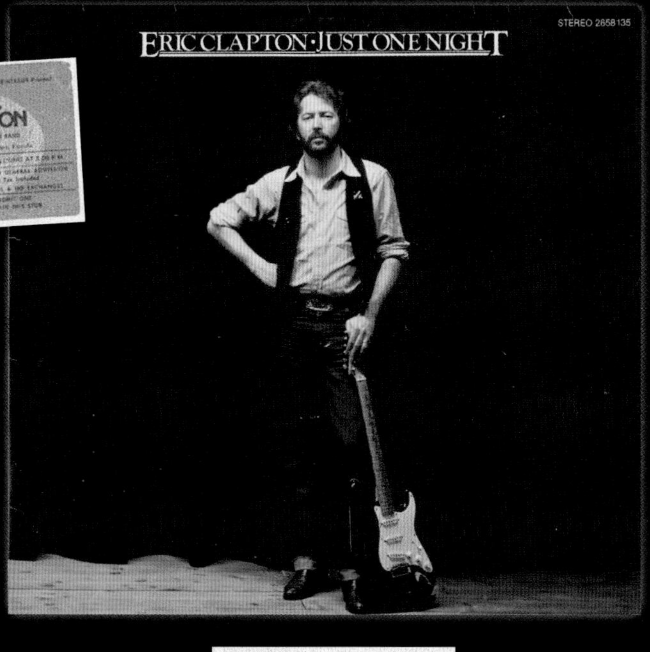

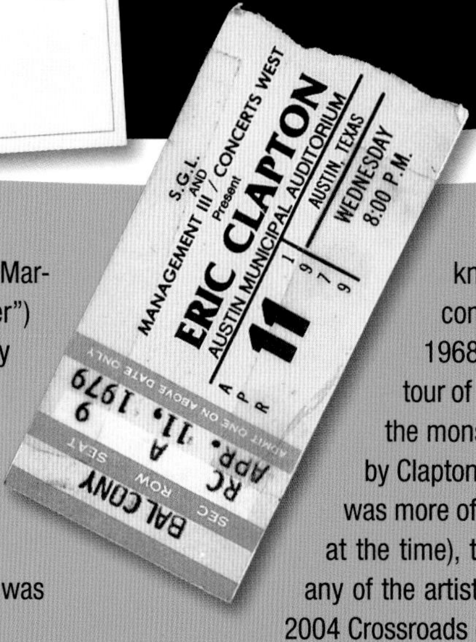

blues-rock when the star rammed it through a cranked Marshall 1962 combo (forever after known as a "Bluesbreaker") and warned the recording engineer that he intended to play loud. The result was one of the first widely chased guitar tones in the history of rock, and from thence forward, the previously underappreciated Les Paul Standard was a well appreciated guitar indeed. Clapton himself, however, was forced to evolve somewhat, due to the theft of said Les Paul in the summer of 1966 while he was rehearsing for Cream's first shows.

After that, Clapton gigged and recorded with a few borrowed Les Pauls but, unable to find one that he liked as much as his lost "Beano" guitar, eventually settled in with a Gibson SG and an ES-335 for the majority of his work with Cream. The SG, a 1964 or 1965 model, became famous for the paint job given to it by the Dutch artists collectively known as The Fool, a name also given to the guitar itself. When Clapton owned the guitar, the remains of the framework of its original Maestro "lyre" vibrato tailpiece could still be seen. Todd Rundgren acquired the SG in 1974, and its bridge, tailpiece, and paint job were updated some time after. It is currently on loan to the Hard Rock Café in San Francisco. Despite the SG's memorable appearance, the cherry-red ES-335 that Clapton used toward the end of the Cream era and early on with Delaney and Bonnie is arguably more memorable in a tonal sense, at least in the ears of many fans. This 1964 ES-335 with small-block fingerboard inlays is perhaps best known for its appearance at Cream's farewell concert at London's Royal Albert Hall in November 1968, but was also used throughout Cream's U.S. tour of 1968 and on several studio recordings, notably the monstrous "Badge" from *Goodbye*. Purchased new by Clapton during his tenure with the Yardbirds (though it was more often seen in the hands of bandmate Chris Dreja at the time), the red ES-335 has had the longest tenure of any of the artist's guitars to date and was surrendered in the 2004 Crossroads guitar auction, where it sold for $847,500.

The end of the 1960s signaled Clapton's movement, by and large, from Gibson to Fender. "Jimi was playing [a Strat] while I was still playing an SG. I didn't get to it then, but I got to it right away afterward," he explained. But still, finding the perfect Strat remained difficult.

"What I would always look for on a Strat was a maple neck that had been worn out," he remembered. "That was the thing: if it looked brand new [shakes his head]. It was like a restaurant: if it has lots of people in there, it's got to be good food. I just thought that if it had all those worn-out patches, it meant that it had been well favored."

He found such a Strat for the equivalent of $400 at the Sound City music shop in London on May 7, 1967, just a few days before Cream flew to New York to record its second album, *Disraeli Gears*. The guitar was serial no. 12073, a 1956 sunburst with an alder body and suitably worn maple fingerboard. He christened it "Brownie" and used it during much of the early 1970s, especially on his solo debut, 1970's Eric

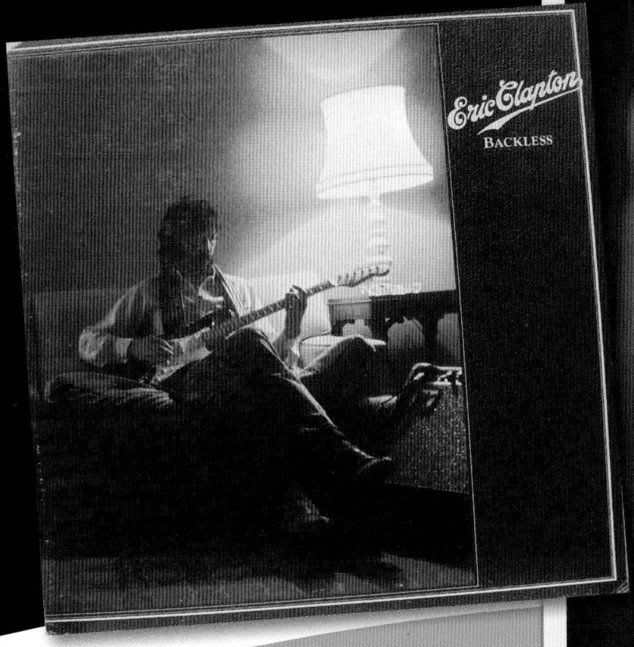

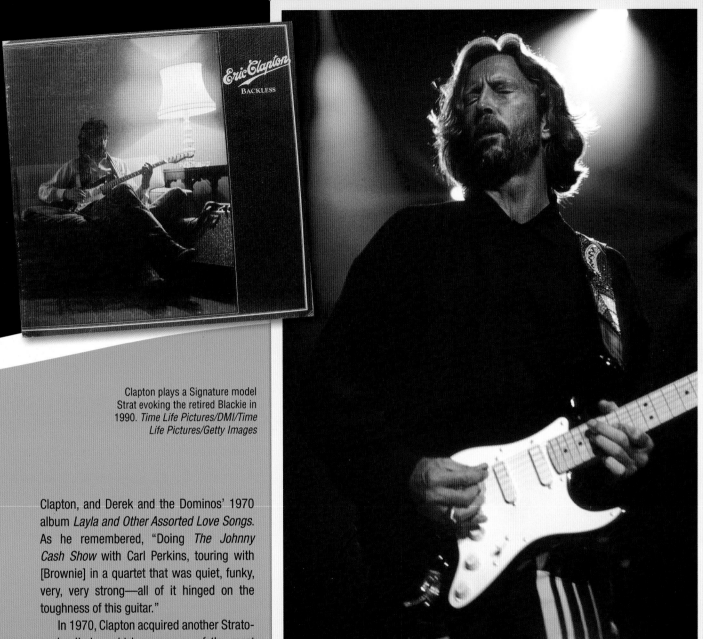

Clapton plays a Signature model Strat evoking the retired Blackie in 1990. *Time Life Pictures/DMI/Time Life Pictures/Getty Images*

Clapton, and Derek and the Dominos' 1970 album *Layla and Other Assorted Love Songs*. As he remembered, "Doing *The Johnny Cash Show* with Carl Perkins, touring with [Brownie] in a quartet that was quiet, funky, very, very strong—all of it hinged on the toughness of this guitar."

In 1970, Clapton acquired another Stratocaster that would become one of the most famous electric guitars of all time.

"The problem was trying to find the maple necks [fretboard]," he said. "All the models that were current had the rosewood fingerboards. They [the maple-fretboard Strats] had kind of gone out of circulation, on this end of the scene [in England] anyway. It wasn't until I went through the States on tour that I started picking them up in pawnshops and guitar shops for a *song*. I'd buy four or five at a time."

At a guitar store in Nashville, Clapton purchased six late-1950s Strats and combined the best elements from his favorite three of the bunch; the other three were given to Pete Townshend, George Harrison, and Steve Winwood. This "parts guitar" he named "Blackie," and after 1971, Brownie served as a backup instrument.

Blackie was unique, blending elements from three '56 and '57 Strats, the modifications and repairs required to keep it serviceable over the years, and plenty of wear, sweat, and mojo from Clapton's own hands. The guitar was heavily used, from its first live appearance at the 1973 Rainbow Concert until its semi-retirement around 1985.

Clapton sold Brownie for $497,000 at a 1999 fundraising auction. Blackie was the star of the same auction that saw the sale of Clapton's '64 ES-335 in 2004 and fetched the highest price paid for a guitar at auction to date, going to Guitar Center for $959,500.

—Dave Hunter and Michael Dregni

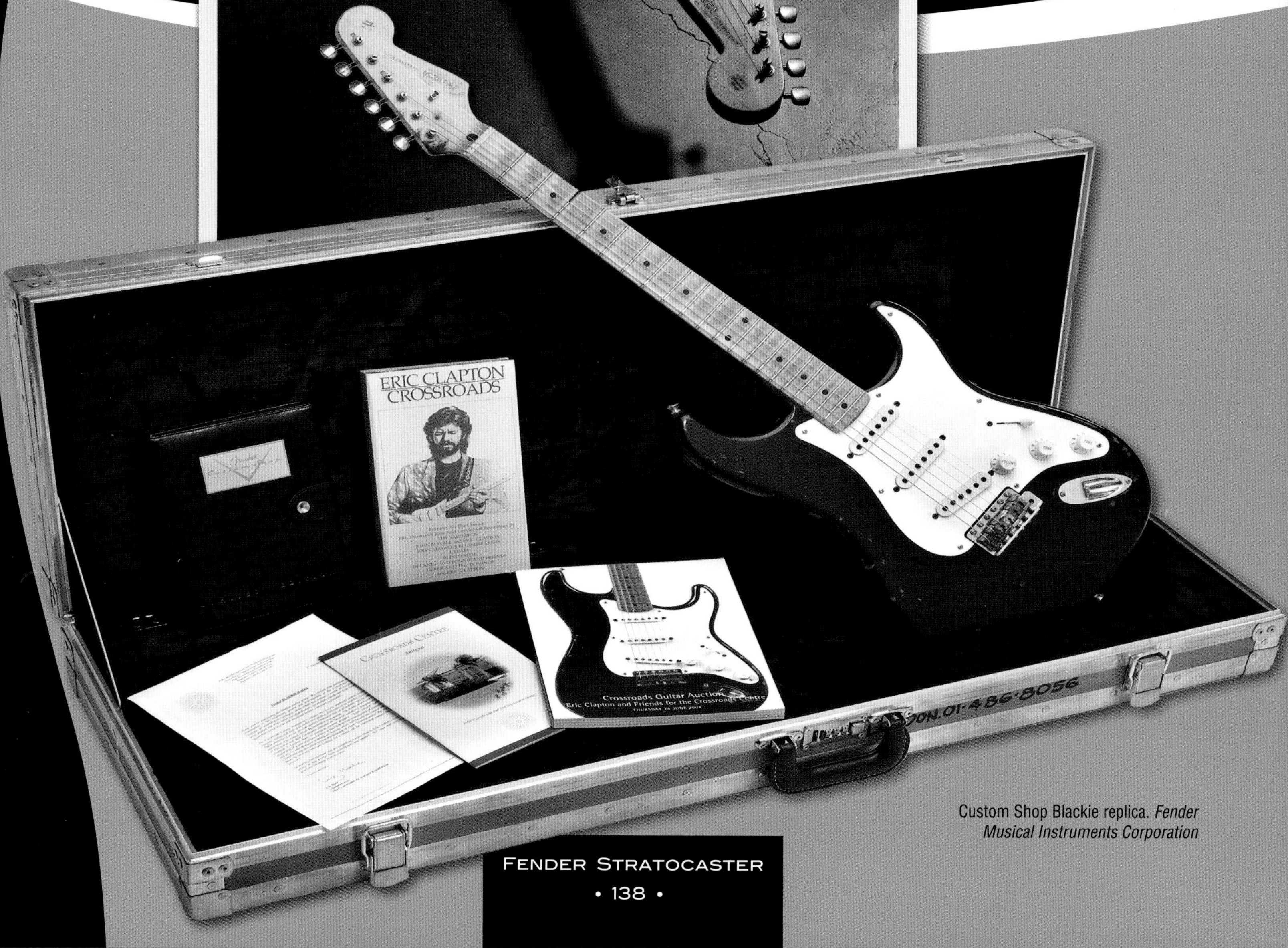

Custom Shop Blackie replica. *Fender Musical Instruments Corporation*

2009 Eric Clapton Signature Daphne Blue and Grey Stratocasters. *Fender Musical Instruments Corporation*

ERIC CLAPTON
SIGNATURE AMPLIFIERS
& STRATOCASTER® GUITAR
Fender
MAKE HISTORY

George Harrison

George Harrison plays his Strat, Rocky, onstage with Delaney and Bonnie in 1969. *Jan Persson/ Redferns/Getty Images*

It's always a little heartwarming, somehow, to recall what gearheads the Beatles remained, even through careers graced with unfathomable levels of fame and recognition. They were, after all, musicians first and foremost, and the equipment used to make that music continued to be vitally important to them right up through the end of the band's run and beyond. When both George Harrison and John Lennon acquired Fender Stratocasters early in 1965, their childlike glee was virtually palpable. As revealed in Andy Babiuk's strenuously researched *Beatles Gear* (Backbeat Books, 2001), Harrison in particular had enjoyed trying a fellow musician's Stratocaster in Hamburg in 1960 and had been beaten out by a rival guitarist in an effort to purchase a used example in 1961. His subsequent use of Gretsch and Rickenbacker guitars through the early years of the band's success might have been a rebellion of sorts at his failure to acquire the original object of his desires: "I was so disappointed, it scarred me for life," the Beatle said in the TV documentary *The Story of the Fender Stratocaster*. When Don Randall sent a representative to New York to try to woo the Beatles to Fender mid-1964 during the band's U.S. tour, the effort apparently never made it past an underling in the Fab Four camp. Yet around February 1965, both Lennon and Harrison decided to tap that jones for what was then arguably the world's most popular solidbody

George Harrison's 1964 Stratocaster, Rocky.
Nigel Osbourne/Redferns/Getty Images

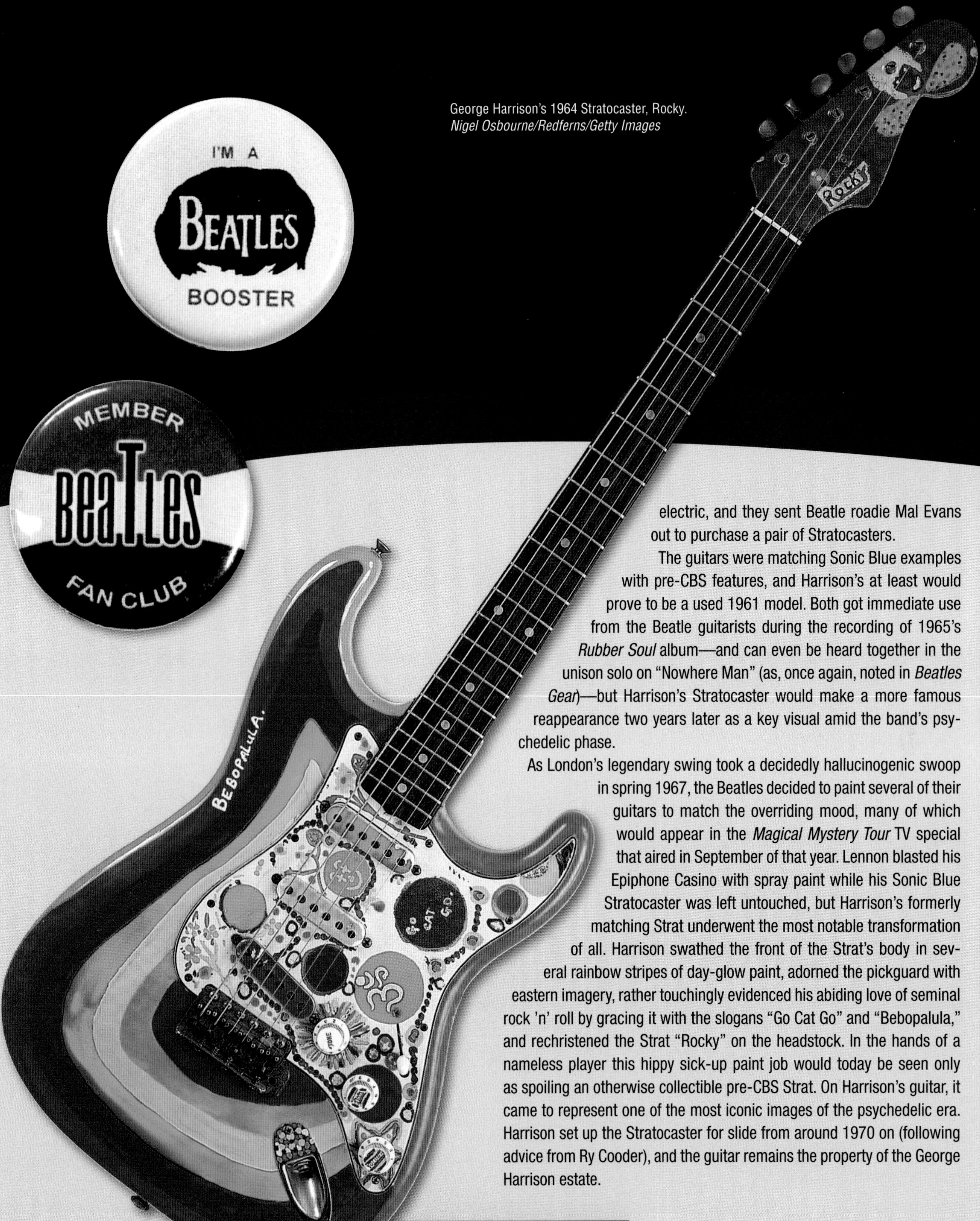

electric, and they sent Beatle roadie Mal Evans out to purchase a pair of Stratocasters.

The guitars were matching Sonic Blue examples with pre-CBS features, and Harrison's at least would prove to be a used 1961 model. Both got immediate use from the Beatle guitarists during the recording of 1965's *Rubber Soul* album—and can even be heard together in the unison solo on "Nowhere Man" (as, once again, noted in *Beatles Gear*)—but Harrison's Stratocaster would make a more famous reappearance two years later as a key visual amid the band's psychedelic phase.

As London's legendary swing took a decidedly hallucinogenic swoop in spring 1967, the Beatles decided to paint several of their guitars to match the overriding mood, many of which would appear in the *Magical Mystery Tour* TV special that aired in September of that year. Lennon blasted his Epiphone Casino with spray paint while his Sonic Blue Stratocaster was left untouched, but Harrison's formerly matching Strat underwent the most notable transformation of all. Harrison swathed the front of the Strat's body in several rainbow stripes of day-glow paint, adorned the pickguard with eastern imagery, rather touchingly evidenced his abiding love of seminal rock 'n' roll by gracing it with the slogans "Go Cat Go" and "Bebopalula," and rechristened the Strat "Rocky" on the headstock. In the hands of a nameless player this hippy sick-up paint job would today be seen only as spoiling an otherwise collectible pre-CBS Strat. On Harrison's guitar, it came to represent one of the most iconic images of the psychedelic era. Harrison set up the Stratocaster for slide from around 1970 on (following advice from Ry Cooder), and the guitar remains the property of the George Harrison estate.

Jeff Beck

Jeff Beck performs in 1973. *Robert Knight Archive/Redferns/Getty Images*

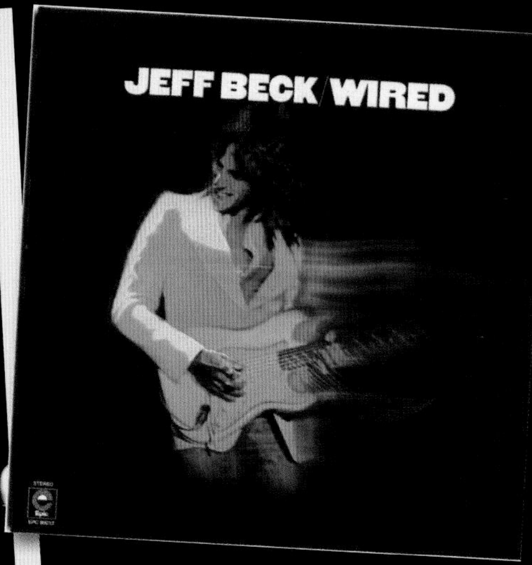

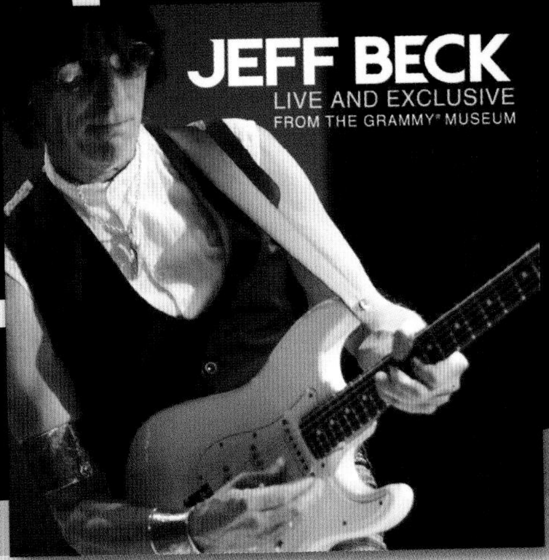

Among the several classic blues-rockers who evolved through the popular fat humbucker tones of the 1960s to more nuanced styles and sounds courtesy of the Fender Stratocaster, Jeff Beck is arguably one of the most masterful. Where others make admittedly good use of the instrument as a whole, Beck wields the Strat's versatile vibrato bar virtually as an instrument in itself and has taken the model as a whole to new heights of jazz-rock fusion in doing so.

The British guitarist made a big name for himself right from the start, after stepping into very big shoes in the Yardbirds as Eric Clapton's replacement, then splitting off to form the Jeff Beck Group with Ron Wood and Rod Stewart in 1967, all before he'd reached the age of 25. Upon joining the Yardbirds, he at first inherited the red Fender Telecaster with rosewood fingerboard that Clapton had frequently played, which had been a "band guitar" of sorts, then set about acquiring his own, the now-famous Blonde Esquire with black replacement pickguard and sanded-down forearm contour. Come the 1970s, though, Beck became synonymous with, first, a humbucker-loaded Telecaster, then a '54 or '55 Gibson Les Paul that had been refinished in a dark oxblood color and had its original P-90s replaced with humbuckers. While the thick, creamy, sustaining Les Paul tones for a time seemed a Jeff Beck calling card, particularly as heard on *Blow By Blow*, this artist was ever striving for deeper expression from his work, and he finally found it in the emotive tremors of Leo Fender's original "Synchronized Tremolo Action."

Beck came out big time as a Strat fanatic on the 1976 album *Wired*, lacing the album with a newfound dexterity that would come to be his trademark and which was acknowledged by his appearance on the cover wielding an Olympic White example of his new love (in a rare photo in which Jeff Beck did *not* display his bare biceps). For many fans, frenetic vibrato bursts of the album track "Goodbye Pork Pie Hat"—a tune written by Charles Mingus as a tribute to Lester Young—best define Beck's move to the Stratocaster, and it certainly acts as a catch-all for his technique on the instrument. Through the course of the 1980s Beck further developed his style by dropping the pick in favor of using the fingers of his right hand to attack the strings, adding another distinctive characteristic to the guitarist's arsenal of snarling eruptions and quivering denouements. Following the overtly commercial *Flash*, an album Beck has frequently rejected as record-label pabulum, Beck recorded another of his classic Strat-fueled outings in *Jeff Beck's Guitar Shop*, the cover of which blended his love of hotrods and guitars in an illustration that showed a Beck-like character working beneath the "chassis" of a giant Stratocaster up on the lift in an auto garage.

Rather than fawning over vintage models, Jeff Beck has long favored contemporary Fender Stratocasters, particularly those with the updated two-post vibrato and stainless-steel saddles. Fender's Jeff Beck Signature Stratocaster has gone through several incarnations and currently carries the noiseless ceramic single-coil-sized pickups and roller nut that Beck also favors.

Jeff Beck's array of Strats—and one Tele—backstage during a 1980s tour. *Rick Gould*

2004 Jeff Beck Signature Surf Green Stratocaster. *Fender Musical Instruments Corporation*

1972 Tangerine Sparkle hardtail Stratocaster. *Chicago Music Exchange, www.chicagomusicexchange.com*

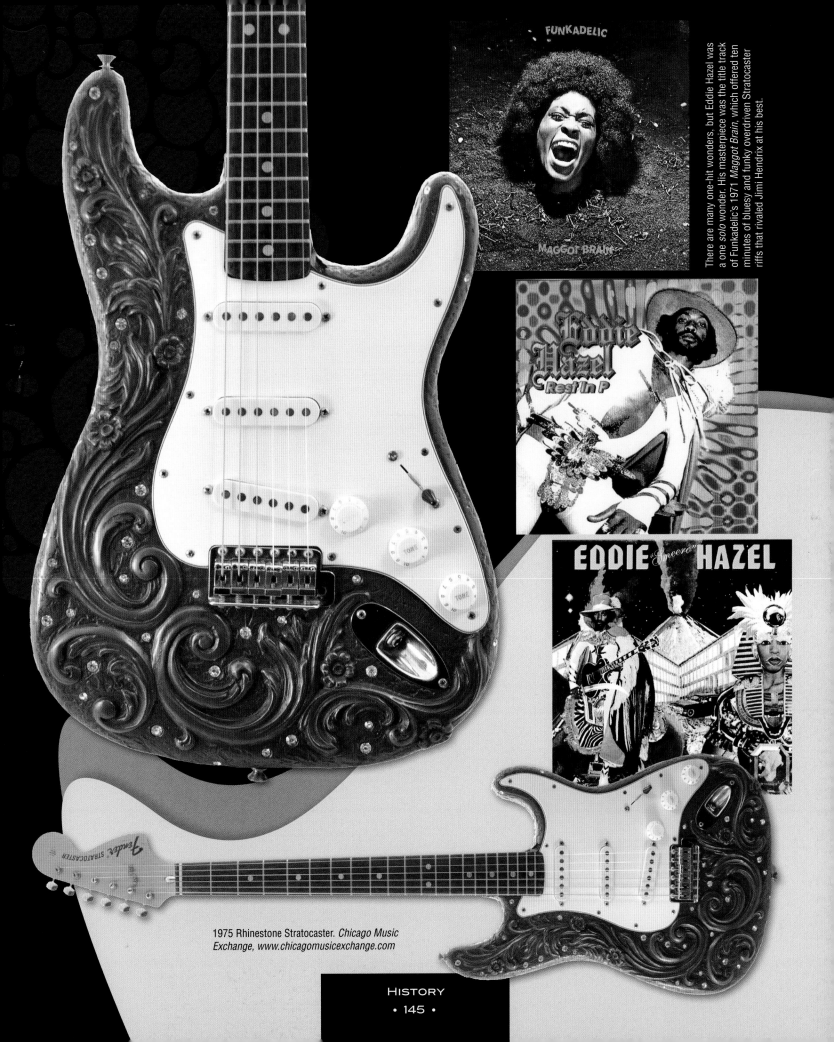

There are many one-hit wonders, but Eddie Hazel was a one *solo* wonder. His masterpiece was the title track of Funkadelic's 1971 *Maggot Brain*, which offered ten minutes of bluesy and funky overdriven Stratocaster riffs that rivaled Jimi Hendrix at his best.

1975 Rhinestone Stratocaster. *Chicago Music Exchange, www.chicagomusicexchange.com*

1978 Antigua Stratocaster.
Nigel Osbourne/Redferns/Getty Images

Jerry Garcia of the Grateful Dead plays his Natural Stratocaster at the Tivoli Concert Hall in Copenhagen, Denmark, in 1972. *Gijsbert Hanekroot/Redferns/Getty*

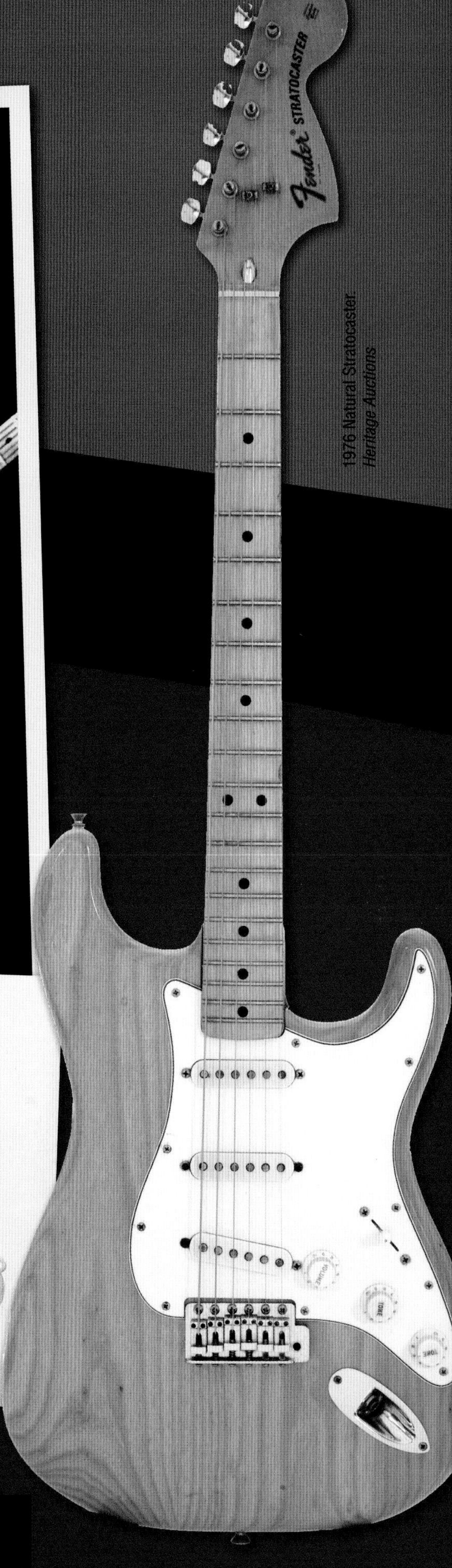

1976 Natural Stratocaster.
Heritage Auctions

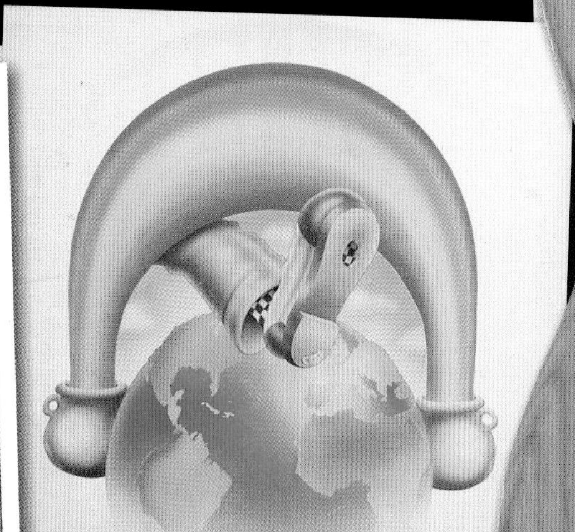

Ritchie Blackmore

Ritchie Blackmore and Deep Purple perform during their 1974 U.S. tour. *Fin Costello/ Redferns/Getty Images*

Often touted by devotees of the form as the original god of the über-metal solo, Ritchie Blackmore kept the Fender Stratocaster in the fold when most stadium rockers were turning to the fatter tones of Gibson Les Pauls, SGs, and Flying Vs to pound their Marshall stacks into submission. First with Deep Purple in the early 1970s and then with Rainbow after 1975, Blackmore established himself as the dark master of the Stratocaster, while also firming the foundations of a lead-heavy, medieval-influenced vein of hard rock and metal that has perpetuated to this day.

Like so many topflight artists, Blackmore modified his instruments considerably. He favored large-headstock, post-CBS Strats, mainly the early 1970s models with the "bullet" truss-rod adjustment points behind the nut and is most noted for giving these a scalloped fingerboard. Created by filing away the wood between frets to create a concave fingerboard surface, the scalloped neck is said to aid speed and finger vibrato. Blackmore preferred a graduated scallop, which was fairly shallow up to the seventh fret and somewhat deeper thereafter. He also disconnected the middle pickup, which he never used; glued the necks in place, rather than relying on his Fenders' bolt-on attachments; and modified the vibrato tailpieces to achieve some up-bend in addition to the standard down-bend by removing some of the wood in front of the trem's inertia block in the back of the body. After they became available, Blackmore also added Seymour Duncan Quarter Pound Strat-style replacement pickups to the bridge and neck positions of his guitars. These are retained in Fender's artist model, the Ritchie Blackmore Stratocaster. During Rainbow's heyday, Blackmore also took to smashing plenty of Strats, usually as the grand finale to an explosive set, which would often culminate in a dummy amp stack bursting into flames after being assaulted with the unfortunate instrument. Rather than destroying one of his painstakingly modified guitars, though, he would usually inflict such punishment on a Strat copy that would be pieced back together for further abuse night after night.

Blackmore selects from his arsenal of Strats backstage in 1974. *Fin Costello/Redferns/Getty Images*

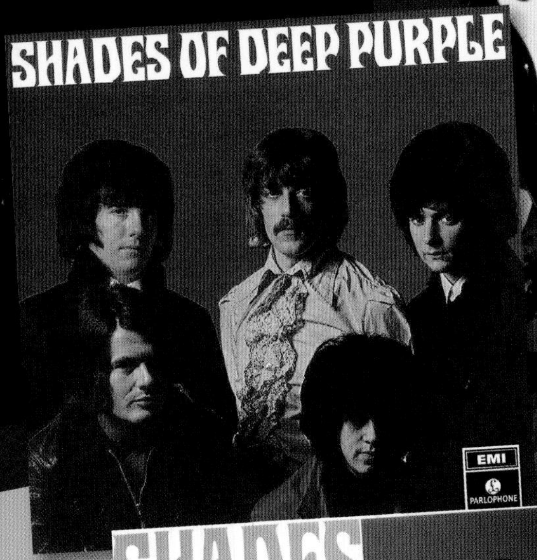

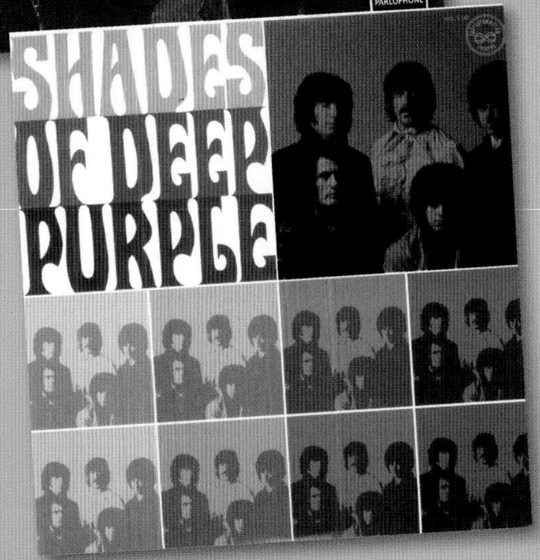

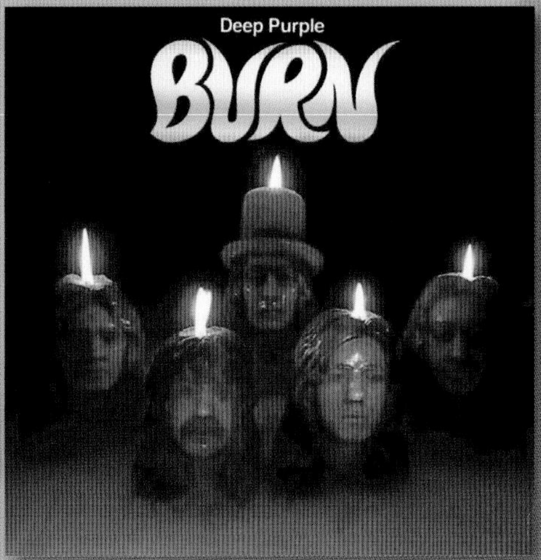

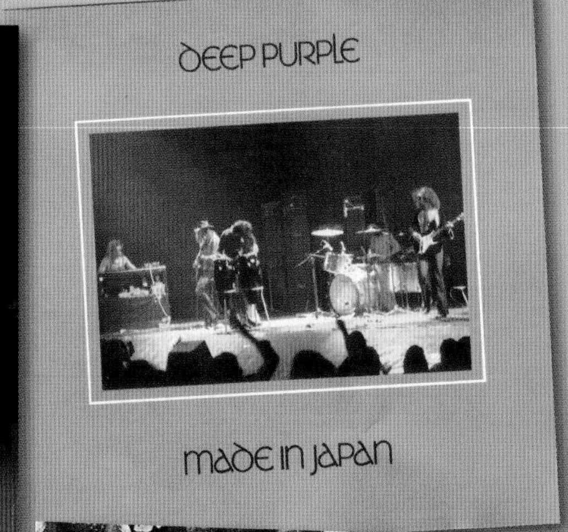

Translating Blackmore's six-string hellfire and fury to a 20,000-strong arena crowd obviously required some gargantuan amplification, and all needs were ably met with a pair of 200-watt Marshall Major heads, each of which ran through two 4x12-inch speaker cabs. To induce these extremely robust tube amps into early distortion, and to warm up the tone of the otherwise bright Strats, Blackmore played through an Awai reel-to-reel tape recorder, which he set to "pause" and used purely as a preamp.

In his more recent adventures with the Baroque-influenced outfit Blackmore's Night, Blackmore plays a range of acoustic instruments, although for his electric excursions he has lately taken to endorsing a model by German-made Engl amps, the E650 Ritchie Blackmore 100W.

Ritchie Blackmore

Blackmore tests the famed durability of his Strat during Deep Purple's 1974 U.S. tour. *Fin Costello/Redferns/Getty Images*

Ritchie Blackmore's 1974 Stratocaster. *Christie's/Bridgeman*

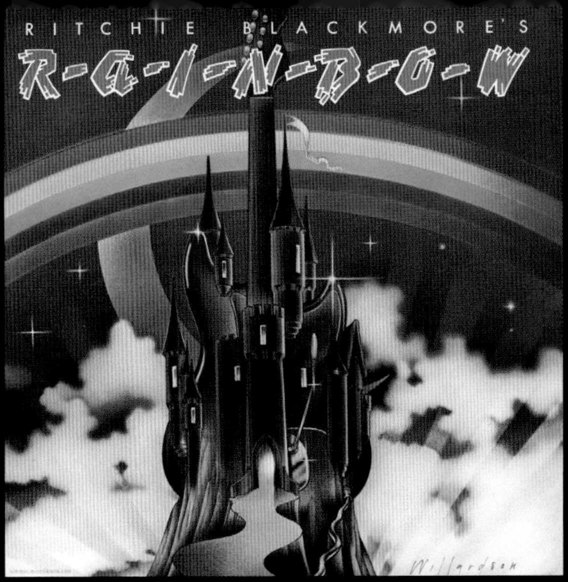

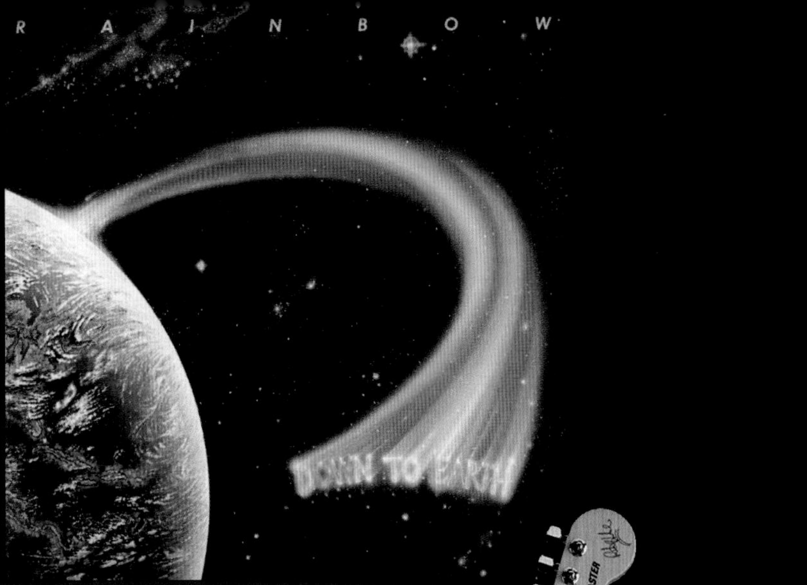

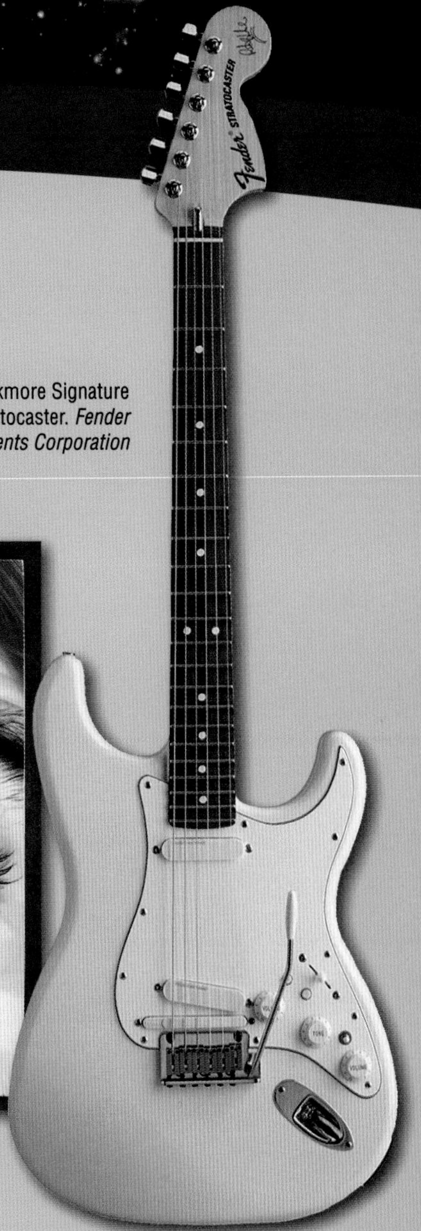

2004 Ritchie Blackmore Signature Olympic White Stratocaster. *Fender Musical Instruments Corporation*

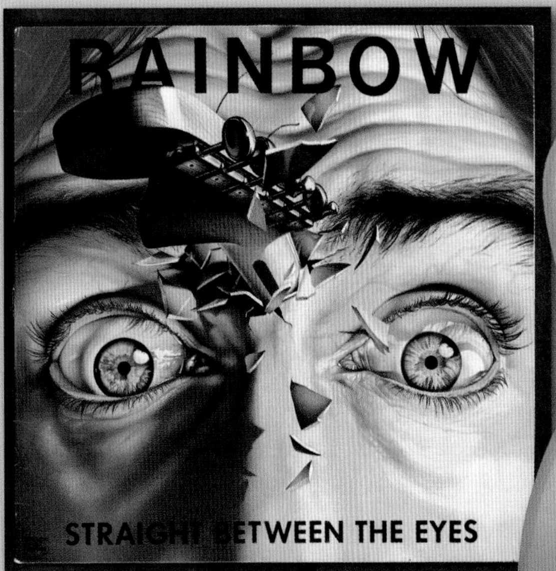

David Gilmour

Dave Gilmour of Pink Floyd performs at the Miller Strat Pack concert on September 23, 2004, at Black Island Studios in London. *Jo Hale/Getty Images*

Some are born with great guitars, while others have great guitars thrust upon them. So it was, to some extent at least (and with Shakespeare's forgiveness), with David Gilmour, who made plenty of standout music with Pink Floyd on other instruments before acquiring a certain 1954 Strat toward the end of the 1970s. Historic in its own right, now doubly iconic for its use on several classic Pink Floyd recordings, Gilmour's 1954 Stratocaster is a very early example of that model and carries the serial number 0001 on its neck plate, although these two facts don't have any real correlation.

This '54 Stratocaster, with a neck made in June of that year and a body dated in September, is certainly an early one (the Stratocaster was only released early in 1954 following several prototypes made in 1953), but is not actually *the* first Strat made, as the serial number implies. Gilmour's Stratocaster wears a nonstandard finish that is sometimes referred to as Desert Sand or faded Olympic White but is not quite like either of those two later Fender custom colors. It also has a gold-plated vibrato unit and jack plate and a gold-colored anodized aluminum pickguard like those that would later appear on the Musicmaster, Duo-Sonic, and Jazzmaster. The common wisdom in vintage-Fender camps is that the eye-catching serial number was used to denote a special-order model, indicating this perhaps *was* the first Stratocaster with gold-plated hardware, seen more often on Blonde Mary Kaye Stratocasters that

David Gilmour's 1954 Stratocaster guitar, serial number 0001. *Nigel Osbourne/Redferns/Getty Images*

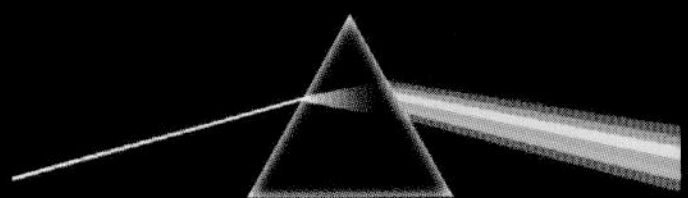

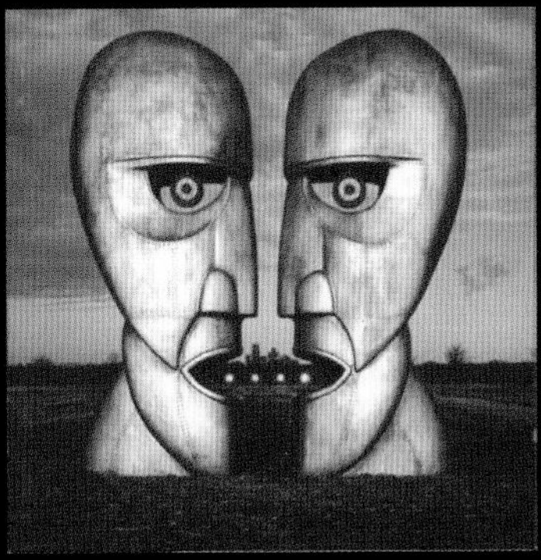

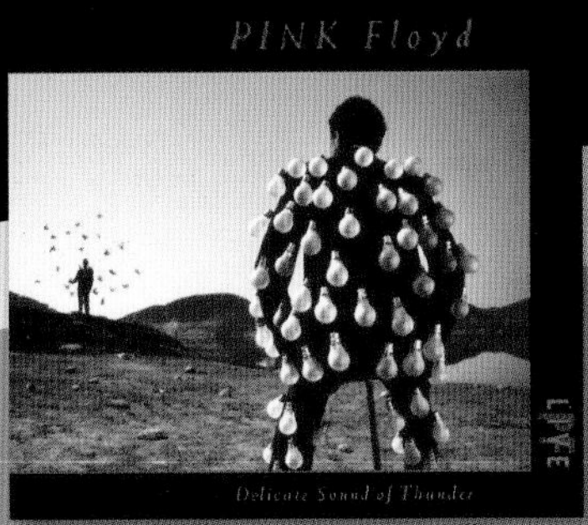

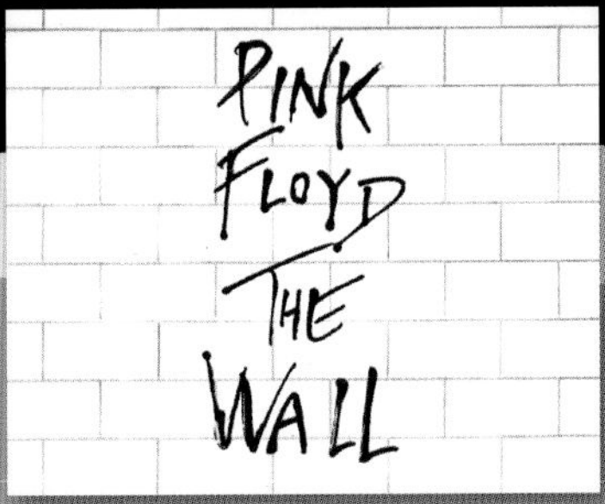

became popular a couple of years later. In any case, Stratocasters made before Gilmour's have been seen wearing higher numbers, so the 0001 most likely wasn't intended to denote the guitar's chronology—at least not among all Strats.

Gilmour's 0001 Strat followed a rather circuitous route into his loving hands. Owned at one time by pickup maker Seymour Duncan, the Strat was purchased by Pink Floyd guitar tech Phil Taylor in the mid-1970s for a reported $900 (possibly from Pete Townshend's guitar tech, Alan Rogan, who is credited in some versions of the history as having owned it between Duncan and Taylor). A couple of years later, Gilmour pried the instrument from Taylor by offering the tech the cash he was seeking toward the down payment on a house. The 1954 Strat was often used in the studio from around 1977 onward on several Pink Floyd recordings and on work Gilmour did for Paul McCartney and Brian Ferry. One of the easiest ways to see and hear it simultaneously, though, is to watch the video of the fiftieth anniversary concert for the Fender Stratocaster filmed at Wembley Arena, London, in 2004, when Gilmour picked up this legendary guitar for live renditions of "Coming Back to Life" and "Marooned."

2008 David Gilmour Stratocaster.
Fender Musical Instruments Corporation

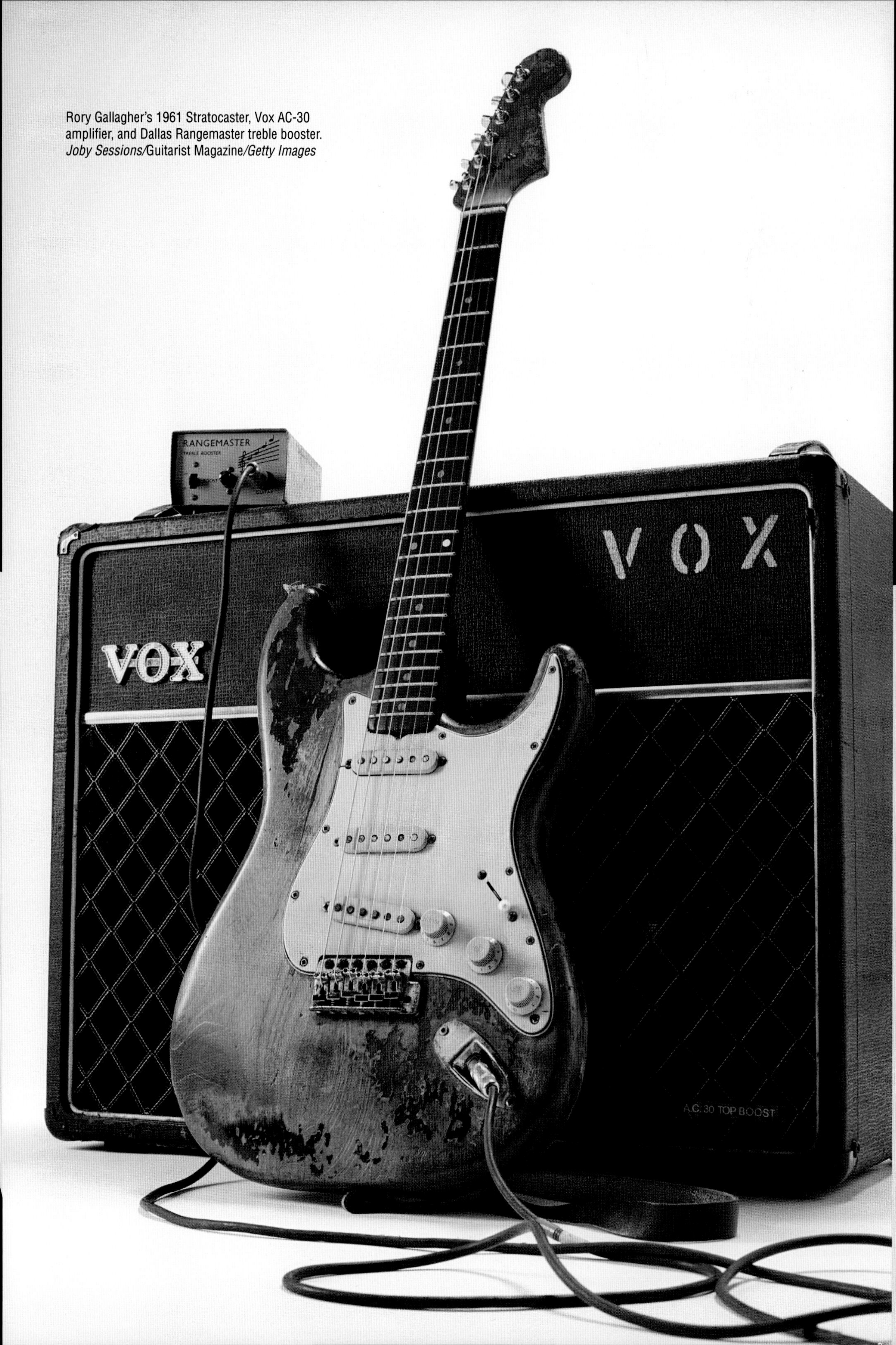

Rory Gallagher's 1961 Stratocaster, Vox AC-30 amplifier, and Dallas Rangemaster treble booster. *Joby Sessions/*Guitarist Magazine*/Getty Images*

Amid all the battered Strats that have made their marks in the annals of the electric guitar, Rory Gallagher's leaves a bolder impression than most. This road-worn 1961 Stratocaster epitomizes the instrument of the hard-traveling, hard-playing, hard-living blues rocker and will eternally remain associated with the late Irish musician. Gallagher bought this guitar in 1963. It was not only the first Stratocaster he had ever seen, but it was believed to have been the first Strat imported into Ireland. It was ordered for another local guitarist who thought he was buying a red Stratocaster (as recently popularized by Hank Marvin in England). When a sunburst instrument arrived, he played it for a time then decided to pass it along to Gallagher and wait for a new red Strat. A fortuitous decision: Rory Gallagher and this passed-over Strat produced a mountain of fiery, emotive, heartfelt blues and helped to establish a Fender-based blues-rock tone that is idolized to this day.

In addition to its famous disappearing finish, Gallagher's Strat shows evidence of the wear and tear that will overcome any hard-gigged electric guitar. Its replaced tuners (mismatched, with five Sperzels and one Gotoh), single white-plastic fingerboard dot in place of one absent clay twelfth-fret marker, rewound pickups, and replaced potentiometers are all repairs of pure necessity, undertaken by an artist who made this his main instrument throughout his career. (Gallagher owned but rarely played one other Strat, a 1957 Sunburst with maple neck bought as a backup, as well as a Telecaster, a Gretsch Corvette, and a handful of other guitars.) Mike Eldred, the head of Fender's Custom Shop, who examined the original item in the course of creating Fender's Rory Gallagher Tribute Stratocaster, relates that there were many further modifications under the hood too. "Inside it was pretty trashed. Replaced wood, bad wiring job, bits of rubber. It was a mess," Eldred told Patrick Kennedy for *Strat Collector* in 2004.

The most notable aspect of Gallagher's '61 Strat's decay, however, was not the result of abuse (Gallagher doted on the instrument and cared for it lovingly), but of its owner's body chemistry. According to brother Donal, who now owns the guitar, Rory had a rare blood type that gave his sweat extremely acidic properties. Gallagher sweated *a lot* in the course of any performance, and his Strat's sunburst finish paid the price. (The artist himself spoke of having to remove the waterlogged neck to dry it out, sweat having penetrated the wood after wearing away the clear nitrocellulose lacquer from the maple.) The amount of bare wood on this legendary '61 Stratocaster has helped propagate the belief that guitars with thinner (or no) finishes resonate more freely and have a better tone than those with thick, nonbreathable finishes. There might be something to this theory, but it's also a reasonable assumption that the magic that Rory Gallagher and his battered Strat made together had less to do with absent lacquer than it did with the artist's unchained heart, head, and hands.

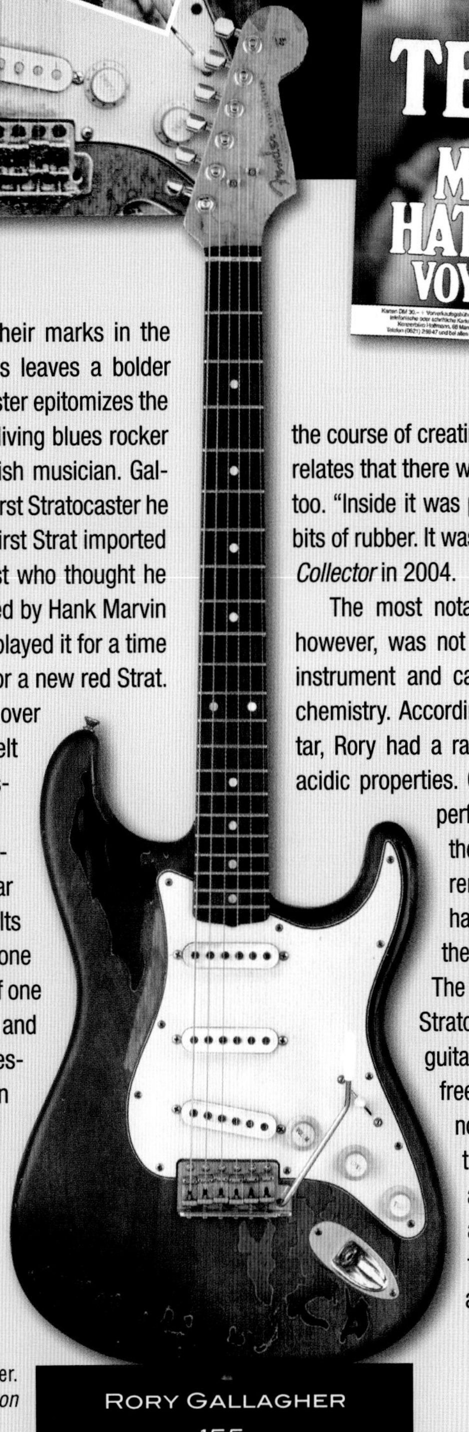
2004 Rory Gallagher Tribute Stratocaster.
Fender Musical Instruments Corporation

Robbie Robertson

Robbie Robertson of the Band plays alongside Bob Dylan at Madison Square Garden on January 29, 1974. *Gijsbert Hanekroot/ Redferns/Getty Images*

Robbie Robertson's bronzed 1954 Stratocaster that he played at *The Last Waltz. Rick Gould*

Music fans who are unfamiliar with the intricacies of Robbie Robertson's career tend to know him primarily as the guitarist with the Band and Bob Dylan, and to picture him, if at all, with the odd monster of a Stratocaster that he wielded in much of the concert documentary *The Last Waltz*. Dig just a little deeper, though, and you quickly find that this understated artist boasts a career that stretches virtually from the roots of rock 'n' roll to span many of the high points in the history of popular music. The guitarist was born Jaime Royal Robertson in Toronto, Canada, in 1943 to a Canadian father and a mother of Mohawk descent. He learned the guitar at an early age during visits to his mother's relations on the Six Nations Reserve, and he was an active professional musician around the Toronto scene while still in his teens.

Robertson joined formative rock 'n' roller Ronnie Hawkins and his band, the Hawks, in 1960 and toured the United States and Canada with the outfit until 1964. After a brief stint on their own, Robertson and the Hawks—which included Levon Helm, Garth Hudson, Rick Danko, and Richard Manuel—signed on as Bob Dylan's backup band in 1965, and upon signing to Capitol Records in 1967 as a band in their own right, changed their name to the Band. They would release several successful albums of their own into the middle of the following decade, while returning time and again to their collaboration with Dylan.

Known as more of a Telecaster player through the early years of the Band, Robertson acquired a pre-CBS Stratocaster along the way, took to playing it more frequently, and decided to transform it to a sort of monument in honor of the Band's

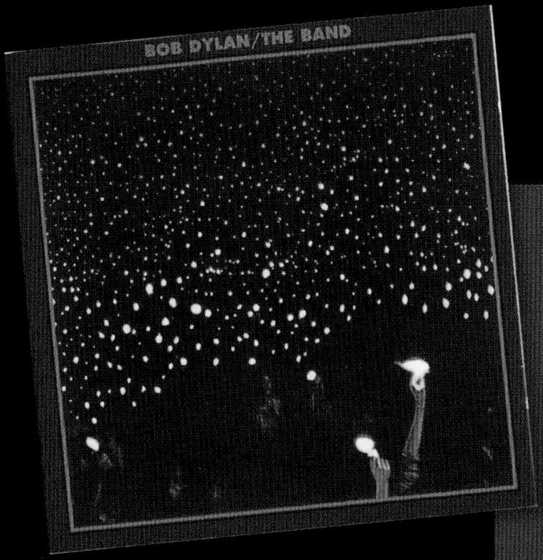

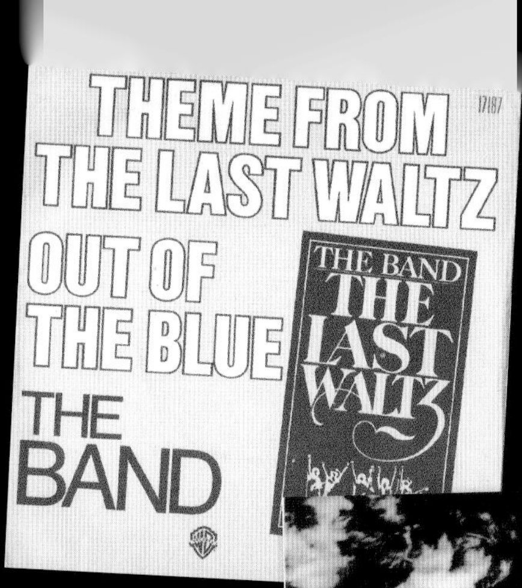

final concert together, documented by Martin Scorsese in the film *The Last Waltz*, which is still considered among the best concert films ever made. "I've had this souped-up old Stratocaster quite a while," Robertson told *Musician* magazine in 1987. "It has number 0254 on the back. You can tell it's old 'cause the neck's a little thick. Before I used it in *Last Waltz*, I had it bronzed, like baby shoes." To clear up some picking space for the fingerpicks he habitually used, Robertson also had the Strat's middle pickup moved back alongside the bridge pickup, a mode that makes the guitar look like it carries a humbucking pickup, but it's actually the two single-coil Strat pickups. Robertson has often said this guitar was a 1958 Stratocaster, although the thicker neck profile, the round string guide on the headstock, and its 254 serial number might suggest an older guitar from 1954, although the interchangeability of Fender parts makes this virtually impossible to determine without disassembling the guitar. While he used this freshly bronzed pre-CBS Stratocaster throughout much of *The Last Waltz*, the bronze shell, in addition to giving it "a very thick, sturdy sound," also added considerable weight to the guitar. At times, Roberts lightened the load by switching to what appears to be a '57 Stratocaster in two-tone sunburst, although it's unclear whether this was his guitar or Bob Dylan's (certainly Dylan plays it on the finale, "I Shall Be Released"). Robertson later added a "double-locking" Washburn vibrato unit to the Stratocaster, taking it even further from its Leo-certified origins.

Bronze Strats aside, Robertson's wry, spare playing style has made him a true guitarist of note, and he has been admired by many prominent names in the music industry, in addition to legions of fans, for his rootsy tone and tasteful fills. Turning once again to the live documentary film, there are few better examples of his sound, or his musicality, than the performances on "The Night They Drove Old Dixie Down," "Ophelia," and "The Weight," the latter a Band classic written by Robertson himself.

Fender has recently issued a Custom Shop Robbie Robertson Stratocaster available in the artist's preferred Moonburst finish as well as a lacquer-based bronze, and he has recently been seen playing one of two Fender Custom Shop Strats decorated by the Apache artist Darren Vigil Gray.

"I've had this souped-up old Stratocaster quite a while. It has number 0254 on the back. You can tell it's old 'cause the neck's a little thick. Before I used it in *The Last Waltz*, I had it bronzed, like baby shoes. That gave it a very thick, sturdy sound. A Stratocaster has three pickups: I had the one in the middle moved to the back with the other and tied them together. They have a different sound when they're tied together, and I don't like having a pickup in the middle, where you pick. I've got a Washburn whammy bar on that guitar."

—Robert Robertson, *Musician*, 1987

Wayne Kramer

2010 Wayne Kramer Signature Stratocaster. *Fender Musical Instruments Corporation*

The MC5 roared out of 1960s Detroit like a big-block V8 with open headers. Fueled by the twin guitars of Wayne Kramer and Fred "Sonic" Smith, their supercharged take on rock 'n' roll mixed garage, R&B, and psychedelia, with a boost of Sun Ra for good measure, and pushed the contemporary boundaries of volume and furor to the redline. The MC5 was also known for their political leanings and were one of the only bands of the era to talk the talk and walk the walk, holding the Grant Park stage in Chicago during the 1968 Democratic convention, for example, and escaping moments before the Chicago PD took over proceedings. (Rumor has it the Grateful Dead and Jefferson Airplane, though billed, were no-shows.)

Given their antiestablishment leanings, it might seem odd to some that Kramer's most iconic guitar was this "Stars and Stripes" Stratocaster, though as the guitarist explained upon Fender's release in 2011 of a heavily relic'd Signature Series model (complete with its "This tool kills hate" neckplate), "When I painted the guitar with this motif it was really to claim my patriotism in spite of what the country was doing at the time."

Certainly, performance was a part of the equation as well. "The [MC5's] performance was on all levels," Kramer explained. "I had clothes made up out of these exotic materials and the rest of the people in the band did as well,

Wayne Kramer bends a note on his trademark Strat while performing with MC5 in Mount Clemens, Michigan, in 1969. From left, drummer Dennis "Machine Gun" Thompson, Kramer, Fred "Sonic" Smith, and Rob Tyner. *Leni Sinclair/ Michael Ochs Archives/Getty Images*

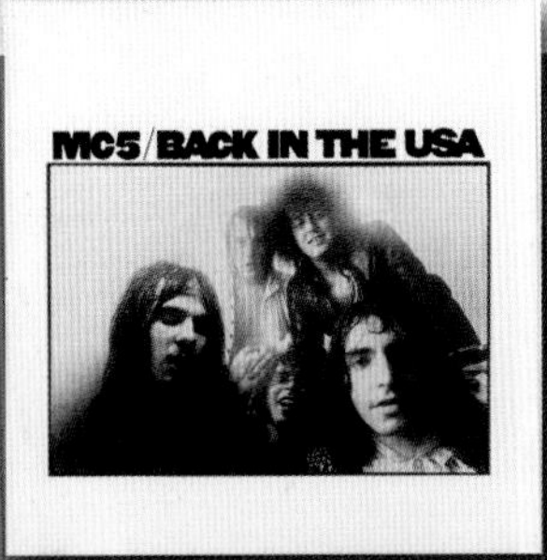

and I thought maybe the guitar itself could be part of this, kind of, total assault on the culture."

Little is known of the original guitar, other than the fact that it's a CBS-era instrument and must have been fairly new when Kramer acquired it. Given its new vintage and the MC5's balls-out sonic assault, it doesn't seem a stretch to assume that Kramer—who also played Epiphones and Gibsons with the MC5—had the humbucker installed in the middle position. What Kramer has offered in regard to the Stars and Stripes Strat, however, is that it was the instrument he wielded on the evenings of October 30 and 31, 1968, when the MC5 recorded the incendiary performances at Detroit's Grande Ballroom that became the touchstone protopunk LP *Kick Out the Jams.*

The MC5 disbanded in 1972 and Kramer did two years in federal prison for selling cocaine to an undercover agent in 1975 (an incident immortalized in The Clash's "Jail Guitar Doors"). Upon release he formed the abortive Gang War with Johnny Thunders before going on to enjoy a solo career and work scoring television and films. Over the years, he and surviving MC5 bandmates have reunited to perform with members of The Cult, Motörhead, Mudhoney, and other acts that they influenced. Kramer has also continued to spread his political beliefs through music, including his work with Jail Guitar Doors, a nonprofit that provides musical instruments to prisoners in the United States and Great Britain. *—Dennis Pernu*

Lowell George of Little Feat at the Beacon Theatre in New York on April 7, 1978. *Richard E. Aaron/Redferns/Getty Images*

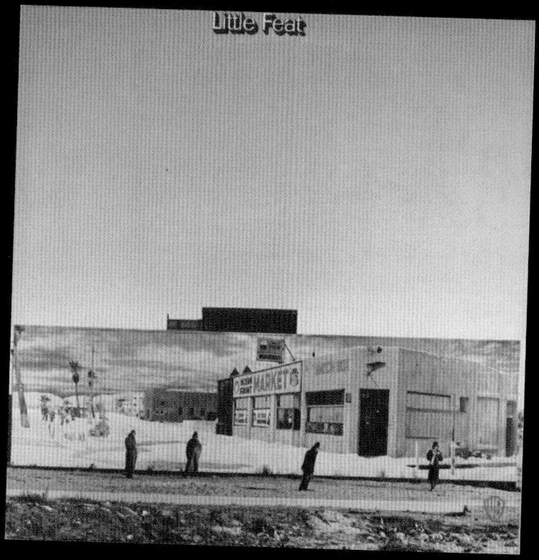

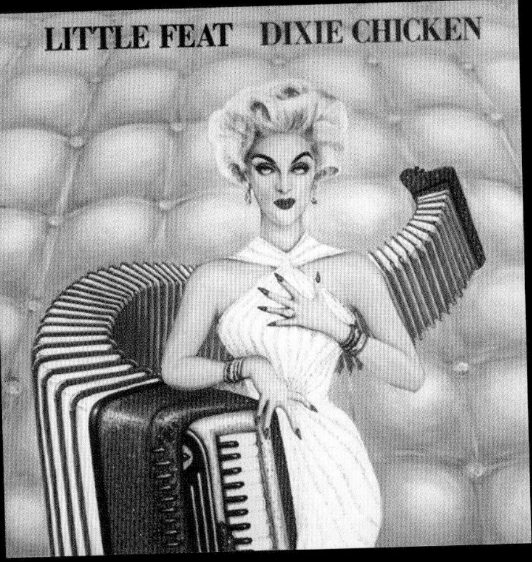

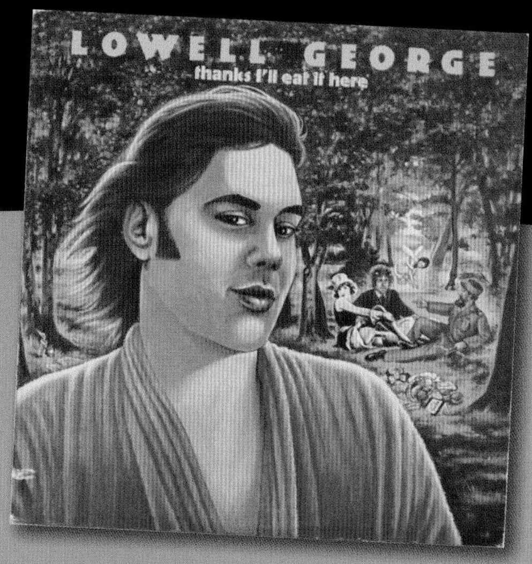

From his early days with Frank Zappa and the Mothers of Invention in the late 1960s, to the formation of his own band, Little Feat, to his short-lived solo career, Lowell George was well on course to becoming a significant hero of the Stratocaster before his untimely exit from the scene on June 29, 1979. Check out any of Little Feat's landmark 1970s recordings and, alongside that soulful voice, George's guitar tone stands out as one of the most distinctive of the era. When George told *Guitar Player* interviewer Dan Kening in 1976 that he always preferred "to buy a stock guitar so if it gets stolen I can replace it easily," that really only told a fraction of the story of what went into creating that distinctive voice. Looked at another way, the guitar that he often turned that "stock guitar" into might be considered something entirely different from a standard Stratocaster.

Having had several guitars stolen on the road, as he also told *Guitar Player* magazine, George had taken to buying standard, off-the-shelf 1970s Stratocasters at the peak of his success, but the best known of these had several modifications that helped it achieve his signature tone. While the Strat's standard neck pickup served his mellower moments well, he put a slightly fatter Telecaster pickup to the bridge position for extra punch, which was given a serious goose by the addition of an Alembic Blaster preamp, housed in a replacement output-jack plate. Add to the brew a set of heavy-gauge flat-wound strings, put it in open-A tuning (like the more common open-G, but a whole step up), slip a Sears Craftsman 11/16 socket wrench on your little finger for slide, and pump it all through a custom-made Dumble amplifier, and you're there. A long way from "off-the-shelf Strat" for sure, and George's tasteful slide work deserves a modicum of the credit too.

Lowell George had at least two similarly equipped '70s Stratocasters, one with a natural finish and another in blonde, as witnessed in photos and live concert footage from the era, but he likely owned several over the years. Not all had the Tele pickup or the Alembic preamp at all times, but they tended to evolve toward that ideal as he carted them out on the road and back into the studio again. Any of the great studio albums exhibit the tone that this mighty concoction brought forth, but it might arguably best be heard on Little Feat's live album from 1978, *Waiting for Columbus*, which eventually became their best selling record. Dig the blistering slide tones on tracks such as "Fat Man in the Bathtub," "Dixie Chicken," and "Rocket in My Pocket" (its girth aided by some judicious delay)—and note, just as crucially, how important the use of restraint, and silence, is to his playing style too—and you know it can be none other than Lowell George. All the more tragic, then, that he left us at the age of 34 after dying of heart failure just two weeks into his solo tour.

Mick Mars of Mötley Crüe picks his well-traveled Stratocaster.
Ebet Roberts/Redfern/Getty Images

1988 XII Stratocaster twelve-string.
Nigel Osbourne/Redferns/Getty Images

1979 25th Anniversary Stratocaster.
Nigel Osbourne/Redferns/Getty Images

1981 Gold C Series Stratocaster with 24-karat gold hardware. *Nigel Osbourne/Redferns/Getty Images*

Guitarist Homer Haynes teamed with Jethro Burns on a long run of country music hits and sendups.

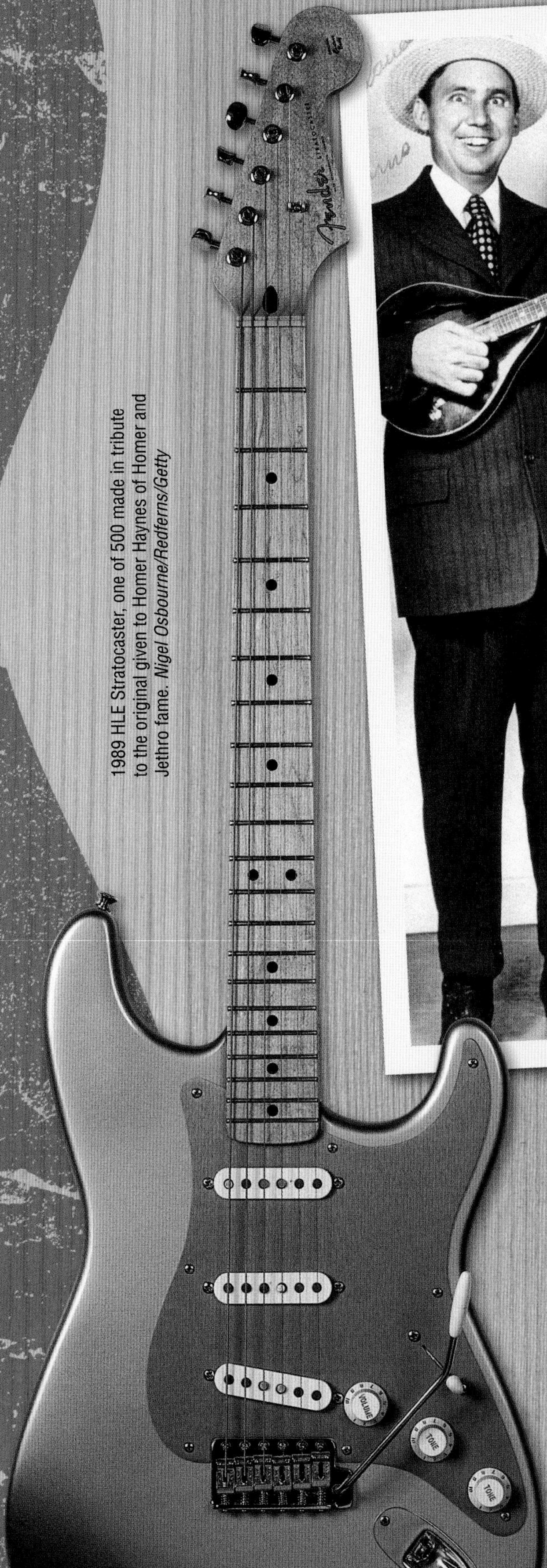

1989 HLE Stratocaster, one of 500 made in tribute to the original given to Homer Haynes of Homer and Jethro fame. *Nigel Osbourne/Redferns/Getty*

Ry Cooder picks his Coodercaster, a hot-rodded partscaster based on a Strat body and neck. Cooder fitted the guitar with a cheap '60s Teisco Gold Foil pickup he got from David Lindley in the neck position and a Valco pickup from a Hawaiian guitar in the bridge position. *Morena Brengola/Redferns/Getty Images*

1995 Freddy Tavares Aloha Stratocaster, one of 152 diamond dealer models with an inlaid diamond at the tip of the headstock and a hollow aluminum body. *Brunk Auctions*

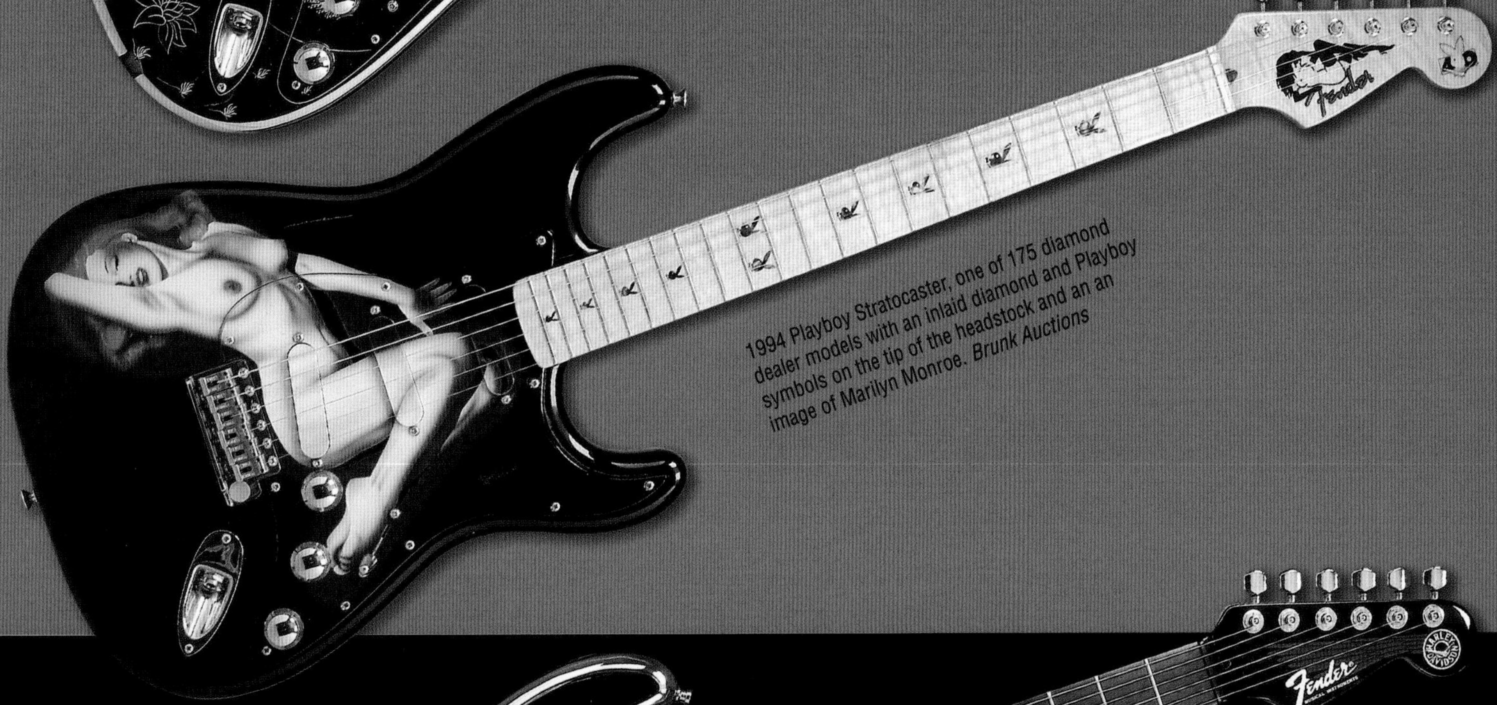

1994 Playboy Stratocaster, one of 175 diamond dealer models with an inlaid diamond and Playboy symbols on the tip of the headstock and an an image of Marilyn Monroe. *Brunk Auctions*

1993 Harley-Davidson Stratocaster, one of 109 diamond dealer models with an inlaid diamond at the tip of the headstock and a hollow aluminum body with chrome finish. *Brunk Auctions*

Lenny Kaye jams on his Strat with the Patti Smith Group in 1973.
Jody Cavaglia/Lenny Kaye collection

Lenny Kaye's 2006 60th Anniversary Stratocaster, customized by guitar tech Barre Duryea into a "Unicaster."
Lenny Kaye

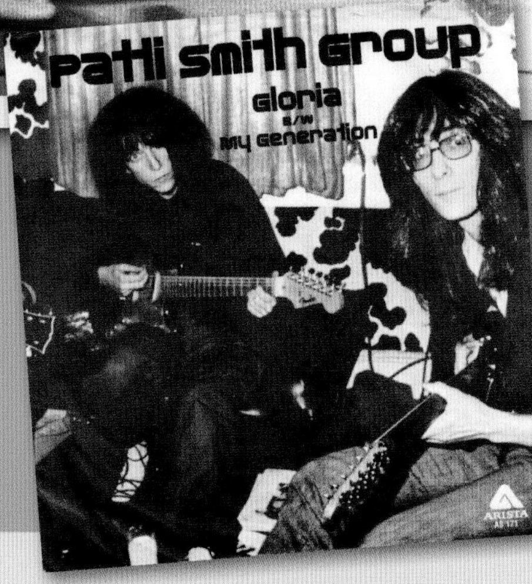

"I mostly play the Fender Stratocaster. I like its body shape, the sense of manipulation, its clarity. I've been playing Strats pretty much my whole life. I've gone through many—many which have vanished into the ozone through sticky-fingered backstage people. What I play now is a fairly unique instrument that I call a Unicaster. The joke in the band is that I would always play the middle pickup wide open and hardly ever switch. So one day I came to the rehearsal room and my guitar tech had removed all the other pickups and cut me a pickguard so I would just have the middle pickup and a volume knob. It's a hijacked 60th Anniversary Strat, but it's really served me well. I try to make the different sounds come out of my fingers."

—Lenny Kaye

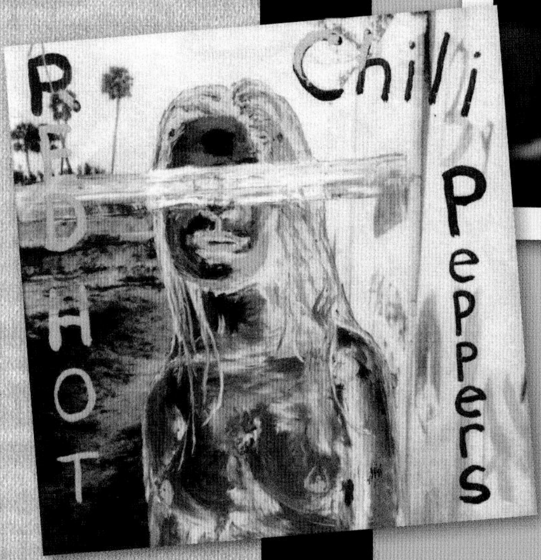

John Frusciante and the Red Hot Chili Peppers play Jones Beach, New York, on September 12, 2003.
KMazur/WireImage/Getty Images

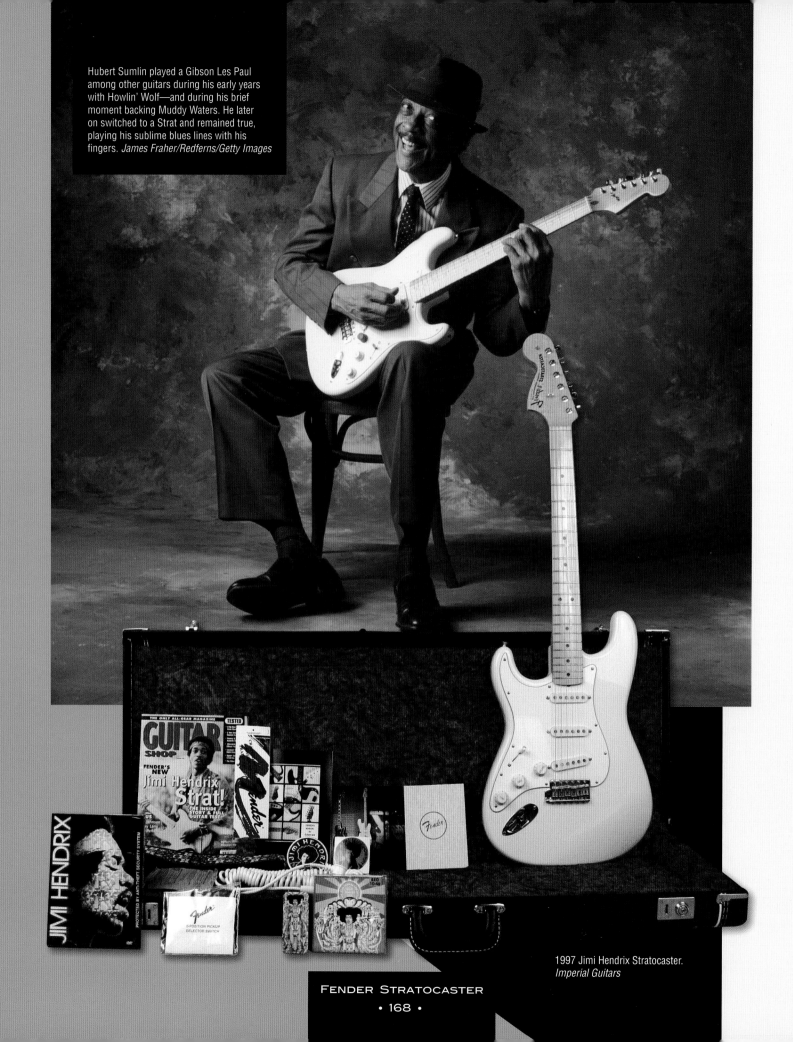

Hubert Sumlin played a Gibson Les Paul among other guitars during his early years with Howlin' Wolf—and during his brief moment backing Muddy Waters. He later on switched to a Strat and remained true, playing his sublime blues lines with his fingers. *James Fraher/Redferns/Getty Images*

1997 Jimi Hendrix Stratocaster. *Imperial Guitars*

Dr. Feelgood guitarist Wilko Johnson's Stratocaster and 1962 Telecaster in his trademark black-and-red color scheme. *Kevin Nixon/Guitarist Magazine/Getty Images*

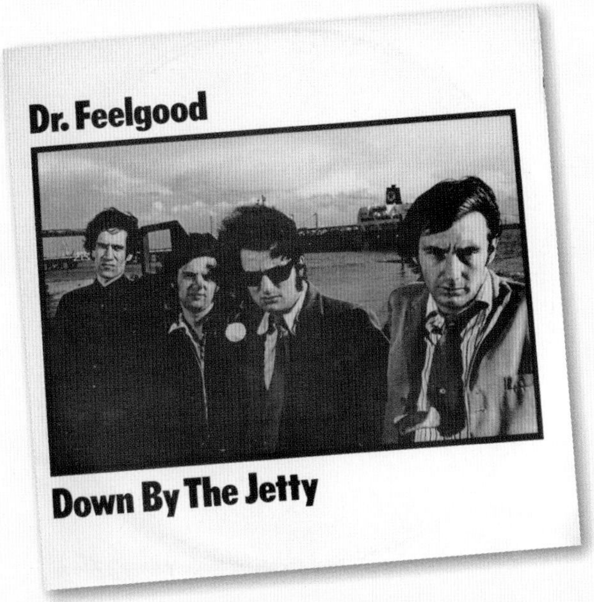

Moto Custom Shop Stratocaster and Blues Deluxe amplifier, one of 250 sets made. *Brunk Auctions*

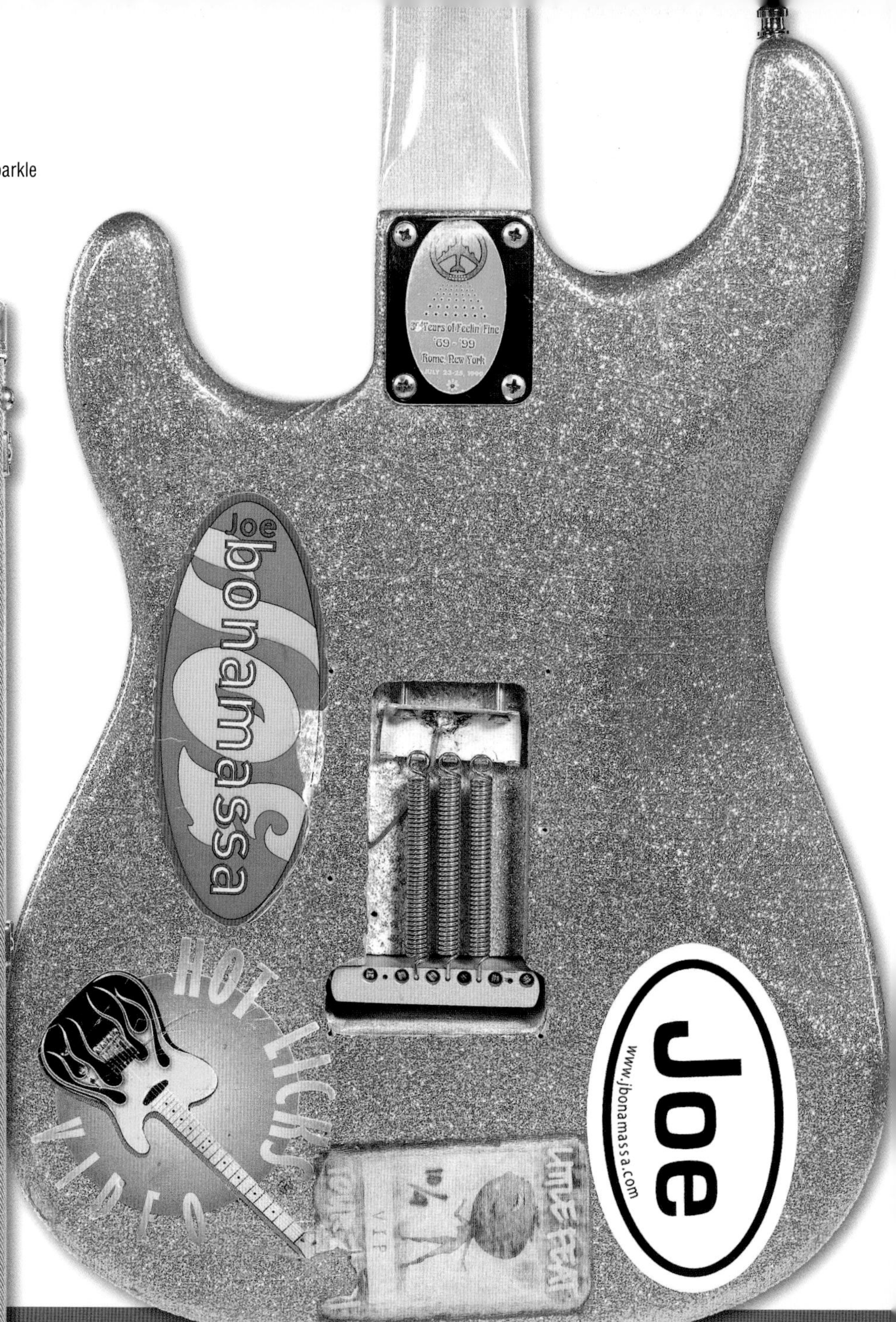

Joe Bonamassa's Gold Sparkle Stratocaster. *Bonhams*

"This Gold Sparkle Stratocaster has been part of my music since I was 17 years old. There was a time in my very early twenties that I wasn't sure if I wanted to continue pursuing music as a profession. I had grown tired of the grind and the task ahead of me to even make a modest living seemed monumental. I sold off all my guitars except one. For some reason or another I kept the gold Stratocaster that I assembled from various vintage parts. I have always and will always have great affection for that guitar down to the pin-up girl sticker that I found in an Omaha antique shop for the grand sum of $5. This is the guitar that inspired me to pull myself up by my boot straps, refocus, and go on to have a successful decade of making solo albums."

—Joe Bonamassa

2004 50th Anniversary Aztec Gold Stratocaster.
Fender Musical Instruments Corporation

Randy Bachman

Randy Bachman and his Strat power Bachman-Turner Overdrive.
Michael Ochs Archives/Getty Images

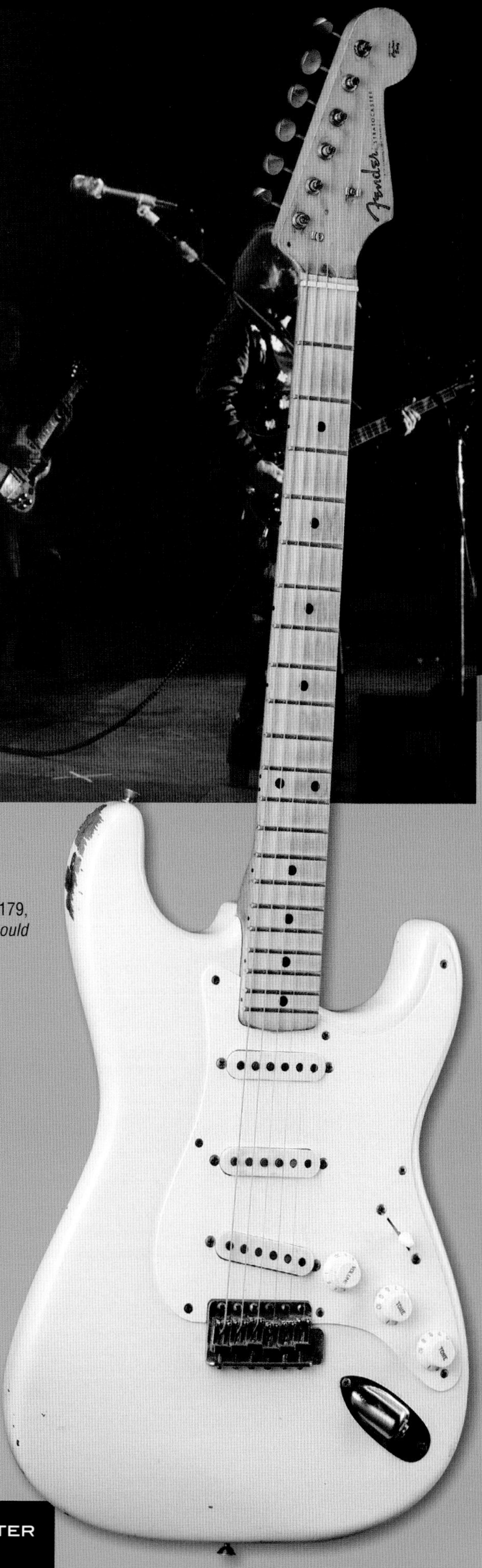

Randy Bachman's 1955 Stratocaster, serial number 7179, that he played with BTO. *Rick Gould*

There's a saying among hot rodders that anyone can build a hot rod, but it takes a real man to cut one up. This old adage refers, of course, to the act of taking torch and hacksaw to rare, vintage tin with the intention modifying it to do things that Henry Ford never intended. When it comes to guitars, Randy Bachman is a first-class hot rodder.

Though he often has been seen taking care of business with a Gibson Les Paul and is known as one of the world's foremost collectors of Gretsch instruments, Bachman is also closely associated with the Fender Stratocaster, thanks to a guitar known as "The Legend." Bachman, founder of Canadian rock giants The Guess Who and Bachman-Turner Overdrive, obtained The Legend in the late 1960s. It had already been modified a bit by a previous owner, but Bachman was fearless when it came to laying the thing down on his workbench and applying chisel, saw, and sundry other tools, all in an effort to make the guitar do what he wanted it to do—things Leo never intended. As Bachman told photographer Rick Gould:

"Originally a black '59 Strat, the Legend was stripped to bare wood. The upper horn had my name in rub-on decals as well as a round metal Titano

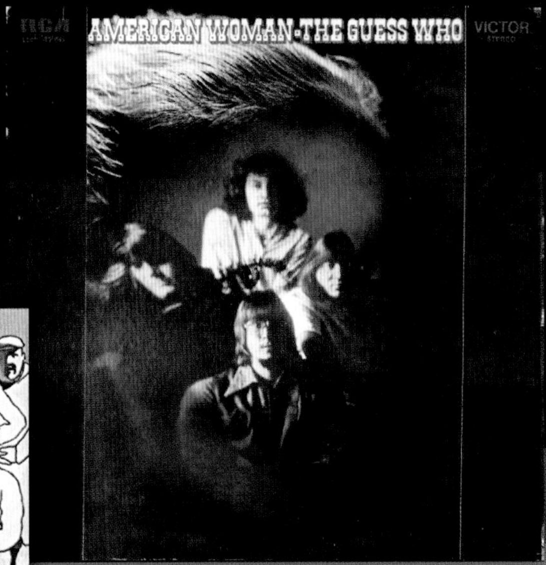

accordion logo. The guitar had been modded to be a 9-string and had extra tuners on it, which I took off, leaving three extra holes in the headstock. Also, the big curved part on the headstock had broken off when I threw the guitar into a speaker cabinet à la Pete Townshend. I also broke off the wang bar and had to redrill the tremolo block to accommodate a bigger screw-in arm that I had made by a blacksmith. It was a 'T' with an arm to grab over the pickups and a big one that went out back past the strap attachment. This allowed for extreme Hendrixian wang-bar tactics with feedback.

"In the back, I chiseled out a long channel, thinking I could create my own B-bender by cutting out the B saddle, stabilizing the trem block, and keeping just one spring on the cutout B saddle. Then I found out I couldn't hacksaw the trem block so I just left it.

"When the nut broke to pieces, I didn't have a replacement so I used my mother's metal knitting needle. It didn't have grooves and it was cool how the strings slid around for low bending. I sanded and steel-wooled the back of the neck like a violin neck with no finish, which made playing such an ease.

"I reversed the inny jack to be an outy, which I thought Fender always should have done anyway because it allows bigger jacks and L jacks to be easily used."

If it seems like all this gouging and soldering made The Legend a Stratocaster in name only, you ain't seen nothin' yet. Reportedly, the guitar also featured a swapped-in rounder-profile Fender Jazzmaster neck and three on-off pots in place of the usual three-position selector, allowing Bachman to combine any two pickups, including the bridge and neck units.

Bachman: "My bridge pickup was a '50s Tele that was held to the pickguard with clear bathtub caulking, which prevented feedback and squeal. I had a Rickenbacker pickup at the neck for a while and then a '59 Humbucker. The last mod was three off/on pickup switches that allowed for an amazing combination of pickups—neck and bridge, all three, bridge and middle, neck and middle, et cetera. Problem? Yes. I was too wild onstage and would hit them all. Of course the guitar would have no sound because all the pickups had been switched off."

"There's something about the Strat sound that just rings out," Bachman wrote in his book, *Vinyl Tap Stories*. "If you take that same guitar and run it through a small tweed Fender amp cranked right up, you get a really great bluesy sound."

As for The Legend, sadly it went the way of many other hard-touring rock 'n' roll axes: Bachman reports that it was stolen. "It would be the thrill of a lifetime to get the guitar back, but it was just a wreck, so unless someone knows what it is . . ." he said. "But what a sound and monster it was." —*Dennis Pernu*

Randy Bachman's 1960 hardtail Stratocaster that he played with BTO. *Rick Gould*

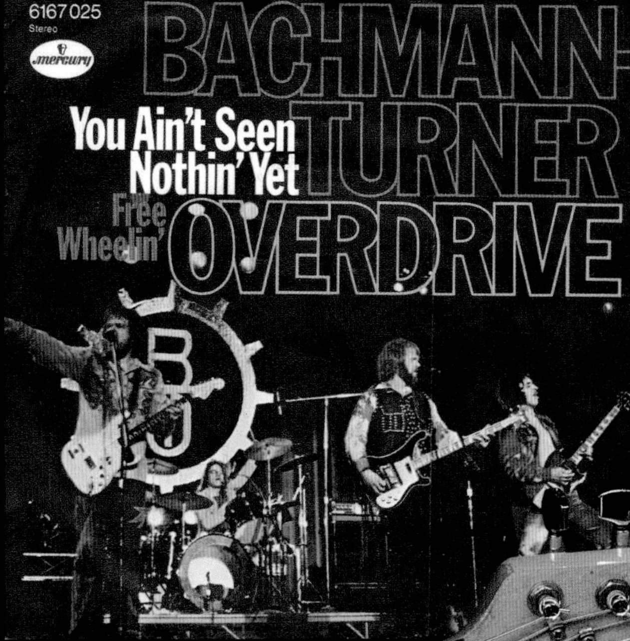
6167 025
Stereo
mercury
BACHMANN-TURNER OVERDRIVE
You Ain't Seen Nothin' Yet
Free Wheelin'

[redacted]

Fender
STRATOCASTER

BACHMAN-TURNER OVERDRIVE

BACHMAN · TURNER OVERDRIVE NOT FRAGILE
NOT FRAGILE

BACHMAN-TURNER OVERDRIVE II

Ronnie Wood

Ronnie Wood and Rod Stewart front the Faces in 1974.
Mick Gold/Redferns/Getty Images

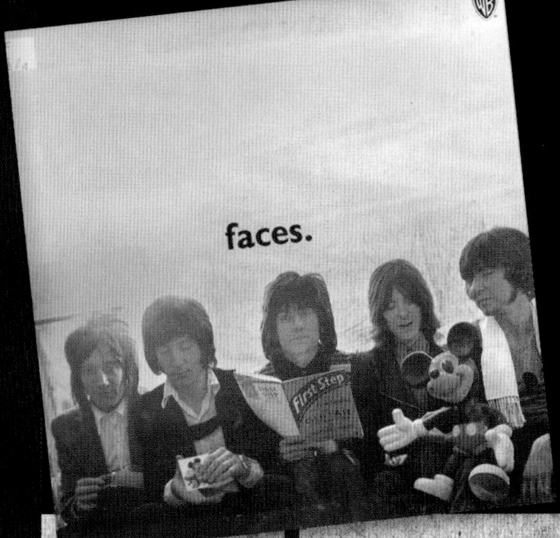

Playing the guitar with the Faces, then separately with Rod Stewart, then the Rolling Stones—with several notable side projects and solo ventures laced throughout—pretty much gives you your choice of any guitar out there. Yet time and again Ronnie Wood has turned to the workmanlike Fender Stratocaster. And while archive shots of Wood in concert will often show the more unusual, arguably more dramatic metal-fronted Zemaitis models or his Lucite-bodied Dan Armstrong, a prized vintage Stratocaster has long been his go-to guitar, both on stage and in the studio.

For many years Wood owned and played an original 1955 Stratocaster in two-tone sunburst, with a similar-looking 1956 Strat as backup. Entirely stock, the '55 is far and away the single guitar most seen in his Stones performances of recent decades and remained a major

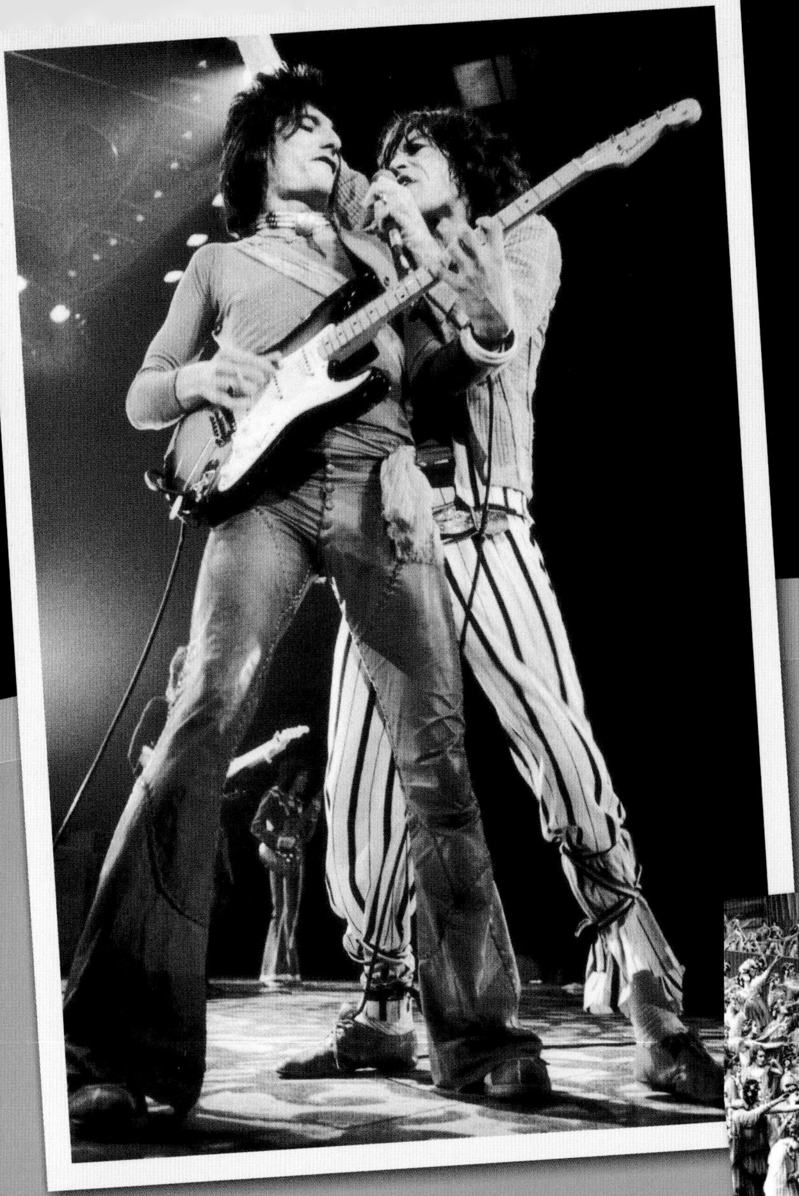

Wood and Mick Jagger share the mic during the Rolling Stones' 1975 Tour of the Americas. *Christopher Simon Sykes/Hulton Archive/Getty Images*

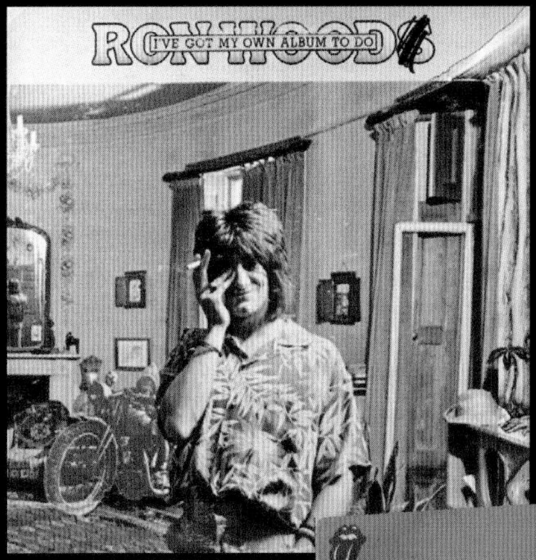

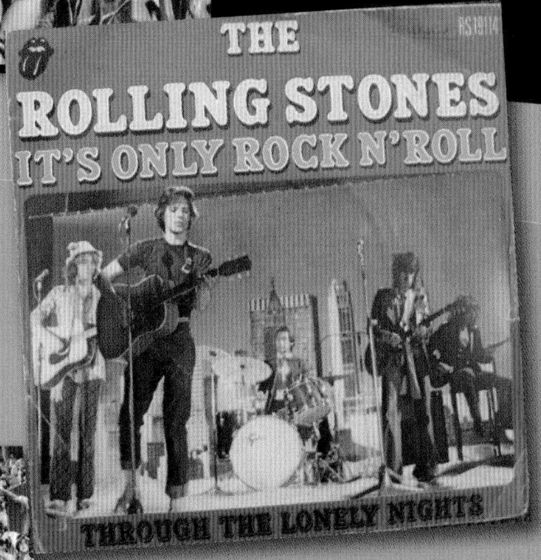

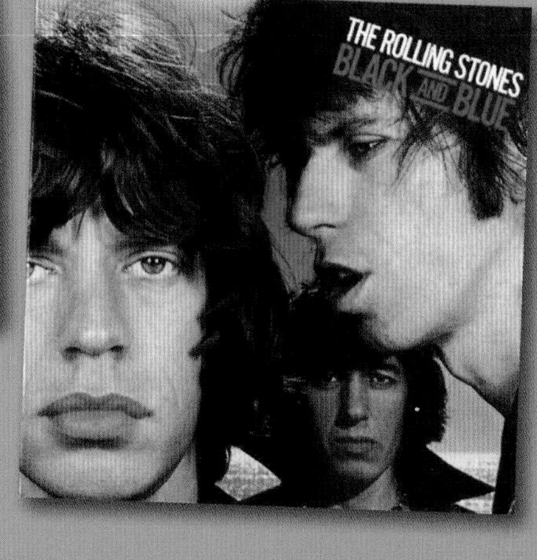

ingredient in the recording of his 2010 solo album, *I Feel Like Playing*, which features collaborations with Billy Gibbons, Slash, Flea, and several other artists. As Wood told *Premier Guitar* magazine while promoting the album, "I think, like wine, the matured sound of a '50s Strat is more or less a stable part of my diet—like with Jeff Beck and Jimmy Page and Eric Clapton. They're just very comfortable. You get that reliable sound that comes from a '50s amp and a '50s guitar."

For many, Keith Richards's guitar tone might define that Rolling Stones sound, but watch any Wood-era Stones concert footage and you quickly appreciate how much he contributes to the band. Although he name checks Beck and Clapton in reference to the timelessness of the Stratocaster's appeal, his is quite a different approach to the instrument: he came up amid Britain's blues-rock scene of the late 1960s and early 1970s, sure, but for Wood the emphasis was always more on rock 'n' roll. Give him a Stratocaster and a tweed amp and he'll come out sounding more like a cranked-up Buddy Holly than a Buddy Guy. That said, his appearances at the 2010 Crossroads Festival showed him ably hanging with the diehard blues crowd. Whatever he's playing, though, Wood always seems to make it appear an easy, casual affair, hitting his stride in tasty, laid-back riffs and behind-the-beat rhythm chops, defining a groove that has long kept pace with the Stones, certainly, but was also right in step with his other great British rock 'n' rollers, the Faces and Rod Stewart. Nailing the groove, nailing the tone, and nailing the vibe—and doing it, more often than not, on a Stratocaster.

Robin Trower

Robin Trower bends a note on his Strat in 1975.
Colin Fuller/Redferns/Getty Images

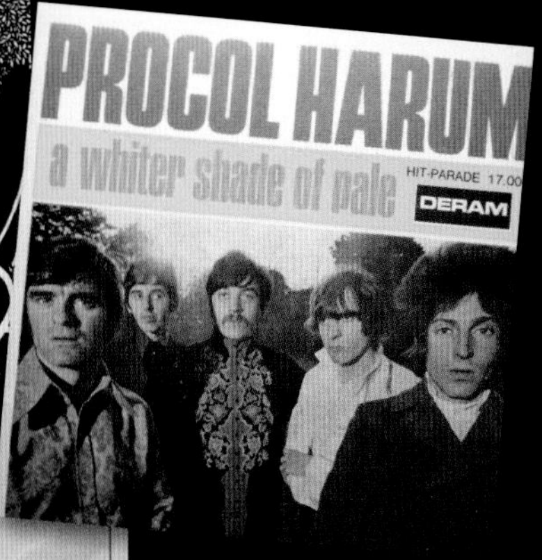

Not unlike both Eric Clapton and Jeff Beck, British blues-rocker Robin Trower made the leap from playing a Les Paul with Procol Harum from 1967 to 1971 to being a Stratocaster fanatic in his own solo work from 1971 on. What he did with that Strat, though, was quite different from either Beck or Clapton and is perhaps more often associated with the playing and tone of Jimi Hendrix than with his British compatriots. In fact, Trower is a name that frequently came up alongside that of Hendrix in the boutique effects pedal world's Uni-Vibe renaissance of a few years back: if a Uni-Vibe cloner mentioned Hendrix's "Machine Gun" or "Star-Spangled Banner," they were going to name drop Robin Trower's "Bridge of Sighs" in the next breath. For all the Hendrix associations, however—and Trower himself has frequently said that he isn't copying Hendrix, as such, but trying to carry on in his footsteps—it wasn't his admiration for the deceased legend that prompted his switch to the Stratocaster but simply a "feel thing."

As Trower told Steve Rosen in *Guitar Player* magazine in 1974, he was struck by the Strat revelation upon arriving early for a sound check one day in 1971 while Procol Harum was on tour with Jethro Tull. He picked up Tull guitarist Martin Barre's Strat (a guitar that Barre had set up for slide), plugged it in, and yelled, "This is it!" Trower continues: "I then switched to Strat. Up to then, I had been playing Les Pauls. I always felt there was something missing on Les Pauls. They had a good fat sound, but they never had that 'musical' sound. When I played a Strat I realized it had that strident chord." As legendary as the PAF-loaded Les Paul has become, Trower's comments on the "musicality" of the Stratocaster echo the feelings of many other guitarists who have made it their choice through the years and reflect a recognition of the clarity and harmonic depth that Leo's pickups, wood choices, build technique, and the 25.5-inch scale length all bring to the table.

Trower first acquired a black Stratocaster that he would later deem "unplayable," which he demoted to backup status, making a white Strat from around 1973 or 1974—large headstock, bullet truss-rod adjustment, maple fingerboard—his main instrument through much of that decade. The artist dipped into the well-respected Squier JV series Stratocasters in the 1980s and has largely played contemporary Stratocasters since that time. Whichever Strat he straps on, though, he continues to prove that old truism that a true artist will sound like himself whatever gear he chooses to get the job done. That being said, a Fuzz Face, Uni-Vibe, and Vox or Tycobrahe wah-wah (or recent Fulltone equivalents) all run through a pair of 100-watt Marshall heads might also be part of the equation. The Fender Custom Shop has issued a Robin Trower Stratocaster made to the specs of his favorite 1970s model.

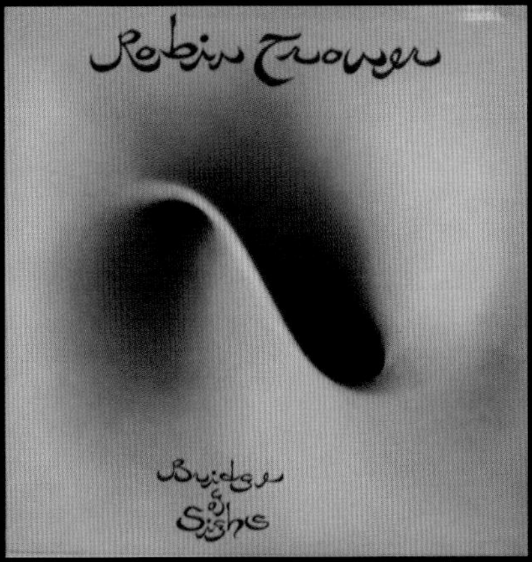

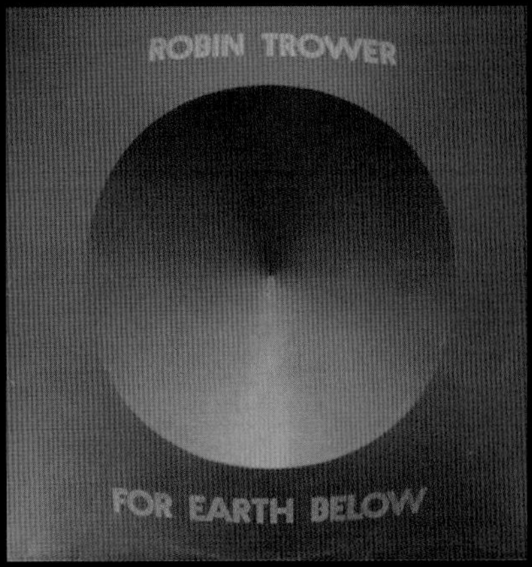

2009 Robin Trower Signature Midnight Wine Burst Stratocaster.
Fender Musical Instruments Corporation

Dave Murray, back right, leads Iron Maiden's three-Strat assault at Earls Court, London, in 2003. From left, Adrian Smith, bassist Steve Harris, Murray, and in front, Janick Gers. *Jo Hale/Getty Images*

In the late 1970s, whilst acts like Zeppelin, Sabbath, and Deep Purple lounged poolside, content amid sacks of money, the New Wave of British Heavy Metal (better known as NWOBHM, natch) looked to blaze a fresh trail for metal. However, one guitarist in the movement's leading band did manage to bring a piece of rock history along for the ride.

In 1976, Iron Maiden's Dave Murray answered an ad in U.K. music mag *Melody Maker* purporting to offer the Stratocaster that once belonged to recently deceased Free guitarist Paul Kossoff. After double-checking the serial numbers, Murray laid down the equivalent of $1,400 for the axe—a princely sum for a working-class bloke. "[Kossoff] used that guitar on a lot of Free," Murray explained to www.gear-vault.com in 2009. "I actually saw him many years ago using it during a Free performance of 'My Brother Jake' on an English television show called *Top of the Pops*. They were one of my favorite bands, and I had to have that guitar because it belonged to Kossoff."

The Stratocaster, comprising a 1957 body and a 1963 rosewood-board neck, is immediately recognizable for its unconventional H/S/H configuration. Murray reported that he added the DiMarzio 'buckers to obtain a thicker sound. The humbucker in the bridge position definitely does something to the lines of the guitar, canceling the sense of movement that is aided by the normally angled bridge pickup.

Regardless, the purchase and the modifications proved savvy: the Stratocaster appeared on Iron Maiden's first eight albums and was a constant sidekick to Murray on tour. "It was my main guitar," he said, "and I played everything with it: lead and rhythm, clean stuff, heavy stuff. It was real versatile."

One point of debate concerning this guitar appears to be whether it's the same white-with-mint-pickguard Stratocaster that appeared on the cover of Kossoff's *Back Street Crawler* solo LP released in 1973. Some maintain that Murray had the guitar painted; others claim that it was already black when it came to him. Given Murray's admiration of Kossoff and his understanding of the instrument's significance, as well as the substantial financial sacrifice he made to obtain it, it seems doubtful he would have had the guitar painted after obtaining it.

After endorsing ESP and Jackson in the late '80s and early '90s, Murray returned to Fender in 1995, and in 2009 his black Strat with loads of provenance was honored with a Signature Series model. Murray has retired the original '57/'63 from the road, but one of his main guitars since 2010 has been a Sunburst California Series Stratocaster loaded with Seymour Duncan Hot Rail blade-type pickups and a Floyd Rose tremolo system. —*Dennis Pernu*

Born in California to a musical family, Bonnie Raitt began exploring the blues at an early age and set out to perform on her own in the late 1960s and early 1970s, doing acoustic coffeehouse gigs in and around Cambridge, Massachusetts, while enrolled as a student at Harvard/Radcliffe. The blues soon bit her good, and she left her dual major in social relations and African studies to amp up and hit the road full time. She has never looked back. The electric Bonnie Raitt that we know today is one of the blues' most respected slide players, and the instrument of choice is the Fender Stratocaster, specifically a rag-tag and road-weary 1965 Strat, a guitar from a turning point in Fender's history.

Raitt acquired her stripped and heavily gigged example, which wasn't going to be anyone's prize, back before "vintage" Strats had much cache even in the best condition. The body and headstock had lost their paint and logos, respectively, as if awaiting a refinish, and the former had taken on a ruddy, natural brown stain. The pickups remained, though, and the guitar was otherwise functional and, it would seem, a tonally superior example of the breed, as Raitt has proven over the course of many years and nine Grammy Awards. Other than its scruffy looks, this Stratocaster is exemplary of the "transition period" represented by early post-CBS Strats. It carries the large headstock that CBS execs purportedly introduced so the iconic electric guitar would be more recognizable on TV, the pearloid dots that were seen as an upgrade of the former clay dots in the rosewood fingerboard, and the three-ply white plastic pickguard characteristic of the era. Otherwise, the '65 Stratocaster differs little from its pre-CBS predecessors of at least a couple of years before.

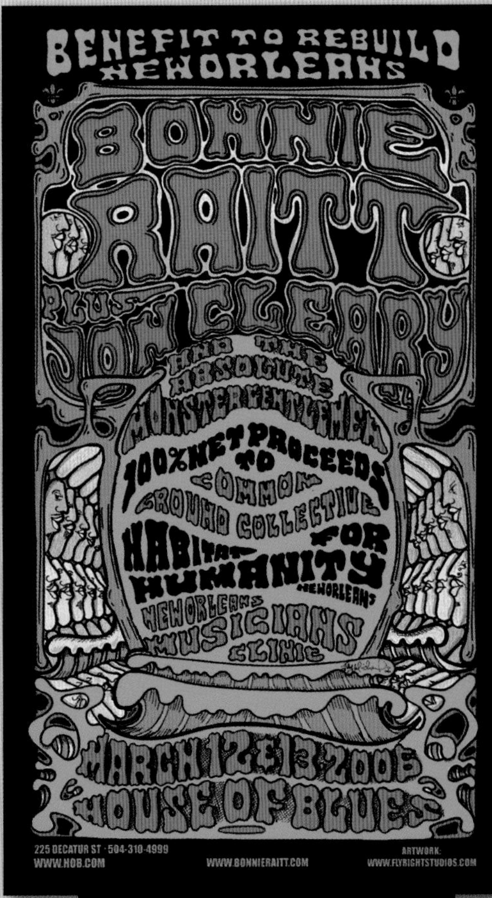

Raitt's fluid style and sweet-yet-biting tone have helped make her playing instantly recognizable among myriad slide guitarists. She tunes her Strat in open G (D-G-D-G-B-D low to high) and uses a custom-cut glass wine bottle neck on her middle finger while attacking the strings with a clear plastic thumb pick and the bare (though fingernail-aided) fingers of her right hand. The seeming simplicity of many of her lead lines belies an innate melodic sensibility and an ability to hit straight at the hook of the tune, qualities that have helped her become one of few hardcore blues-slide players to cross over into mainstream success. Even on the major hits, songs like "Love Sneaking Up on You" and "Something to Talk About," that slinky, sweet slide oozes in and stamps Raitt's signature all over the tune just as assuredly as do her distinctive vocals.

Mark Knopfler

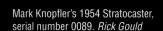

Mark Knopfler fingerpicks his Strat onstage with the Dire Straits in 1980. *Mike Prior/Redferns/Getty Images*

Mark Knopfler's 1954 Stratocaster, serial number 0089. *Rick Gould*

For many people, Mark Knopfler's tone on late-1970s Dire Straits tracks like "Sultans of Swing," "Lady Writer on the TV," and "Down to the Water Line" virtually defines the sound of the Stratocaster played "clean with a little hair on it." Close your eyes and picture the source of that tone, and the image has just got to be one of a pair of red early 1960s Stratocasters that served as Knopfler mainstays through the early part of his career. Knopfler's first "real Strat," the one with the maple neck, was initially believed to have been a '61 or '62 model refinished in Fiesta Red, an homage to British Strat hero Hank Marvin. Its neck carried a maple cap fingerboard, which would have made it either extremely rare for its day or a later modification; as revealed by Knopfler himself to Willie G. Mosely in *Vintage Guitar* magazine in 2001, the artist now believes this guitar to have been a Japanese copy. It has since been sold at auction for charity.

In 1977, Knopfler bought his second red Strat as a backup, this time a *real* '61 with a rosewood fingerboard, and it soon made its way into the first string. Acquired used with a stripped-natural finish, Knopfler also had this one refinished in Fiesta Red. Around 1980, though, he declared his pre-CBS Stratocaster too precious to take on the road and moved to a series of Strat- and super-Strat-like guitars made initially by Schecter, then by Rudy Pensa and John Suhr of Pensa-Suhr in California, and later by Pensa alone. Regardless, he has always remained a "Strat guy" in most fans' estimations

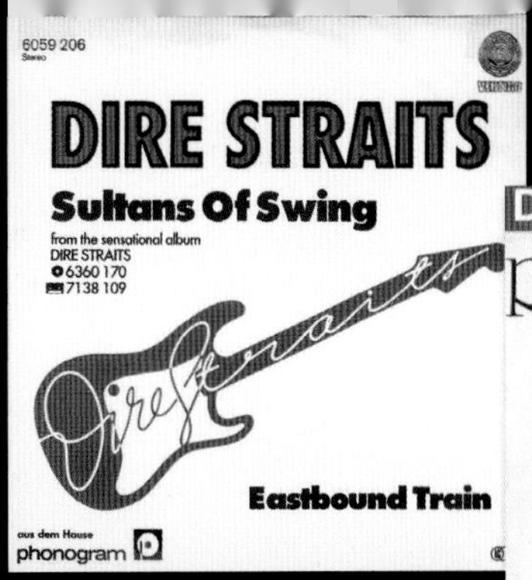

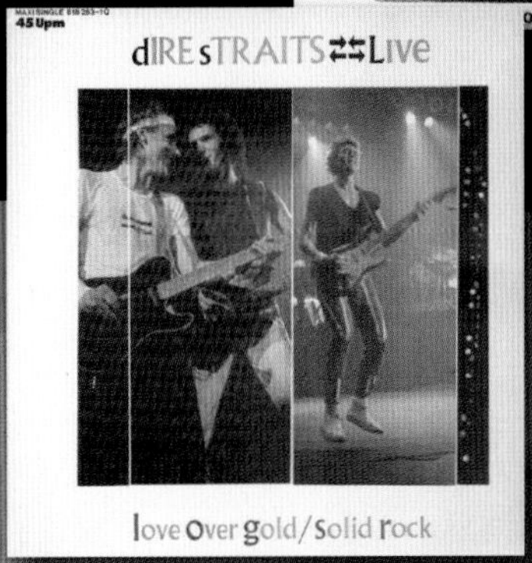

(despite, perhaps, a brief transition through the "Money for Nothing" Les Paul phase) and has even returned to the pre-CBS fold in recent years, sporting a genuine 1954 Stratocaster with the early serial number 059, a guitar given to him by friend Paul Kennerley.

While Knopfler's musical adventures have segued through several avenues—from Mississippi Delta–influenced National guitar, to Chet-style country-jazz picking, often on a Monteleone Custom archtop guitar—it all seems to come back home to a common ground when you put a good Stratocaster in his hands. Pipe it through a brown-face early '60s combo with just a little compression in the front end, attack the strings fingerstyle with the right hand, and set that selector switch between the bridge and middle pickups for extra quack, and it's a tone that'll take you "South Bound Again" every time. Fender's Artist Series Mark Knopfler Stratocaster is based on the Fiesta Red '61 refin with rosewood fingerboard.

2004 Mark Knopfler Hot Rod Red Stratocaster.
Fender Musical Instruments Corporation

Yngwie Malmsteen

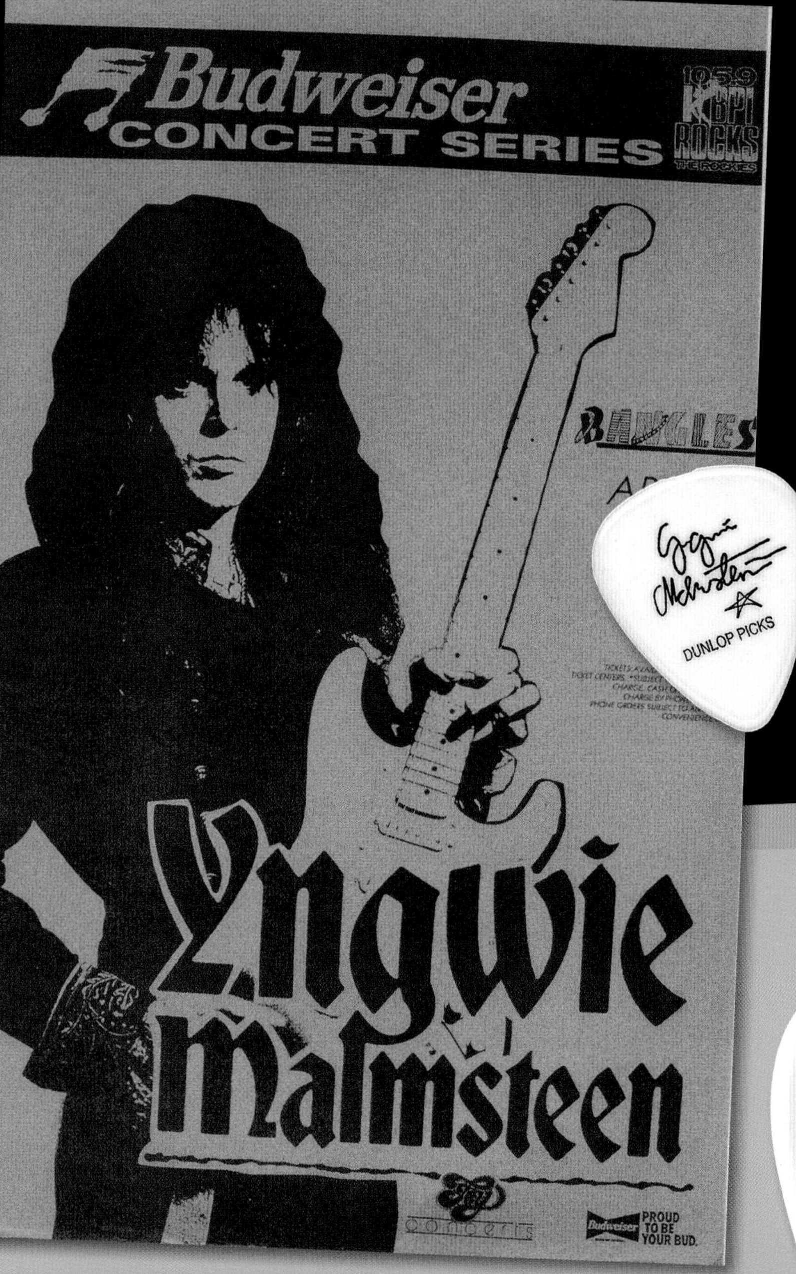

2011 Yngwie Malmsteen Vintage White Stratocaster with scalloped fretboard. *Fender Musical Instruments Corporation*

Like the birth child of some cloning experiment that accidentally melded the DNA of Eddie Van Halen, Ritchie Blackmore, and Niccolo Paganini, Yngwie Malmsteen brought a distinctive new voice to the shred-rock arena when he arrived on the scene in the early 1980s. Rather than indulging in the tapping and hammer-ons of Van Halen and others, Malmsteen displayed a fluid, legato-like alternate picking technique and an impressively vocal vibrato that enabled him to roll out neoclassical runs at breathtaking speeds, and found him hailed as the single-handed founder of a new classical-metal genre. And while his early work with the bands Steeler and Alcatrazz, as well as his 1984 solo debut, *Rising Force*, helped him ascend the ranks of poodle-haired, Superstrat-toting virtuosi, Malmsteen did it all on a plain old (if uniquely modified) 1972 Fender Stratocaster, the first serious guitar he ever acquired as an aspiring teenage guitar hero in Stockholm, Sweden.

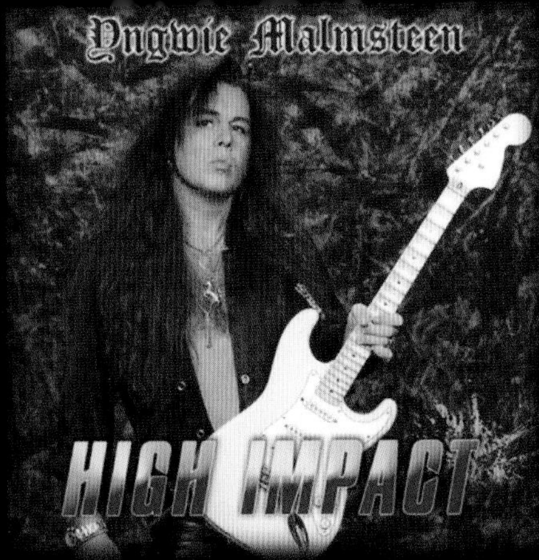

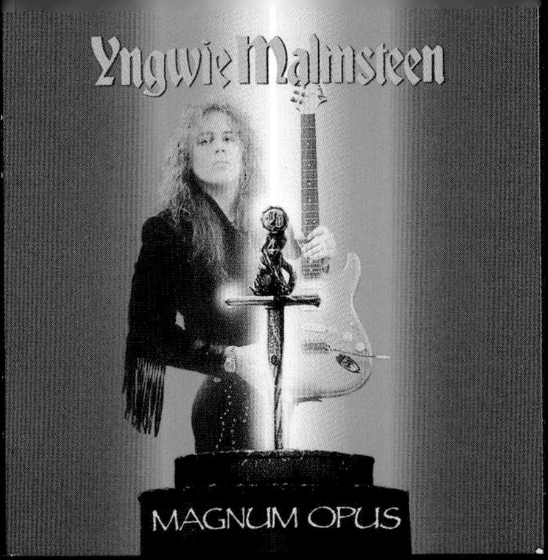

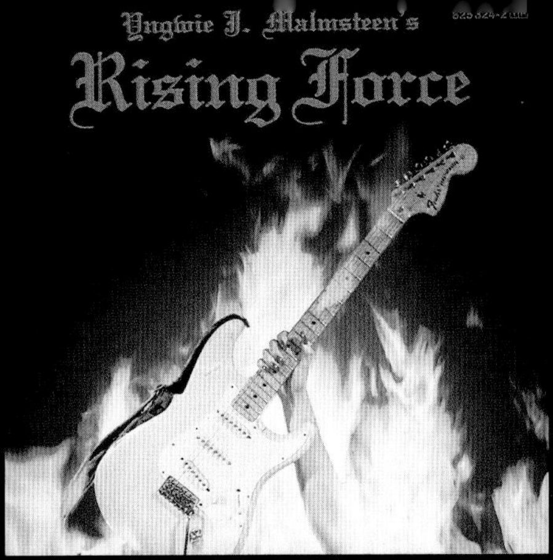

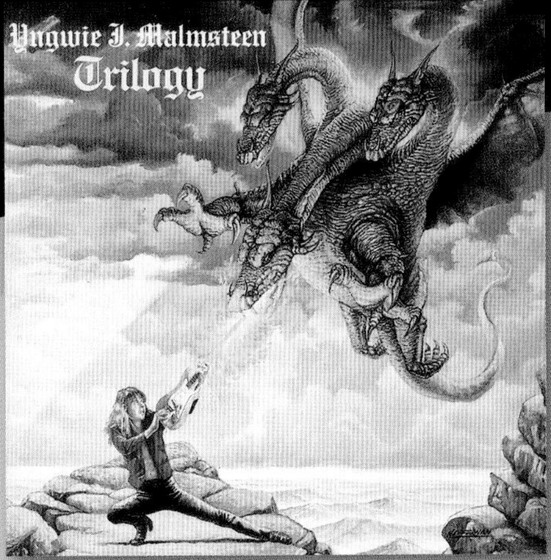

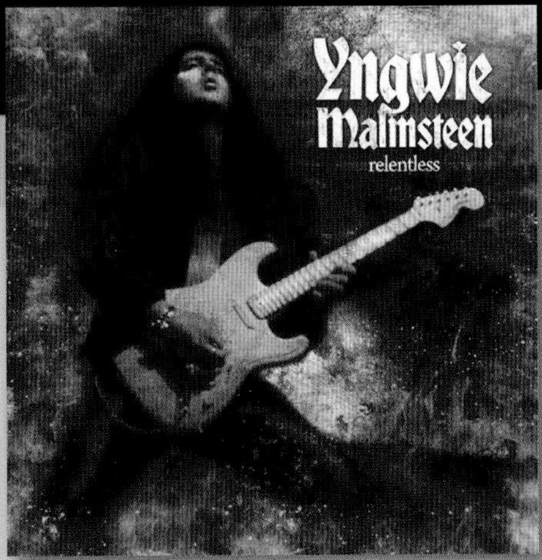

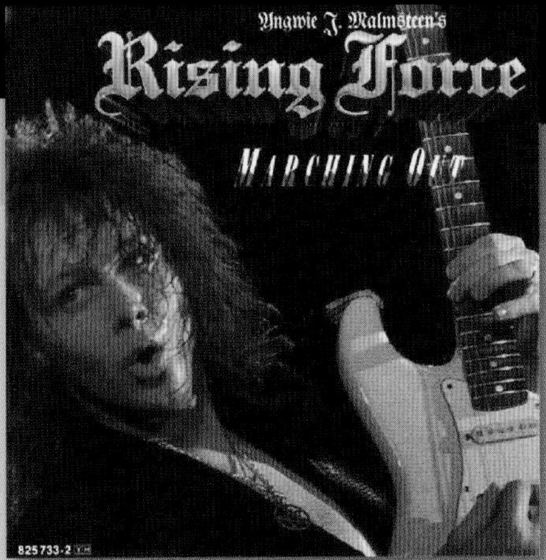

In 2005, Malmsteen told Hugh Ochoa of stratcollector.com that he first decided the course of his life at the age of seven in 1970, while watching a documentary on the death of Jimi Hendrix. The show ran a clip of Hendrix burning his Stratocaster at Monterey, and although the young Malmsteen couldn't even see just what kind of guitar was aflame, he knew he had to have it. A year later, on his eighth birthday, Yngwie's sister gave him Deep Purple's *Fireball* album and he discovered that Ritchie Blackmore played a Stratocaster, the same guitar Hendrix had played and burned. American-made guitars were rare and prohibitively expensive in Sweden in the 1970s, but Malmsteen eventually acquired a white 1972 Strat, and the instrument clicked for him right from the start.

Malmsteen created the famous "scalloped" divots in his Strat's fingerboard himself, after observing such construction on an old lute that had come in for work in a repair shop in which he apprenticed as a teenager. He tried the technique on a few of his own cheaper guitars, then, finding it appealed to him, took the file to his prized Strat. The Swede wasn't the first to perform on a scalloped fingerboard (his hero, Ritchie Blackmore, had been using the technique for some time), but his pyrotechnics on the instrument helped popularize the mod among the shred crowd. Although Malmsteen now has a large collection that includes many pre-CBS 1950s and early-1960s Strats and several Gibsons, he has always expressed a preference for Stratocasters made between 1968 and 1972, largely because he feels the bigger headstock improves the resonance on those models. Unlike his colleagues in the genre during the early 1980s, Malmsteen eschewed Floyd Rose vibrato systems (again, for tonal reasons), and has always retained his stock Fender vibrato units. Other than the scalloped neck and jumbo frets, his '72 Strat, and the Fender signature models based upon it, are largely stock, with other minor modifications, including a DiMarzio HS-3 pickup in the bridge position (alongside standard Stratocaster pickups in the neck and middle positions) and a brass nut. None of these are the high-gain accoutrements one might expect from a shredder like Malmsteen, but ram these clean single-coils through upward of twenty Marshall JMP 50s, and the setup apparently gets the job done.

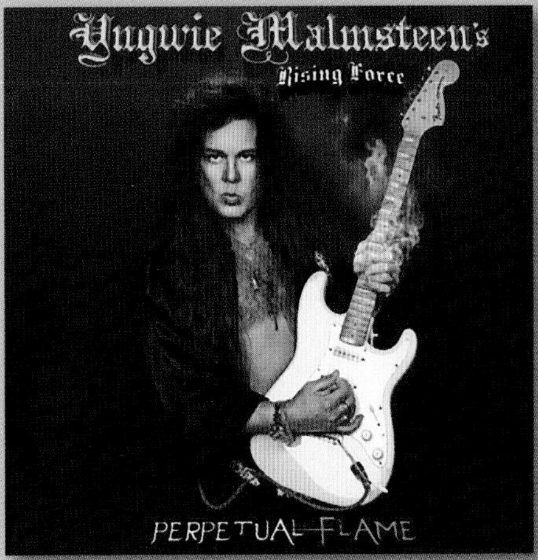

Yngqie Malmsteen shows off his guitar collection. His trademark Strat, the Duck, is seventh from left in the front row.
Rick Gould

Richard Thompson

Richard Thompson picks his Strat in Leeds, England, on March 4, 2013.
Ben Statham/Redferns/Getty Images

Much of Richard Thompson's unique style and tone might seem to come from his transmogrification of fingerstyle acoustic Scottish and English folk music to the electrified genre, but that shouldn't by any means imply that this British artist can't rock with the best of them, and his roots are very much in rock 'n' roll. And while the Fairport Convention guitarist and solo artist has long enjoyed using alternative designs from smaller guitar makers, we will always consider him "a Strat player" first and foremost. Thompson was playing a mid-'60s Stratocaster when he co-founded folk-rockers Fairport Convention in 1967, but he acquired what would be his "No. one" Strat in 1971 around the time of his departure from the band. Although the first solo album that he recorded with it, *Henry the Human Fly*, might be considered both a commercial and critical failure, the 1959 Stratocaster came into its own on 1982's *Shoot Out the Lights*, which *Rolling Stone* magazine declared one of the best rock albums of all time.

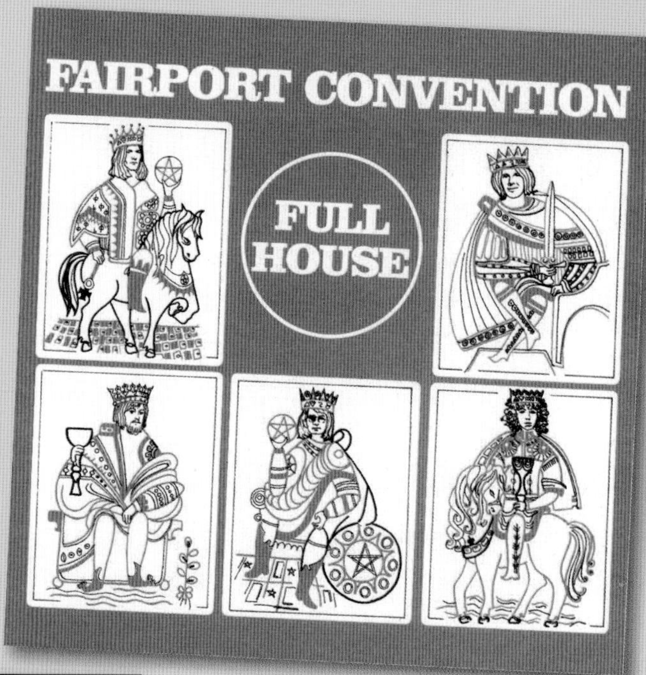

Thompson was born in the Notting Hill neighborhood of London in 1949, although his father, a Scotland Yard detective, was a transplanted Scotsman whose musical tastes would prove a major influence on the young guitarist. Everything from classic jazz and bebop to Scottish folk music seemed to have found free rein in the

Thompson household, and eventually wove its way into the diverse blend that informs the artist's playing style even today. Listen to Thompson's solo work on the title track from *Shoot Out the Lights*, or any of his standout electric playing really, and you'll hear a wiry, angular style that is impossible to define. Although he was raised on rock 'n' roll and hit the stage himself when the London scene really was at its most exciting, both his tone and the riffs he applies it to have leaned more toward an edgily clean eclecticism than toward the heavy, humbucker-fueled blues-rock that was so many players' stock-in-trade in the late 1960s.

In Richard Thompson, we might even hear a player whose acoustic voice and playing style translates more accurately to his plugged-in approach, including his hybrid picking style (using a pick between thumb and index finger and the bare tips of the middle and ring fingers) and his frequent use of open tunings.

In the latter part of his career Thompson has frequently turned to electrics made by California builder Danny Ferrington, which often comprise clever twists on some of the basic Stratocaster specs. Time and again, though, he has returned to his '59, which was played so heavily in its first ten years of ownership that the original neck with rosewood fingerboard would no longer take a refret and was replaced by an all-maple neck from 1955. Thompson also plays a reissue-style Fender Stratocaster in Sonic Blue that his guitar tech, Bobby Eichorn, assembled from select pieces of different Fender guitars.

Fender
VOLUME
TONE
TONE

2007 George Fullerton 1957 Stratocaster with matching Pro Junior amp
Fender Musical Instruments Corporation

2010 Custom Shop 1956 Stratocaster. *Fender Musical Instruments Corporation*

2010 Custom Shop 1960 Shoreline Gold Stratocaster. *Fender Musical Instruments Corporation*

(Continued from page 107)

Marvin of the Shadows received what is widely considered to be the first Stratocaster brought into the United Kingdom. The Fiesta Red Strat with gold hardware was brought to him by Cliff Richard (a singing star with whom the Shadows performed as backing band, in addition to logging several hits as an instrumental outfit), and quickly became a major part of Marvin's sound. Blending proto-surf and twangy pop stylings, Marvin's riffs were peppered with emotive vibrato bends and trills, and made a real feature of Leo's marvelous "Synchronized Tremolo."

Back in the United States, while Fender's Jazzmaster—and soon, Jaguar—would be more heavily associated with the surf scene, Dick Dale was laying down seminal surf riffs played by surfers, for surfers, on a gold 1959 Stratocaster dubbed "the Beast," given to him by Leo himself. Otherwise, in addition to thriving in the genres in which it was conceived, the Stratocaster was proliferating on the pop-rock scene in the early 1960s but would prove a tool of even more adventurous artists a little later in the decade. Even so, Stratocaster sales declined slightly in the early mid-1960s, a fact likely attributable to the plethora of competition at the peak of the guitar boom, both from other makers and from other models of Fender. Some might have assessed the Strat at this point and declared that it had "had a pretty good run" for its first decade and simply wasn't the new kid on the block anymore. They wouldn't have been inaccurate, as such, despite missing the fact that this guitar's heyday was very much still ahead of it.

Bob Dylan's use of a Stratocaster in his infamous "gone electric" moment at the Newport Folk Festival in 1965 marked it as a rebel, but it was Jimi Hendrix who took that image over the top, sonically as much as visually, with his groundbreaking playing as a solo artist in 1967 and beyond. Where the heaviest players in rock so far had mostly rediscovered Gibson's discontinued Les Paul Standard with humbucking pickups, Hendrix showed what the Stratocaster's crystalline single-coil pickups could do when cranked to the max through a Marshall stack and tickled with some inventive whammy abuse. Up to this point, the Stratocaster had ascended rather steadily through the ranks of solidbody electric guitars in its thirteen years on the planet, but many would argue, and with just cause, that Hendrix's use of the guitar was what finally punched it through into the stratosphere.

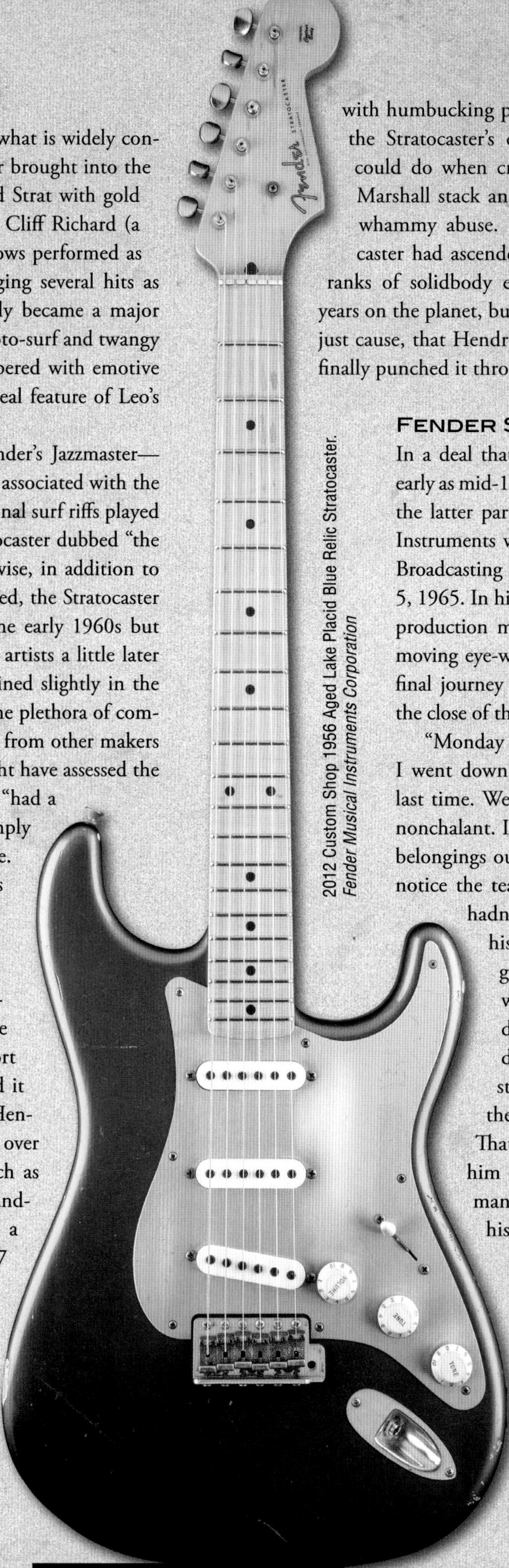

2012 Custom Shop 1956 Aged Lake Placid Blue Relic Stratocaster.
Fender Musical Instruments Corporation

Fender Sells Up to CBS

In a deal that had been pursued at least as early as mid-1964 and negotiated throughout the latter part of that year, Fender Musical Instruments was officially sold to Columbia Broadcasting System Inc. (CBS) on January 5, 1965. In his book *Fender: The Inside Story*, production manager Forrest White offers a moving eye-witness account of Leo Fender's final journey home from work as owner at the close of the previous workday:

"Monday evening, January 4, 1965, I went down to see Leo in his lab for the last time. We both found it difficult to act nonchalant. I helped him carry his personal belongings out to his car, pretended not to notice the tears in his eyes, and hoped he hadn't noticed mine. He got into his car and I walked to the side gate. He stopped briefly on his way out, paused and said, 'I don't know what I would have done without you.' . . . He stepped on the gas and was out the gate before I could answer. That was the last time I would let him out the gate as I had done so many times before. I watched until his car was out of sight."

Leo Fender's quest to sell his company began midway through 1964, when he instructed Don Randall to quietly begin searching for a suitable buyer. Randall turned to the investment firm Merrill Lynch for introductions to companies that might be looking to invest in the musical instruments market, and CBS eventually was put forward. Looking to expand its portfolio, CBS was eager to acquire a leading electric guitar and amplifier manufacturer during a boom time in that industry. A deal to purchase both Fender Electronic Instruments and Fender Sales was hammered out, and the price, a staggering $13.5 million, was the highest paid to date for a musical instrument manufacturer. The head honcho's desire to sell wasn't based purely on the notion of hitting it big on the company he had built from nothing, though, but was inspired by what then had seemed more pressing personal needs. Having been unable to shake a strep infection contracted in the mid-1950s that continually aggravated his sinuses, Leo Fender had, by the mid-1960s, been feeling more and more rundown from his illness and further exhausted by the effort of running the ever-expanding business, which usually kept him at the office far later than the eight-hour workday. By 1964 Fender employed approximately 500 workers, in a premises that had expanded to 27 buildings in Fullerton. Business was good—business was great, even—but Leo Fender himself just wasn't up to it.

When the sale was completed in February 1965, CBS changed the long-standing name Fender Electronic Instruments to Fender Musical Instruments, now a division of Columbia Records Distribution Corp. under CBS. Don Randall was named vice president and general manager, the title Forrest White had held in recent years, while White was made plant manager again, a position he had held in the mid-1950s. Fender had hired guitarist Bill Carson in 1957 to work in quality control. Having been promoted to guitar production foreman in 1959, Carson also stayed with Fender through the sale to CBS and would move over the Fender Sales in 1967. Among other formative Fender employees that stuck it out with CBS, for the time being at least, were George Fullerton and Freddie Tavares, although Dale Hyatt left around the time of the sale's completion. As part of the sales agreement, Leo Fender was retained as a consultant in research and development for five years, with a "noncompete" clause of ten years that was intended to prevent him from starting his own company. The consultation role seems to have been largely a token gesture on CBS's part, and Leo's input apparently carried relatively little weight as the corporate owner set about maximizing the bottom line.

Some reports, though unconfirmed, indicate that Leo Fender's doctors had him believing that perhaps he didn't have long to live and that his sale of Fender was a clear move to get out from under the burden of the company and enjoy what time he had left. In any case, three years after selling the company that he had built from the ground up over the course of twenty years to become one of the world's most successful musical instrument manufacturers, Fender finally found relief from his affliction. "About 1968, I found a doctor who knew the appropriate treatment for the infection," he told *Guitar Player* magazine in 1971, "and I haven't been bothered with it since."

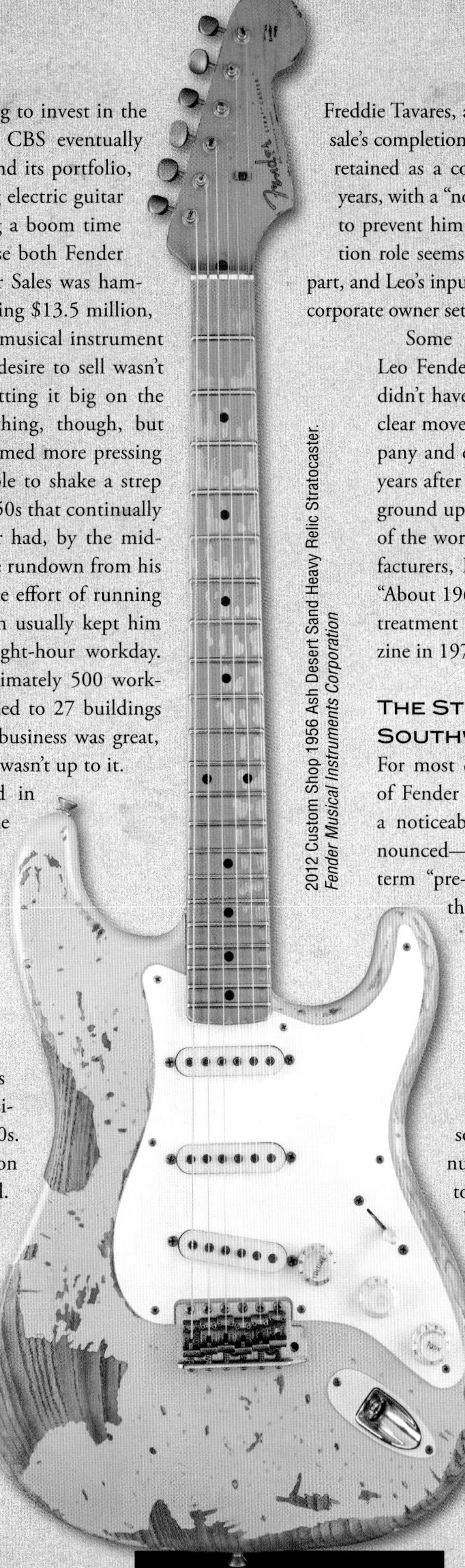

2012 Custom Shop 1956 Ash Desert Sand Heavy Relic Stratocaster. *Fender Musical Instruments Corporation*

The Strat Slides Southward Under CBS

For most diehard Fender aficionados, CBS's acquisition of Fender serves as a demarcation point for the start of a noticeable decline—at first gradual, then more pronounced—in the quality of Fender guitars. As such, the term "pre-CBS" has come to stand as an identifier of the more valuable and collectible vintage Stratocasters (and other Fenders), with post-CBS indicating less desirable later examples. To be fair, though, the quality of the instruments certainly wasn't impacted the second that the ink dried on the contract, or even for several years after. Fender, under CBS, continued to produce plenty of excellent Stratocasters for some time, although the days—or years—were numbered, and the change of owner pointed toward a future where the Strat would one day be but a shadow of its original self.

The thicker, more modern-looking Fender logo that had begun to appear on Stratocaster headstocks in late summer 1964 is often considered the first sign of the post-CBS guitars, even though the sale of Fender to CBS had not yet been completed, and the guitars themselves—other than the change of that thin, water-slide decal—were much the same as they had been earlier in the year, in a firmly pre-CBS era. The new logo, initially a bold gold logo within a thin black outline, was joined by a broader headstock shape at the end of 1965, which essentially bookended the era of the "transition Strat," which ran from late 1964 until that time. By then, as of the winter of 1965, the clay of the fingerboard position markers had been changed to pearloid dots, and the greenish celluloid pickguard was changed for a white three-ply guard made from actual plastic. (For some other minor changes in pickup construction see the "Tone & Construction" chapter.)

Following the transitional mid-1960s changes, in late 1967 Fender replaced the Stratocaster's Kluson tuners with sets made for them by Schaller and stamped with the trademark reversed Fender "F" on the gear housing. In 1968 the coloring of the Fender headstock logo was essentially reversed to a more visible bold black lettering with gold outline and a much bolder model name. By this point, the "late-1960s pre-CBS Stratocaster" had fully arrived. In 1967 the "maple-cap" neck was officially introduced (made with a glued-on maple fingerboard, rather than being a one-piece maple neck as used on guitars of the 1950s). This option gives plenty of late-1960s Strats more of the look of those made from late 1954 to mid-1959, although these lacked the dark wood "teardrop" behind the nut and the "skunk stripe" at the back, since the truss rod was installed from the front before the maple fingerboard was glued on, just as it had been for necks with rosewood fingerboards. Among the more detrimental changes of the late 1960s, however, was the move to polyester finishes around 1968. This "thick-skinned" finish, with its resilient, plasticy feel, was achieved with as many as ten to fifteen coats of polyester paint and is believed by many players to severely choke the tone of any guitar that carries it.

Many of the changes made from the mid- to late 1960s were purely cosmetic and should not have made a late-'65 Stratocaster "sound any worse" than, for example, an early-'64 Stratocaster. Given how greatly guitars produced even on the same day can vary, there are certainly Strats from throughout the 1960s that sound outstanding and plenty from the pre-CBS era that simply don't sound all that good. Regardless, the changes mark the most significant turning point in Stratocaster desirability for collectors, whatever wonderful music players might have made with post-'65 guitars. The laws of supply and demand have also made early CBS guitars more collectible than late CBS guitars, while the "law of Jimi Hendrix" has helped to make anything up to the end of the decade more prized than what came after.

Even so, it can't be denied that more significant issues of declining quality control, driven by increased production and an eye more on raw sales figures than the quality of the instruments, were beginning to take their toll on Fender quality by the late 1960s and certainly the early 1970s. Just a year after CBS's Fender acquisition the factory had increased its guitar and amplifier production by approximately 30 percent, though with no noticeable decline in quality as of yet. In 1966, however, CBS completed construction on an enormous new facility at 1300 S. Valencia Drive, adjacent to the previous site at 500 South Raymond Avenue in Fullerton. Soon after the move into the new premises, production increased another 45 percent, and the first signs of what would be a steady decline in quality in general began to be apparent.

Several of the old guard that had transitioned to CBS from the former Fender Electronic Instruments expressed increasing displeasure with the large company's emphasis on production numbers over all else. As the new decade approached, it also became apparent that CBS was bleeding the profits from the continued business success of Fender Musical Instruments (now officially called CBS Musical Instruments Division other

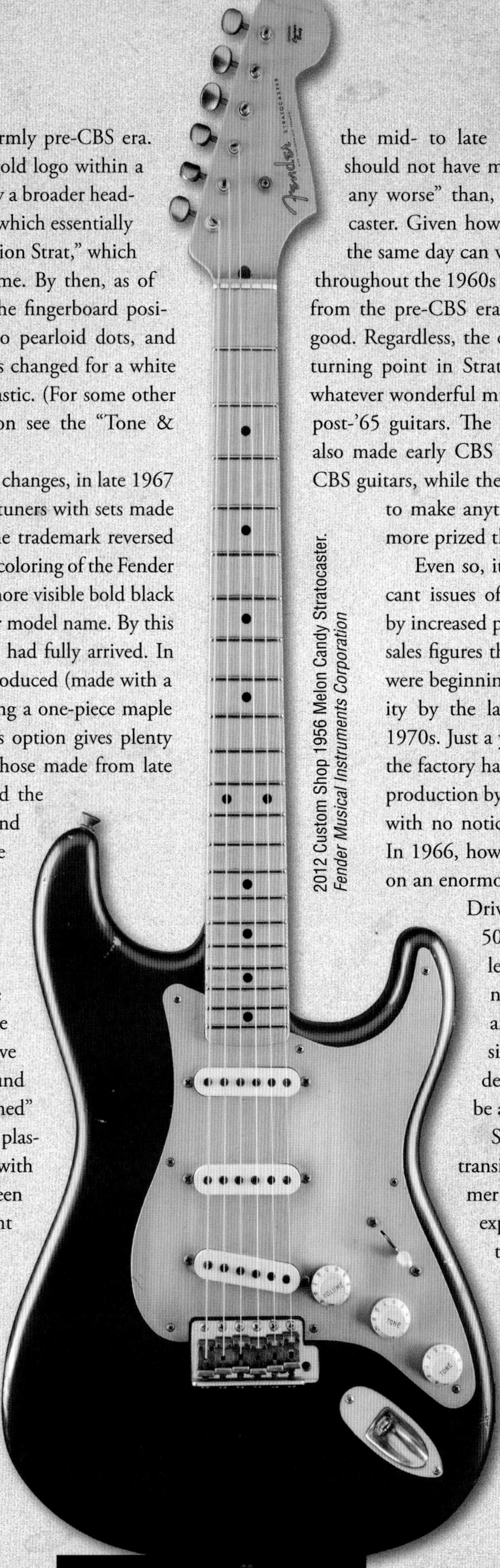

2012 Custom Shop 1956 Melon Candy Stratocaster. *Fender Musical Instruments Corporation*

than in the brand line used on the instruments and amplifiers themselves) to offset losses from other divisions. Division head Don Randall, who was on the same five-year contract term as an executive given to Leo Fender as a consultant, was also dissatisfied with the way the business was going under CBS by this time. Randall departed in 1969, well before the official end of his tenure, and in 1971 he set up his own company, Randall Instruments.

Several other Fender stalwarts would voice their concerns about the detrimental effect of CBS's corporate mentality on Fender quality. As Freddie Tavares told A. R. Duchossoir in *The Fender Stratocaster* (Hal Leonard, 1994), "We had turned into a big fancy corporation all of a sudden, where all the different departments had got their say in everything and then that was budgets, quotas, and so on. They would try to put out the stuff as fast as they could!" Despite his own dissatisfaction with the run of things, Tavares would stay on at CBS/Fender until his retirement in 1986. Several others, though, were soon disenchanted enough to jump ship.

The End of an Era

In late 1971, several significant changes made to two critical components of the Stratocaster finally, and truly, signaled the end of the era of the guitar in its original form, broadly speaking. Many will point to the change to a thicker finish in 1968 as the first factory-induced detriment to the Stratocaster's tone (aside from the unquantifiable variations in wood resonance, variables in pickup construction, and so forth). When the neck attachment, truss rod, and bridge assembly were radically altered toward the end of 1971 it put the final nails into the coffin of the golden age of the Stratocaster.

In theory, the new Tilt Neck mounting system and bullet-head truss-rod adjustment point could have been seen as a good thing, but their fate as signals of a guitar that was already declining in so many other ways has fated them with a badge of dishonor, of sorts. The former part of this new neck construction involved a new three-screw neck mounting with guilt in neck-angle adjustment plate, that allowed the player or repairman to effect slight changes in the "tilt" of the neck without having to remove it to place a thin shim under the end, as the job was previously achieved. Accompanying this device was a newly designed truss rod with a bullet-shaped adjustment nut protruding at the headstock end of the neck, just behind the nut. The "bullet head" was far more accessible than the previous adjustment point, at the heel end (guitar end) of the neck, but was considered "ugly" by many players and, well, just different from "the classic Stratocaster."

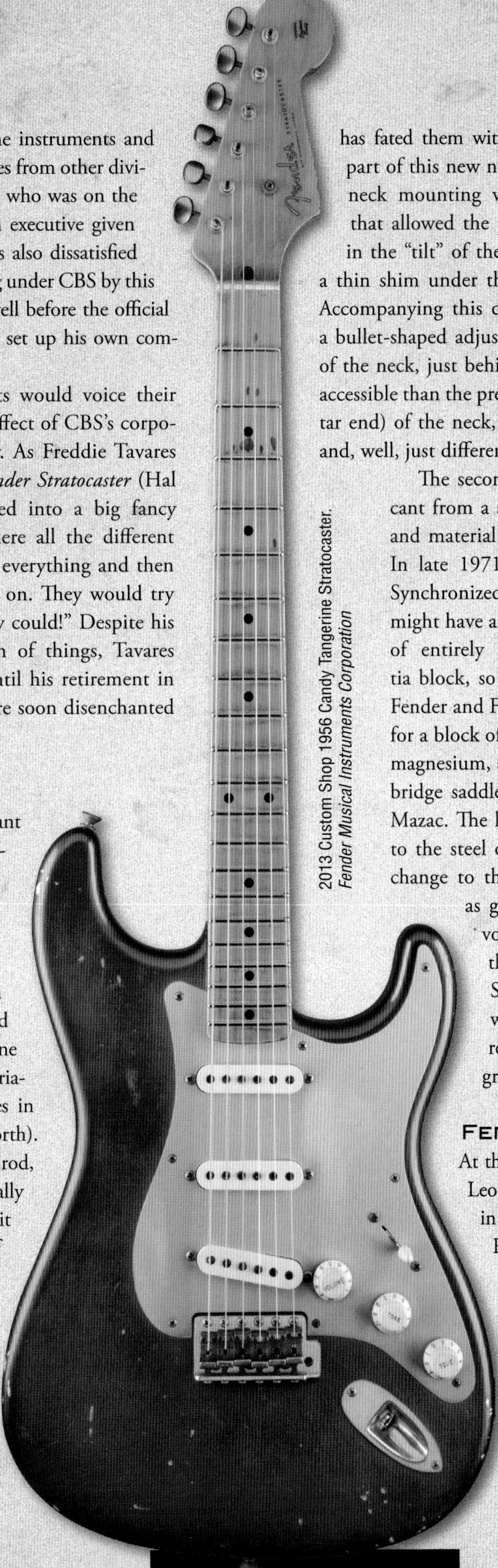

2013 Custom Shop 1956 Candy Tangerine Stratocaster. *Fender Musical Instruments Corporation*

The second major change was arguably more significant from a sonic standpoint, in that it altered the mass and material of the critical anchor points of the strings. In late 1971 Fender entirely reconfigured the original Synchronized Tremolo system, retaining what outwardly might have appeared a similar design but was constructed of entirely different materials. The rolled-steel inertia block, so key to retaining satisfactory sustain in Leo Fender and Freddie Tavares's original design, was changed for a block of die-cast Mazac, an alloy of zinc, aluminum, magnesium, and copper. At the same time, the individual bridge saddles were changed from bent steel to die-cast Mazac. The lesser density of the Mazac, when compared to the steel of the previous components, brought a real change to the Stratocaster's tone, which many describe as giving it a "thinner," "lighter," or "brighter" voice. Once again, it's worth acknowledging that plenty of great music has been made on Stratocasters constructed after these changes were introduced, but they clearly delineate the real bottom that was finally hit in the Strat's gradual decline.

Fender After Fender

At the end of his consultation contract with CBS, Leo Fender established the Tri-Sonic company in 1971 along with Forrest White and former Fender Sales rep Tom Walker. Fender and White began developing ideas for a new line of amplifiers and guitars, with White patenting a design for a bass headstock with three keys on the bass side and one key on the treble that would soon be a familiar new sight on the market. In 1973 the three partners changed the company name to Musitek, then changed it again in 1974 to Music Man, and took old Fender colleague George Fullerton onboard soon after. In 1975, with his noncompete clause completed, Leo Fender stepped forward as president of Music Man, and the company soon hit the ground running with a line of products that had already been in development. Music Man's amps of the mid- to late 1970s, in what were clearly Fender-like configurations but with solid-state preamps and tube output stages, proved fairly successful and were used by major pros such as Eric Clapton and Mark Knopfler. The Stingray bass, with its unusual 3-and-1 headstock, also became a standard of many reputable studio and touring pros, although the six-string guitars were slower to achieve wide acceptance among working musicians. That Music Man guitars, under the latter-day ownership of the company Ernie Ball, were eventually endorsed by Albert Lee, Steve Morse, and for a time, Edward Van Halen, finally put those on the map too.

In 1979 Leo Fender and George Fullerton started G&L—for "George and Leo"—in Fullerton, California, and the pair began to produce a range of guitars in competition with both Fender and Music Man. In 1985 G&L introduced its Broadcaster model, a guitar clearly patterned after the Fender Telecaster, with similar body and headstock shapes, but powered by Leo Fender's newly developed Magnetic Field Design pickups. Fender Musical Instruments, rather ironically, objected to the use of the Broadcaster name—denied them by Gretsch some thirty-five years before—and in 1986 G&L changed the name of its Tele-like model to ASAT (as in the anti-satellite missile). After George Fullerton's interest in G&L was bought out by Leo Fender in the mid-1980s, the company name was changed to "Guitars by Leo"; former Fender employee Dale Hyatt had joined the fold, and Forrest White was soon taken on too. G&L would be Leo's final home as a guitar maker.

Former Fender associates Doc Kauffman and Freddie Tavares died in June and July 1990, respectively. Less than a year later, Leo Fender passed away on March 21, 1991. Six years previous to this, William Schultz, then president of Fender Musical Instruments, along with Dan Smith and a team of other Fender managers and investors, rescued the Fender brand from near extinction under CBS. Under this new leadership, a revitalized Fender Musical Instruments Corporation went about building the brand back into one of the most successful musical instrument manufacturers in the world, and restoring the renowned Fender quality of the 1950s and early 1960s along with it. Following Leo Fender's death, ownership of G&L eventually passed to BBE Sound, which still maintains Fender's final workshop on the premises as a memorial to the man who brought so much to the guitar world.

Gazing Backward to Move Forward

Following a decade of increasing struggle to maintain a foothold in the marketplace, which often found Fender's reputation slipping down between the expectations established by its former glories and the sketchy quality of its current production, a major shift toward the better was in the wind in the early 1980s. In an effort to revive the company's fortunes, CBS brought in John McLaren, Bill Schultz, and Dan Smith in 1981, all young executives from the American branch of Japanese instrument maker Yamaha. Rather ironically (or perhaps not), the new team started production of a Fender line in Japan in order to compete with the cut-price Fender copies that had been coming from that country for some time, and the Squier and Japanese-made Fender series were born.

At the same time, the Smith, Schultz, and McLaren team saw the virtue of returning to Fender's past strengths and launched the company's first-ever reissue-style Stratocasters (and Telecasters) in Japan and the United States in 1982 and 1983, respectively. It was a wise move. The growing success of the reissue lines arguably saved Fender's reputation when the very existence of the company was on the line, and three decades later similar reissue guitars in their various guises have continued to prove the backbone of the lineup.

Shortly after these initiatives, however, twenty years after Leo Fender had decided to sell his company, CBS decided to divest itself of its holdings in the musical instrument industry and, following a search for a suitable buyer, sold up to a group of investors headed by then-Fender president Bill Schultz. The deal, inked in March of 1985, gave the new owners the Fender brand and designs and some stock for $12.5 million, although the Fullerton factories were not included in the bargain (a point which makes it difficult to directly compare the price to the $13.5 million tag on Fender circa 1965, as purchased by CBS in the first place).

After struggling to maintain a place in the market while ramping up production in new premises in the United States and maintaining Japanese production, Schultz and company steered Fender onto a stronger and stronger footing, and did so largely by remembering—and re-creating—what had made the guitars so popular in the company's real glory days of 1950 to 1965. Several contemporary and modified Stratocasters proliferated and found their fans thanks to ever-increasing (or call it "returning") quality and a stronger and stronger brand, the guitars like the American Vintage Reissue Series, the Custom Shop Time Machine series—with their characterful, distressed Relic models—and even the Japanese and Mexican-made guitars produced in the image of models from the early to mid-1950s or early 1960s continue to form the main image in our collective notion of what "a Stratocaster" is or should be. If the Stratocaster is the world's most influential, and most copied, electric guitar, Fender is once again its most successful re-inventor, and the future of Leo's grand design seems more ensured than ever before.

2009 Custom Shop 1956 Desert Sand Stratocaster.
Fender Musical Instruments Corporation

A 1960s Fender advertisement promises that quality and features of Fender instruments meant "confidence."

"Smoother playing, faster action," promises this 1957 fender ad.

PART II

TONE & CONSTRUCTION

WHEN IT CAME TO DEVELOPING THE STRATOCASTER, Fender already had an excellent template on hand in the form of the Telecaster, a burgeoning success in the country market in particular and soon on the blues and rock 'n' roll scenes too. Leo sought to do something quite different with the Stratocaster, of course, adding features and functionality that were gained mainly through the addition of new components, along with a few sexy new twists to the body and headstock styling. Even so, the fundamentals of the chassis—as we might call the body and neck woods—were largely in place, and functioning fine just as they were.

While any guitar's core tone might be shaped by the tonewoods from which it is constructed, it's also worth noting just how certain newly designed components that were added to that chassis to create the Stratocaster considerably shaped, and ultimately differentiated, the sound of the new instrument. If Leo had established his sound with the Telecaster, the Stratocaster certainly attained something that would also be recognizable as "the Fender sound," but was nevertheless quite different in its tonal fine points.

Classic elements of the Stratocaster design are as iconic today as they were in the early days, as shown by this pair of 2005 '70s Stratocasters.
Fender Musical Instruments Corporation

The simple act of adding elements such as the spring-loaded, semi-floating vibrato unit and a trio of similar but slightly different single-coil pickups to the same ash-and-maple construction changed the voice of the Stratocaster in relation to the Telecaster. The alteration might seem subtle in the broad scheme of electric guitar tones, but to aficionados of either breed it is significant enough to render them two entirely different instruments. Otherwise, the ingredients in the Stratocaster still coalesce perfectly toward Leo Fender's original goal of creating a bright, clear, cutting guitar based on the sonic template of the lap steel guitar popular in western swing music at the time, with outstanding resistance to feedback and better sustain than the common hollowbody electrics of the day. Dissect the instrument, and it starts to look extremely simple: the foundation is found in a highly functional and playable bolt-on maple neck (classically with maple fingerboard, but a rosewood 'board alters the formula only slightly) and solid swamp ash body (later alder), all slightly amended by its clever vibrato bridge design with individually adjustable steel saddles. In addition to these, one intangible ingredient—its 25 1/2-inch scale length—also makes an impact on the guitar's final voice. Drastically alter any one of the above, and a Stratocaster becomes an entirely different electric guitar.

Elements of the Stratocaster Design

The key elements in the Stratocaster's basic design have been covered in the discussion of the guitar's development in the "History" chapter, but it's worth summing them up here. By "design" I mean the blueprint, as it were, specifications that are largely intangible, rather than the material ingredients, but which nevertheless contribute to the guitar's sound and function.

The Solid "Slab" Body

This is an obvious ingredient, perhaps, since it forms the cornerstone of the Stratocaster's construction, but its contribution to the tonal formula can't be ignored. Aside from the sonic properties of the common tonewoods used in Stratocaster bodies, which will be

Slab blanks and contoured bodies back up a 2010 Custom Shop 1959 Black Stratocaster. *Fender Musical Instruments Corporation*

Elements of the classic Stratocaster body displayed in a bare body and a 2010 Custom Shop 1967 Aged Olympic White Relic Stratocaster. *Fender Musical Instruments Corporation*

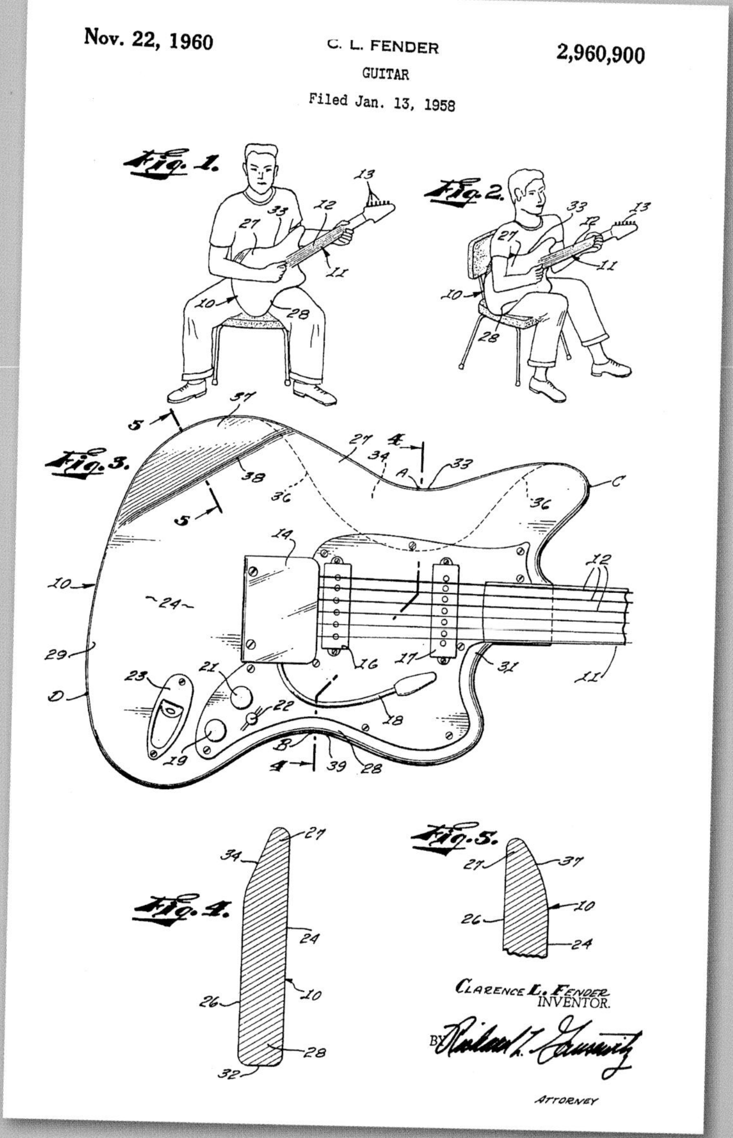

discussed in their own right further along, the sheer method of construction of a guitar with a slab-styled body made from one or two pieces of the same wood, with minimal use of glue and lack of adornments, lends its own tonal characteristics to the instrument. It is difficult to quantify such factors, but suffice it to say that such a design allows a relatively unencumbered vibration of the wood itself, and since there is only one wood involved, it presents the pure characteristics of that wood without the complications of multiwood constructions or heavy adornments. The end result is heard in the Strat's clarity and tonal purity, which is emphasized by other elements of the design, but is certainly anchored here.

Also, while some players will talk of a Stratocaster as "lacking sustain," they are often actually hearing the single-coil pickups, which don't present the "fatness" and perceived sustain of, for example, a higher-gain humbucking pickup when played through the amplifier. Compare both types of guitars unplugged, however, and a good Stratocaster will usually hang in there sustain-wise with any popular set-neck, humbucker-loaded guitar you might put it up against.

The 25 1/2-Inch Scale Length

Whether Leo Fender settled on the Telecaster's (and therefore, Stratocaster's) scale length by happy accident or by conscious design, it certainly worked toward achieving his goals for the instruments. In his lecture to the 1995 convention of the Guild of American Luthiers, guitar maker Ralph Novak stated that, of all factors that affect a guitar's tone, "scale length comes first because the harmonic content of the final tone produced by the instrument begins with the string. Factors such as structure and materials can only act as 'filters' to tone; they can't add anything, they only modify input. Therefore, if the harmonic structure is not present in the string tone, it won't exist in the final tone." Scale length is, therefore, a cornerstone of design for any thoughtful maker and one of the first decisions to be settled when conceiving the voice of an instrument. The fact that Leo Fender settled on the 25 1/2-inch scale seems perhaps to have been serendipitous, but the choice served to emphasize many of the other sonic characteristics that he was hoping to achieve with this guitar.

Put simply, the longer the "speaking length" of any guitar's strings (that is, its scale length, the distance between bridge saddle and nut slot), the more distance there is between the strings' harmonic points. The result is that relatively longer scale lengths have a greater presence of sonic qualities often described as "shimmer" or "sparkle" or "chime." Leo copied the scale length of a Gretsch archtop guitar when designing the guitar that would become the Telecaster, but it turns out that the 25 1/2-inch scale length accentuates the qualities he was looking for more than does the 24 3/4-inch scale that Gibson uses on many guitars, including the Les Paul family, the SG, the ES-175 and several others. With shorter scale lengths, the tighter grouping of the harmonic points create a slightly warmer, "furrier" tone—in short, they don't ring as clearly—which itself is part of the whole Gibson electric tonal mojo.

It so happens that Fender's narrow single-coil pickups, his choice of woods, the steel bridge construction, and the bolt-on maple neck all further accentuate harmonic clarity and high-end presence, so the total package really is working together toward Fender's desired tonal ends. But, as Novak put it, "if the harmonic structure is not present in the string tone, it won't exist in the final tone."

The slightly longer Fender scale length also increases the string tension, making the strings feel a bit firmer to the fingertips, although the springs in the vibrato unit offer some "give" to the playing feel to partly counteract this. The 7 1/4-inch fingerboard radius on vintage Fender guitars (the curve at which the top of the fingerboard is milled) also contributes greatly to the guitar's playing feel and to some extent has always dictated how it was approached. Smaller than the radius used on any other popular model of guitar, this tight circle results in more curve to the surface of the fingerboard and, in one sense, a neck that can feel extremely natural and comfortable in the hand for basic open chords played in the lower positions in particular. The rounder the radius, though, the harder it can be to bend strings on the fingerboard or to do so without "choking out," a phenomenon whereby the curvature of the fingerboard mutes a bent string and causes it to die out prematurely. Obviously, plenty of players do bend strings successfully on the Stratocaster, and it has become the classic choice of several big-bending blues players in particular, such as Buddy Guy and Stevie Ray Vaughan.

The Bolt-Neck Construction

Even if the neck itself and mounting plate and wood screws that hold it in place are all "tangible" components, it is probably best to consider the so-called "bolt neck" *in theory* for its contribution to the Stratocaster's voice, regardless of the wood and hardware that comprise it. Leo Fender adopted the bolt-on neck—which was at first derided by some traditionalists when it appeared on the Telecaster in the early 1950s—for its ease of construction and ease of repair, but this element of the Stratocaster design brings a specific component to the guitar's tone too.

A well-cut and tightly fitted screwed-on neck joint (as the Stratocaster's is, with wood screws rather than actual "bolts") can easily be as tight, and even tighter, than a glued neck joint, in terms of neck-wood-on-pocket-wood pressure. However tight such a joint might be, though, the neck and body woods remain the slightest bit decoupled, thanks to the inevitable presence of tiny air gaps between the two surfaces, due to natural inconsistencies in wood grain, dimples or irregularities in the finish, and other minute voids that would be filled with glue in a glued-in neck joint. In truth, most vintage Fender neck pockets and neck heels are not cut particularly tightly anyway, and these joints are often not as tight as those on guitars made by many skilled contemporary luthiers. In any case, even if it has the potential to be tighter the bolt-on neck is rarely as seamless a joint as a well-executed glued-on neck (or "set neck"). Beyond being merely a preference of construction method, this also leads to noticeable changes in a guitar's tone and response.

As heard in a traditional Stratocaster, some sonic characteristics of the bolt-on neck joint include a certain percussive "snap" and "spank" in the tone, a more clearly defined sense of pick attack in the note, and an increase in that bright, shimmery characteristic that I can only think to define as "jangle" or "chime." While a glued neck joint contributes to an increased sense of warmth and depth on many set-neck guitars—simply put, more "hair" around the note—and a corresponding blurring of the attack and decay, a Stratocaster often exhibits a distinctive "pop" in the pick or finger attack that is heard as if layered atop the body of the note, a sonic entity that is separate from the sound that tails off into the decay of that note. Several other factors contribute to this response, but a big part of it comes to us courtesy of the bolt-on neck joint.

(Continued on page 216)

Leo Fender's 1963 patent drawing for the adjustable bolt-neck design used on the Stratocaster as well as other Fender guitars.

Aug. 4, 1964 C. L. FENDER **3,143,028**

ADJUSTABLE NECK CONSTRUCTION FOR GUITARS AND THE LIKE

Filed Aug. 26, 1963

2 Sheets-Sheet 1

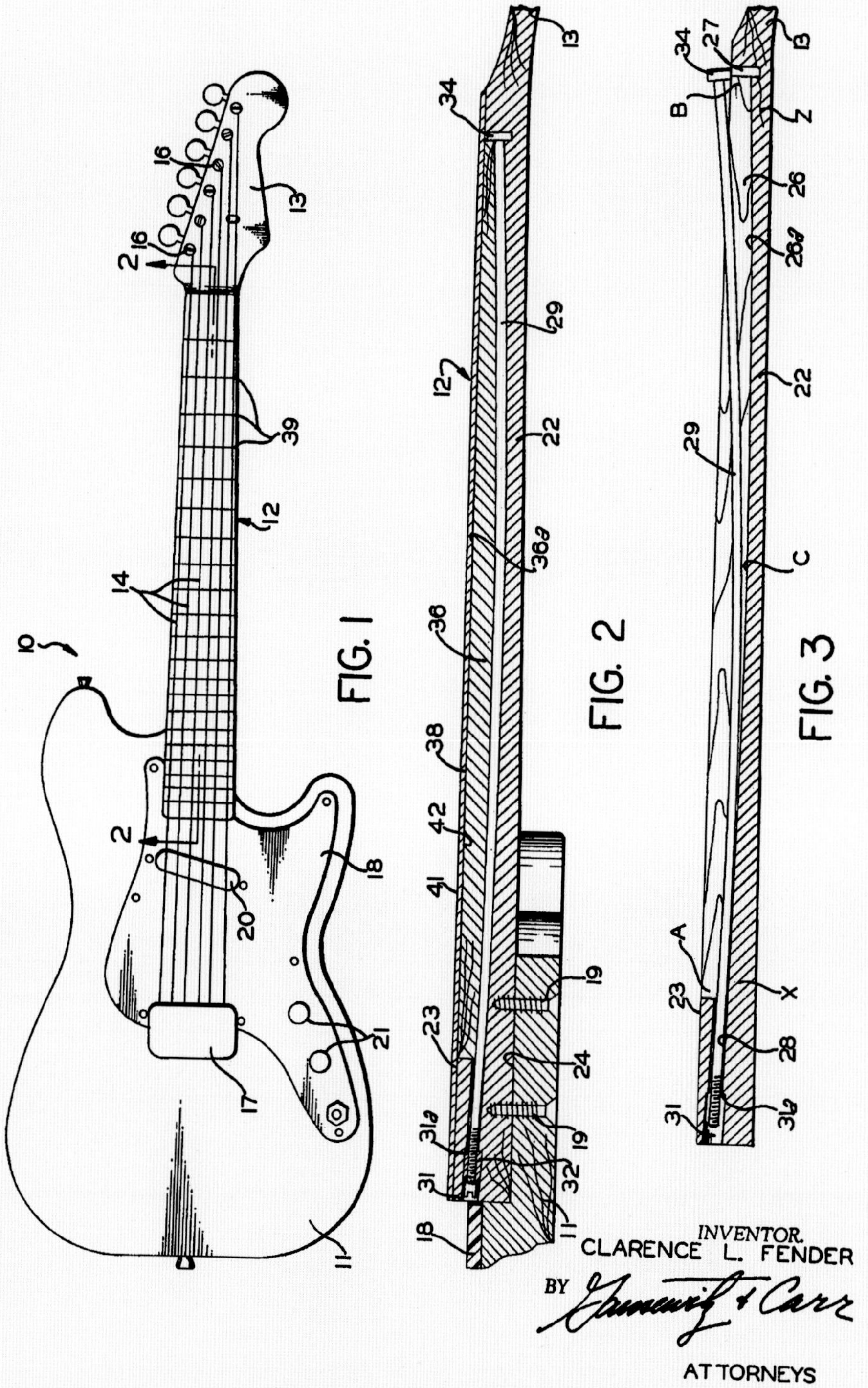

INVENTOR.
CLARENCE L. FENDER

BY Grunewig & Carr

ATTORNEYS

Nils Lofgren

Nils Lofgren hits a high note at the Winterland Ballroom in San Francisco, California, in 1975.
Richard McCaffrey/Michael Ochs Archives/Getty Images

Though he released four stellar albums in the early 1970s with his band Grin, Nils Lofgren got his foot in the door thanks to sessions with Neil Young, who famously drafted the teenaged guitar-slinger to play piano on Young's 1970 solo album, *After the Gold Rush*, despite Lofgren's lack of experience on the instrument. After Grin dissolved in 1974, Lofgren released a string of solo LPs before replacing Steve Van Vandt in Bruce Springsteen's E Street Band in 1984 for the massive *Born in the U.S.A.* tour.

It's through his appearances with Springsteen over three decades that Lofgren's become best known for a particular natural-finish 1961 Stratocaster. As the guitarist explained to *Fender News*, "My first guitar, in the mid-'60s, was a Tele; I got it because Jeff Beck played one. Soon after that, I saw Jimi Hendrix live . . . and the Strat soon became to me—even more than the Tele—the instrument that I was most comfortable with, as far as having different sounds."

Lofgren has actually owned two 1961 models. The first was acquired from a friend in a trade for a 12-string acoustic. The more recognizable Strat, however, came into the Lofgren's hands a bit later. "The other '61 I found in a pawn shop in Berkeley when I was on the road in the late '60s," he told interviewer Peter Walker. "It was this ugly purple thing, but I bought it because it sounded great. I gave it to my brother, Michael, who is a master carpenter, to restore it. He stripped it and dyed it natural wood, and made a beautiful oak pickguard."

Playing for the Boss: from left, Jake Clemons, Gary Tallent, Nils Lofgren, Bruce Springsteen, and Patti Scialfa perform at the Los Angeles Convention Center on February 8, 2013. *Kevin Mazur/WireImage/Getty Images*

This "oakguard" Strat is also notable for its Alembic Blaster preamp unit, visible where the stock recessed output is usually located. When toggled on, the Blaster allows the player to increase volume without affecting tone. A rubber effects pedal knob in place of the traditional skirted Strat volume knob gives Lofgren better control of the volume to use the Blaster to create swirling effects.

Finally, the guitar is outfitted with Bill Lawrence double-blade pickup in the neck position (Lofgren is known to use the pickups, as well as Joe Barden double-blades in other guitars as well). Also noteworthy is Lofgren's technique, which involves a downstroked thumbpick and harmonic-inducing upstrokes with his second and third fingers.

Despite a penchant for aftermarket modifications, Lofgren is an enthusiastic Fender user through and through (on the road, he also uses a Jazzmaster, numerous other Stratocasters, and Fender amps). "I've found that with a Fender, you can lose your finesse and not totally lose it on the instrument, if you can understand that," he told *Premier Guitar* in 2009. "I like to lean into the guitar and use those five settings you can get out of a Strat. I like playing lots of different guitars, but I'll always reach for a Strat. It's the most beautiful electric guitar ever made." —*Dennis Pernu*

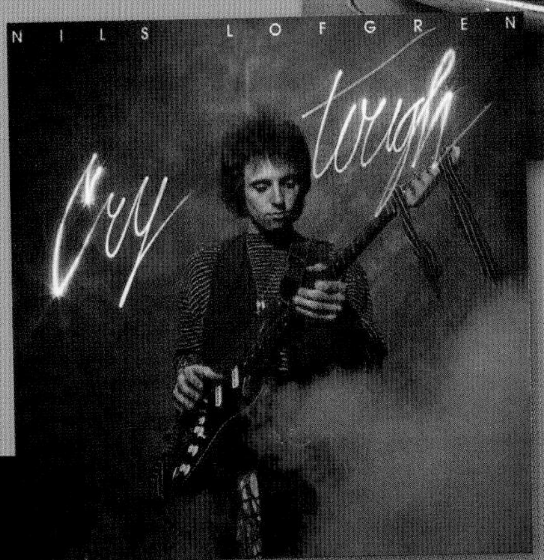

Jimmie Vaughan

Jimmie Vaughan stands proud with one of his Signature Strats relic'ed to mimic his original Olympic White 1963.

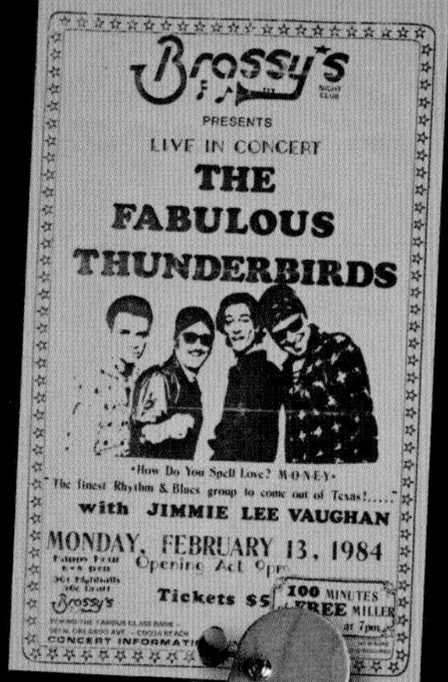

Brossy's
PRESENTS
LIVE IN CONCERT
THE FABULOUS THUNDERBIRDS
with JIMMIE LEE VAUGHAN
MONDAY, FEBRUARY 13, 1984
Tickets $5

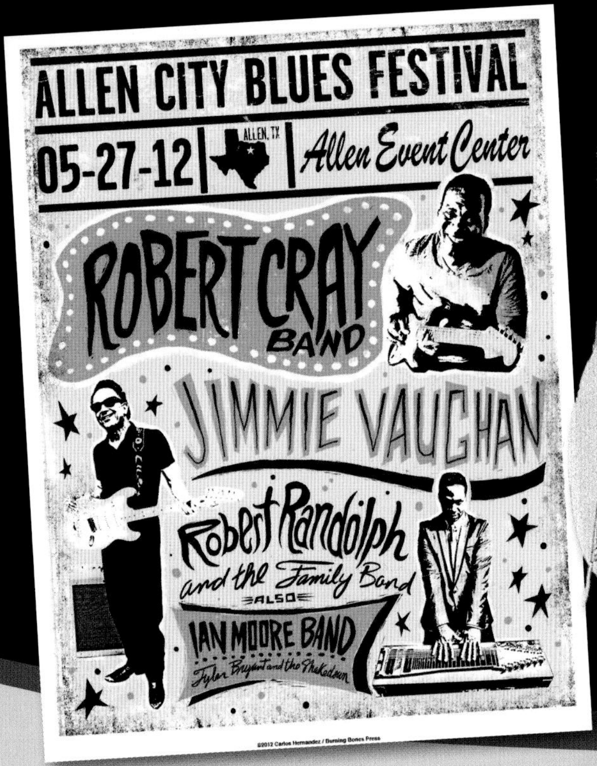

ALLEN CITY BLUES FESTIVAL
05-27-12
ALLEN, TX
Allen Event Center
ROBERT CRAY BAND
JIMMIE VAUGHAN
Robert Randolph and the Family Band
ALSO
IAN MOORE BAND

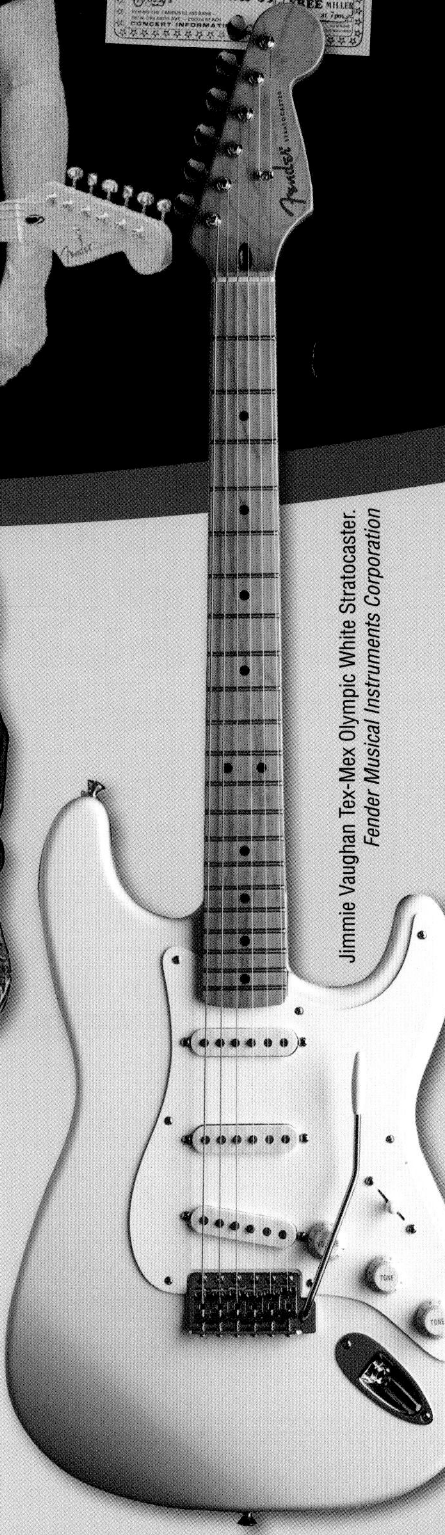

Jimmie Vaughan Tex-Mex Olympic White Stratocaster. *Fender Musical Instruments Corporation*

He really was the reason why I started to play, watching him and seeing what could be done," so said Stevie Ray Vaughan of his big brother, Jimmie. What more really need be said?

Jimmie Lawrence Vaughan was born in March 1951 in Oak Cliff, Texas—T-Bone Walker's old stomping ground, on the edge of Dallas. As he himself relates, Vaughan "was weaned on classic Top 40 radio [which was invented in Dallas], vintage blues, early rock 'n' roll, and the deepest rhythm and blues and coolest jazz of the day, thanks to the sound of Dallas's AM radio powerhouse KNOX and border radio stations like XERB, where personalities like the legendary Wolfman Jack sparked a youth revolution. I never got over that stuff, and I never will."

Sidelined by a football injury when he was 13, a family friend gave Jimmie a guitar to occupy his time during his recuperation. From the moment his fingers touched the strings, he proved himself a natural talent. As his mother, Martha Vaughan remembered, "It was like he played it all his life."

Jimmie launched his first band, the Swinging Pendulums, at 15 and was soon playing Dallas clubs several nights a week. A year later, he joined one of Dallas's top local bands, the Chessmen, which opened shows for Jimi Hendrix. Hearing Muddy Waters and Freddie King play, Jimmie focused on the blues, founding the band Texas Storm in 1969.

In 1974, Jimmie formed the Fabulous Thunderbirds in Austin with singer and harpist Kim Wilson, drummer Mike Buck, and bassist Keith Ferguson. They released their debut album in 1979, *Girls Go Wild*, with a tough blues sound tempered by 1950s rock 'n' roll. With the 1986 *Tuff Enuff*, the title track single, and followup

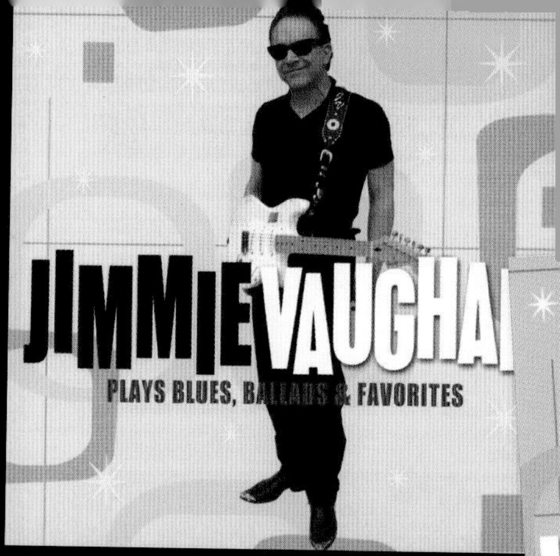

"Mine is the white one that I used on all the Fabulous Thunderbird records and I also made *Strange Pleasure* with it. It's a '63. I customized it a little bit. I put a new neck on it and back then you couldn't get pickups so you had to scavenge them."

—Jimmie Vaughan, 2013

single "Wrap It Up," the Fab Thunderbirds found a widespread, national audience. The album became a Top 40 hit, peaking at No. 10 on the *Billboard* charts.

Shortly after, Jimmie left the 'Birds to play in a duet with his kid brother, which came to a halt following Stevie Ray's death in 1990. The duet album *Family Style* arrived shortly after. Ever since, Jimmie has remained a solo artist.

Jimmie is famed for taste. He's never needed a virtuosic volley of notes to make a statement, relied on effects to find his voice, or hidden behind razzle-dazzle. Instead, he often says his piece with the perfect double stop played with the perfect tone.

He's made music on many guitars, but his well-traveled, beat-up '62 Olympic White Strat has long been his trademark instrument. That Stratocaster has had much surgery with a maple-fretboard neck and plenty of other changes to keep it alive after all its years on the road.

The Jimmie Vaughan sound is a Strat through a Fender narrow-panel tweed Bassman. As Jimmie says, "You can get that sound through a Matchless and several different amps, but it's really basically all the same amp from my perspective—they all came from a Bassman. I mean there's always an exception, but for the most part, a Bassman it is. Tell me what's better than that? I don't know what is." —*Michael Dregni*

Vaughan plays his Strat behind his head with the Fabulous Thunderbirds in 1986. *Ebet Roberts/ Redferns/Getty Images*

Stevie Ray Vaughan

Stevie Ray Vaughan and his First Wife (Number One) at the Oakland Coliseum Arena on December 3, 1989. *Clayton Call/ Redferns/Getty Images*

Few players have done as much to establish the Fender Stratocaster as *the* American blues machine as Stevie Ray Vaughan. Devoted to the Strat, Vaughan owned and played several, but the name he gave his favorite of the bunch—"Number One"—really said it all. Vaughan spent more time on this heavily beaten early 1960s Strat than on any of the others in his collection. Today, it's the guitar most associated with the late blues hero. Although Vaughan referred to the guitar as a '59 Strat, and it did have '59 pickups on it, the body and neck both carried date stamps from 1962, so it appears it originated from that year, although by the end of the star's ownership of the instrument it had really transmogrified into something of a Parts-O-Caster.

Vaughan bought his '62 Strat at Hennig's Heart of Texas Music Store in Austin, Texas, in the mid-1970s, and it possessed a certain magic for him right up until his death in a helicopter crash on August 26, 1990. Store proprietor Ray Hennig, who knew Vaughan as a regular customer, told music writers Joe Nick Patoski and Bill Crawford, "He lived for that guitar. He told me it was the only guitar he ever had that said what he wanted it to say." As much as Number One meant to him, Vaughan nevertheless set about modifying it to his specific requirements almost immediately. The most visible customizations included the reflective "Custom" and "SRV" stickers he added behind the vibrato bridge and on the replacement black pickguard, respectively, but several other alterations had more to do with the feel and playability of the instrument. The addition of a left-handed vibrato unit in the early 1980s is accounted for by two stories, one being that it was the only replacement available in Texas when the original broke, the other that it helped the guitar mirror the upside-down, right-handed Strats of hero Jimi Hendrix (there's nothing stopping both from being true). Vaughan also had

2004 Stevie Ray Vaughan Stratocaster and 2004 Custom Shop SRV Replica prototype. *Fender Musical Instruments Corporation*

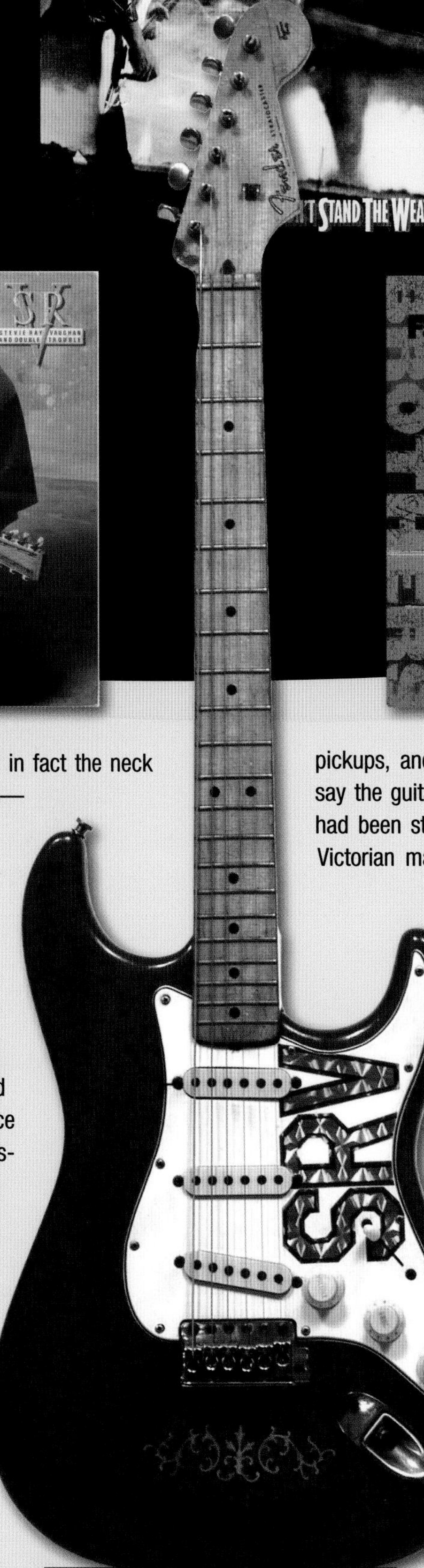

the original frets replaced with jumbo frets, and in fact the neck would be refretted several times over the years—to the extent that, toward 1990, it just couldn't take another refret and was replaced with the original neck from another '62 Strat known as "Red." Also in 1990, Number One was given a whole new set of gold-plated hardware.

Details aside, Number One is really best known for the huge tone Vaughan wrangled from it, which was aided, of course, by a set of pre-CBS pickups that seemed to have been wound slightly on the hot side and the artist's preference for heavy .013–.058 strings, but mostly by a muscular left hand and a ferocious right-hand attack.

If he wasn't playing Number One, odds are Vaughan was playing "Lenny," a Stratocaster he first saw in an Austin pawn shop in 1980. He was unable to afford its $350 price tag at the time, but the guitar was later given to him as a birthday present by his wife, Lenora, and six other friends who all chipped in $50 each. Named in tribute of Lenora, Lenny was an early 1960s Strat that carried its original rosewood fingerboard, pre-CBS pickups, and three-ply white scratchplate—which is not to say the guitar hadn't been modified in other ways. The body had been stripped and stained a rich brown, and a scrolled Victorian mandolin-style inlay had been added beneath the vibrato bridge, which itself was a contemporary replacement unit with die-cast saddles. Vaughan further modified the guitar to suit his needs. First he added the customary reflective "SRV" stickers to the pickguard and then later swapped the original neck for a modern-era all-maple unit given to him by Billy F Gibbons of ZZ Top. Vaughan pressed Lenny into service most notably on the songs "Lenny" from *Texas Flood* and "Riviera Paradise" from *In Step*. When performing the former tribute tune live, he would invariably put down Number One and strap on Lenny, a guitar to which he understandably felt a close bond.

Number One is now in the hands of Stevie's brother, Jimmie Vaughan, while Lenny was sold to Guitar Center for $623,500 in Eric Clapton's 2004 Crossroads Guitar Auction.

Stevie Ray Vaughan's Lenny. *Robert Knight Archive/Redferns/Getty Images*

Eric Johnson

Eric Johnson performs in Hollywood, Florida, on March 14, 2012. *Larry Marano/Getty Images*

2004 Eric Johnson Signature Stratocaster. *Fender Musical Instruments Corporation*

Regarded in guitar circles as a tone freak's tone freak, Eric Johnson is famous for such niggling tweaks as using a rubber band to hold the bottom plate on his Fuzz Face fuzz box because he doesn't like its sound with the standard screws and preferring the performance of his BK Butler Tube Driver when positioned on a wooden block that lifts it above the level of the rest of his effects pedals. Most players would be thrilled with *any* '57 Strat, but with ears like these, and a discriminating sonic sensibility to go with them, you can be sure Johnson isn't likely to settle on just any 1957 Fender Stratocaster. It's well known that even valuable vintage guitars range from poor to mediocre to good to outstanding in the tone and playability stakes—and if Eric Johnson has chosen to ply his trade for years on one particular '57 Stratocaster, you can bet it's a breathtaking instrument. As such, this particular maple-neck sunburst Strat has become legendary among an elite crowd and is a fitting example of everything a great Strat should be.

As iconic a guitar as Johnson's Strat might be, it's no museum piece. Rather, it has been carefully modified to suit the needs of a hardworking and discerning professional. Johnson has the guitar refretted with jumbo wire as often as necessary to keep it feeling meaty and playable. As Johnson explained to Dan Erlewine in *How to Make Your Electric Guitar Play Great!*, rather than having the fingerboard planed down to a flatter radius than the vintage 7.25-inch radius that Fender

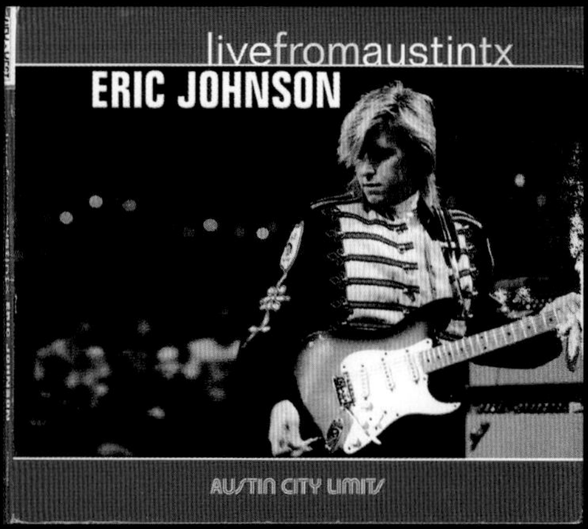

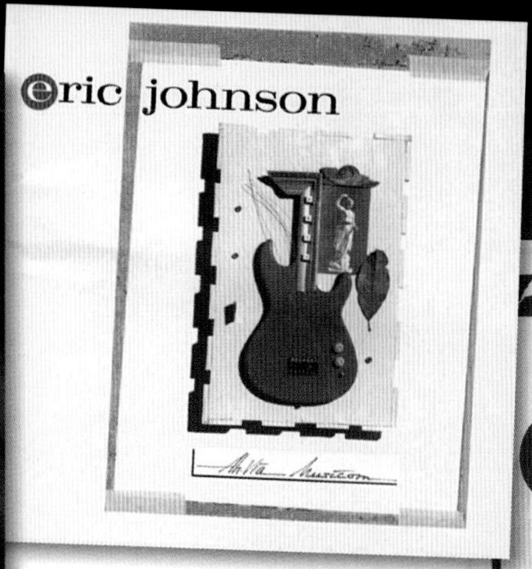

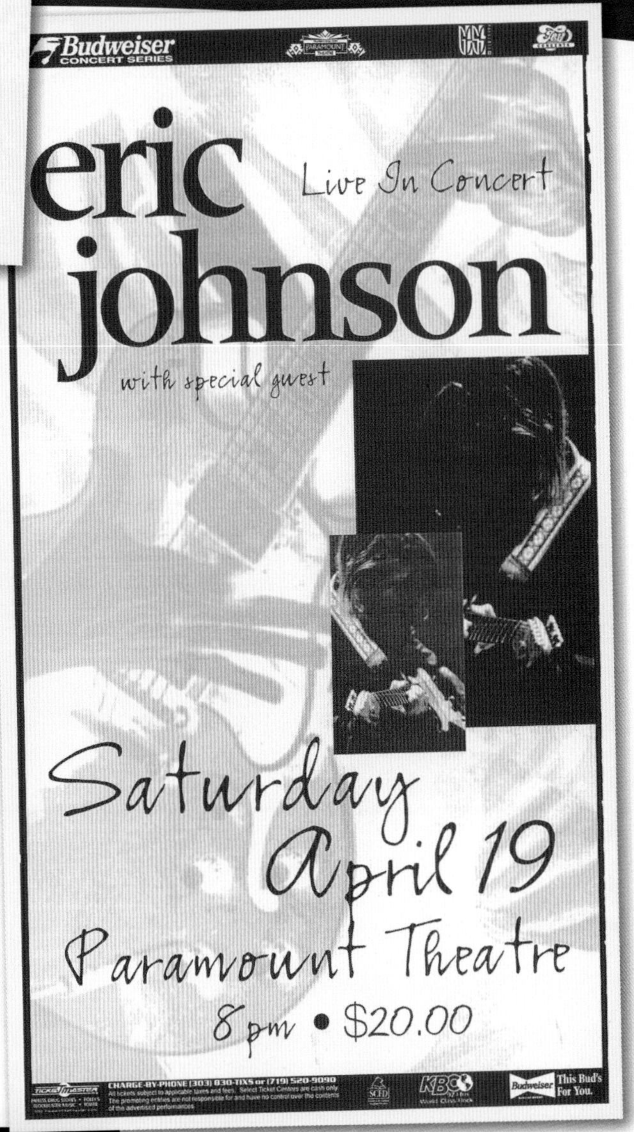

originally used, he has his frets milled down slightly lower toward the middle of the neck so they remain higher toward the edges, making it easier to grip the strings for extreme bends. Johnson famously leaves the cover off the tremolo spring cavity on the back of the guitar because he feels it hampers the tone and has had a nylon insert cut from an old Gibson bridge saddle installed in the high E string's steel saddle to soften its shrillness, a goal further pursued by rewiring the Strat's controls so the bridge pickup passes through a tone potentiometer rather than straight to the output the way a '57 was wired at the factory.

Achieving Johnson's famous "thousand-pound violin" tone involves far more than just the guitar, though, and several other elements of his rig deserve a portion of the credit. The essentials here are really rather simple, but they add up to a mammoth sonic assault. Johnson's guitar signal first runs through his choice of ingredients on a fairly basic but meticulously selected pedal board, including the aforementioned Fuzz Face and Tube Driver, a Crybaby wah-wah, a TC Electronic Stereo Chorus Flanger, and an Echoplex tape-delay unit. From there, Johnson selects between a pair of blackface 1966 Fender Twin Reverb amps with JBL D120F speakers, a 1968 Marshall 50-watt Tremolo head and 4x12 cab, or a 1969 Marshall 100-watt Super Lead and 4x12 cab. A mighty arsenal, yet for all this, we've perhaps got to credit the player's hands for just a *little* of the mighty tone this rig generates.

(Continued from page 204)

Basic Tangible Ingredients

We might be tempted to use the old adage that the tone of any electric guitar is "more than the sum of its parts," and that is true in many ways for the seminal Stratocaster, but an examination of the individual contributions of several of these components does get us a long way toward understanding that sonic "sum." Back in the mid-1950s when the Stratocaster first came together, Fender wasn't always aiming for the highest quality—in the pure and absolute sense—in any of these elements, but sought a marriage of good, robust performance with ease and efficiency of manufacture and repair. Fortunately, a certain unquantifiable magic seemed to reside in the results of this approach, and the pre-CBS Stratocaster gradually established itself as one of relatively few genuine top-tier classics of solidbody electric guitar tone.

Body Woods

The first Stratocasters were made with bodies of ash, the wood used for the Telecasters' bodies at the time. After 1956, that timber remained in use for some Strats, mainly those finished in custom-color Blonde, while alder became the standard wood for the Strat's body. "Swamp ash," as it is known in its more desirable form, is harvested from the lower portions of ash trees grown in the wetlands of the southern United States and is very different from harder, denser northern ash. A good, well-aged piece of swamp ash will exhibit different resonant characteristics and usually be significantly lighter than timber cut from the upper portions of the very same wetlands ash tree.

The tonal magic of a good piece of swamp ash is largely attributable to the porosity of the wood, itself attributable to the conditions in which it grows. Timber below or near the surface of a swamp or wetland absorbs greater quantities of water than higher parts of the tree, which causes the pores to swell. As the wood dries, these pores empty of water, leaving myriad tiny air pockets—and therefore, a relatively low density—in a wood that is nevertheless strong and workable.

"Generally speaking," says Chris Fleming, a Fender Custom Shop master builder, "ash can have a warm, round sound, with a bit of a focused cut to it. It can also be, depending on the guitar,

1954 Stratocaster with an ash body.
Chicago Music Exchange, www.chicagomusicexchange.com

a bit shrill, a bit snarly." As a result, such guitars are "very rich, they're very loud, and they cut through a band very well."

It is clear from Leo Fender's goals in developing the Stratocaster, however, and a solidbody electric guitar in general, that he was nearly as concerned with cost, supply, and ease of manufacture and repair as he was with pure tone. Although he would have valued the fact that swamp ash bodies produced a sound that contributed toward his aims for the guitar, this timber's tonal properties might not have been paramount among his reasons for selecting it. "Being a very frugal and production-minded guy," says Fleming, "he looked for woods that he could get cheaply and sustainably. At that time ash was a good candidate."

Sustainability of supplies was one of the major reasons Fender moved to the second most significant Stratocaster body wood on the majority of guitars made after the middle of the decade. In the late 1950s good ash became more difficult to get. Older, well-dried stocks were being used up, and newer timber was often proving denser and heavier. It made sense, therefore, to save the fewer good swamp ash blanks for blonde guitars, which made the most of exhibiting this tonewood's broad, attractive grain, while the finer, less dramatic grain exhibited by most alder worked just fine under sunburst or opaque custom-color finishes.

The issue also begs a question regarding "classic" Fender tonewoods: If swamp ash is considered the archetypal Telecaster body wood, as well as being the original wood of the seminal 1950s Stratocaster, why didn't the company—adept at promotion even in that innocent age—brag about its use in the guitars? As much as vintage aficionados rave about a great piece of swamp ash, there's no mention of body-wood species at all in Fender promotional literature from the 1950s and early 1960s. To the best of this author's knowledge, in fact, the first mention of body woods appears in the post-CBS Fender advertisements for the "Groovy Naturals" Telecaster Thinline models, noting that they are available either in ash or mahogany.

Regarding the move to alder, and any considerations at early Fender of the tonewoods used for body construction, Chris Fleming speculates: "I think it was more important to have a steady source of acceptable-quality wood to put into their products, and one of the main reasons that they went to alder was that it was probably cheaper and more readily available." Even so, alder does have slightly different sonic characteristics than swamp ash, and tends to have a strong, clear, full-bodied and well-balanced sound, often with muscular lower-mids, firm lows, and sweet highs. In many ways it might be considered a more "open" sounding wood than swamp ash, one capable of producing a guitar with a more versatile and better-balanced tonal palette. Guitarists sometimes have a tendency to latch onto the "first is best" rule regarding so many issues of vintage-guitar specifications, but it seems to make the most sense to simply declare that there are *two* classic Stratocaster body woods. And while the glorious swamp ash might still carry an air of greater romance for many, you need only consider the fact that Jimi Hendrix, Stevie Ray Vaughan, Eric Clapton, and Ritchie Blackmore did most of their notable playing on alder-bodied Strats to see how futile such distinctions can sometimes be, in the "better or worse" sense, at least.

Neck Woods

The Stratocaster's radical, revolutionary body style made it instantly recognizable even from across a dimly lit concert hall, but the most distinctive characteristic of the guitar's construction is arguably its bolt-on maple neck. This entire configuration was high on Leo Fender's list of "easy to manufacture, easy to repair" when he set out to design the Strat's predecessor, the Broadcaster/Telecaster, and we have already discussed the characteristics of the screwed-on joint itself, but the wood from which these necks were made is another significant ingredient in the formula.

Maple is a hard, dense wood, and when used in a guitar's neck contributes characteristics of brightness and clarity to the overall

The classic maple neck with a rosewood fretboard on a 2008 Custom Shop 1960 Surf Green Stratocaster. *Fender Musical Instruments Corporation*

sound of the instrument. In addition to the goals regarding manufacture and repair, the Stratocaster neck therefore also aids Leo's sonic objectives, and does so extremely well. Even beyond their tonal characteristics, maple necks offer elements of response and performance that blend with their sonic contribution, enhancing a Stratocaster in a way that encompasses both the sound and "feel" of the guitar as an instrument. The immediacy of maple's response (merged with the "decoupled" effect of the bolt-on neck joint, as discussed above) helps to give the guitars a perceived "snap" and "quack," along with other characteristics that contribute to the classic twang tone.

As it happens, the maple neck also partners extremely well with an ash body to achieve clarity and articulation. While we might think of these as characteristics of the classic electric country guitar sound—the test-bed into which the Stratocaster was developed—they also give the guitar plenty of cutting power amid more distorted tones, and enhance its distinctive harmonic sparkle and "bloom" amid overdriven sounds. Listen to the way Stevie Ray Vaughan's Stratocaster manages to sound fat and juicy yet simultaneously crispy and articulate on tracks like "Scuttle Buttin'" or "Pride and Joy," the way Jimi Hendrix's playing exudes a marriage of gargantuan girth and delectable clarity on so many of his Strat-based cuts, or the multidimensional sonic complexity in so much of Eric Johnson's Stratocaster work, and you begin to understand what this guitar can do with some overdrive behind it.

Adding a rosewood fingerboard to an otherwise all-maple neck, as Stratocasters featured almost exclusively from mid-1959 until the mid-1960s, does add some warmth, roundness, and smoothness to the guitar's overall tone. These enhancements, however, are typically less pronounced than they are often thought to be—a contribution, many experienced makers will tell you, of perhaps 5 to 10 percent or so of the overall tone. As with any ingredient, though, the picture isn't entirely black and white. "Using different materials for the rosewood," says Fender's Chris Fleming, "Indian rosewood as opposed to Brazilian rosewood—or what we use a lot of now, which is Madagascan rosewood—makes a lot of difference in itself. My favorite rosewood to use on a Fender is Indian. Most [rosewood used by Fender] was Brazilian up until the early '60s, and then it switched to mostly Indian because in the mid-1960s Brazilian began becoming a problem. But Brazilian, in my opinion, is a bit too bright. Once again, though, it depends on the actual piece. Brazilian can be very dense and ringing, which is nice in some combinations, . . . but I'm not wild about Brazilian on maple, although other guys will tell you I'm crazy."

As discussed in the "History" chapter, it is highly possible that Fender changed from maple to rosewood for reasons other than tone. Having clearly been happy to be the rebel at the time of the solidbody's introduction, Fender was perhaps feeling like making a bid for a slightly classier presentation by the late 1950s. The use of a rosewood fingerboard on the Jazzmaster in 1958 seemed *de rigueur* for a guitar aimed at the jazz crowd, while it also fit the direction of the Custom Telecaster, putting it, along with the body-edge binding, in more traditional territory. The impetus by that point was clearly to bring this more traditional look (and the lack of the smudged-looking maple 'board that came with it) to the entire Fender line, and the Stratocaster was graced with this "upgrade" as well.

Neck and Headstock Hardware and Appointments

Since the Stratocaster has traditionally carried no fingerboard binding, no headstock overlay, and only simple dot inlays, there isn't much else to speak of as regards the guitar's austere neck appointments, although the nut, string retainer, and tuners still deserve a mention.

The bone nut used from the start of Stratocaster production is one of the guitar's few nods to guitar-making tradition. Bone is known for its resonance and sustain-enhancing properties and makes an excellent neck-end termination point for the strings' speaking length. As an organic material, it isn't as consistent from one blank to the other as contemporary synthetic nut blanks made from Micarta or Corian might be, and the guitar maker can encounter tiny air bubbles in this finely porous material that will lead to minor irregularities, and therefore slight changes in performance from one nut to the other. On the whole, though, it is a tone-enhancing component nevertheless, does its job well, and can even be impressively long lasting.

For ease of manufacture, Fender necks are created without the back-angled headstocks that many others

1956 Stratocaster headstock with Kluson tuners.
Michael Dregni

use to create adequate string pressure in the nut slots. Necks are carved so that the headstock sits on a slightly lower plane than the fingerboard, so the break angle from the nut down to the first few tuner posts is entirely adequate, but the B and high-E strings in particular (the only unwound strings when the guitar was introduced) have to make a much longer journey to their tuner posts. To correct for this, Fender used a string retainer, which pulled down on the B and E strings slightly to produce adequate pressure in the nut slots and help prevent a droning sound being produced from the dead lengths of these strings between nut and tuner posts. This retainer started out as the same round, slotted disc in use on the Telecaster and changed to a thinner, bent-steel "butterfly" retainer midway through 1956, with a small spacer added beneath it in 1959 to reduce the downward pull on the B and high-E strings, thereby improving return-to-pitch stability when the vibrato was used. Many later guitars from the early 1970s onward carried two "butterfly" retainer clips to achieve the same results on the G and D string pair.

The asymmetrical, six-in-line headstock design is another visual characteristic of the Stratocaster and of all classic Fender guitars. As discussed in the "History" chapter, it has performance benefits in addition to creating a distinctive style for the model. Fender's headstock design enables a straight line for each string from nut slot to tuner post and therefore resists the tuning instabilities that can occur when strings stick or hitch in nut slots from which they must break at angles out toward their respective tuners on wider headstocks, such as those used by Gibson, Gretsch, Epiphone, Rickenbacker, and many others. Such "hitching" is usually compounded further when a vibrato bar is used, which requires a smooth and direct path for the strings' short slide through the nut slots in order to retain adequate return-to-pitch stability. Although the straight string path was already in line on the Telecaster, its functionality proved even more significant on the Stratocaster.

The Kluson tuners loaded onto pre-CBS Telecasters are another part of their classic vibe, and many players and makers will tell you that they have a slightly different "sound" than the heavier replacements by Schaller or Grover, which some players added to their guitars. The design of these tuners' back cover changed slightly over the years, namely in how the brand name was stamped into these gear covers, from a single-line "Kluson Deluxe" to no line (no brand stamp), back to single line, and finally double line—with "Kluson" and "Deluxe" stamped on opposing edges of the cover—by the mid-1960s. In 1967 the Kluson tuners were dropped in favor of Schaller tuners that were made in West Germany to Fender's own design, and stamped with the new, thicker "F" of the Fender logo.

Truss Rod

The Stratocaster's original truss rod was installed through a channel routed in the back of the maple neck, which was afterward filled with a strip of darker walnut, creating a look that has come to be known as the "skunk stripe." From around mid-1959, with the introduction of the rosewood fingerboard, the truss rod was installed through a route made in the face of the neck, which was concealed by the fingerboard when the neck was completed. In both cases, access to the adjustment nut was found at the body end of the neck, requiring that the player either loosen the neck screws to raise the neck heel from its pocket, or dig into the pickguard (usually damaging it slightly) to make changes in neck relief. This would seem one factor that went against Leo's criteria that the Stratocaster (and all of his creations) be easy to service, and Fender did eventually, post-CBS, move the adjustment bolt to the headstock end of the neck in the latter part of 1971. Rather ironically, perhaps, the "bullet head" truss-rod design is loathed by many fans of the vintage (that is, "original") pre-CBS Stratocaster design, and guitars that carry it are often considered, by some at least, to be from the nadir of Fender's Stratocaster production, although usually for several reasons other than (or in *addition* to) this truss-rod bullet.

2008 Robin Trower Signature Stratocaster with a modern version of the 1960s F-logo tuners.
Fender Musical Instruments Corporation

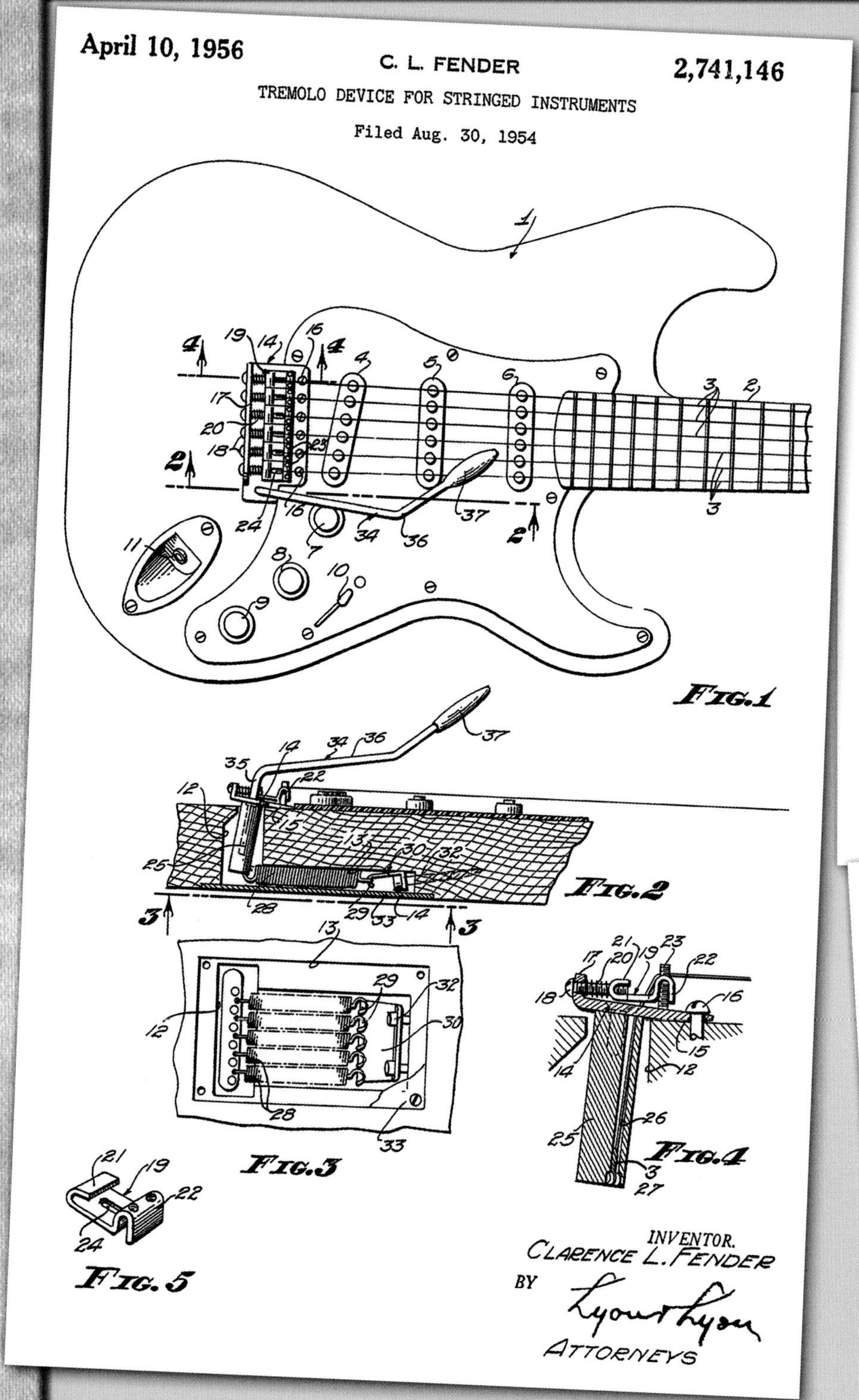

Leo Fender's 1954 patent drawing for the tremolo bridge design used on the Stratocaster.

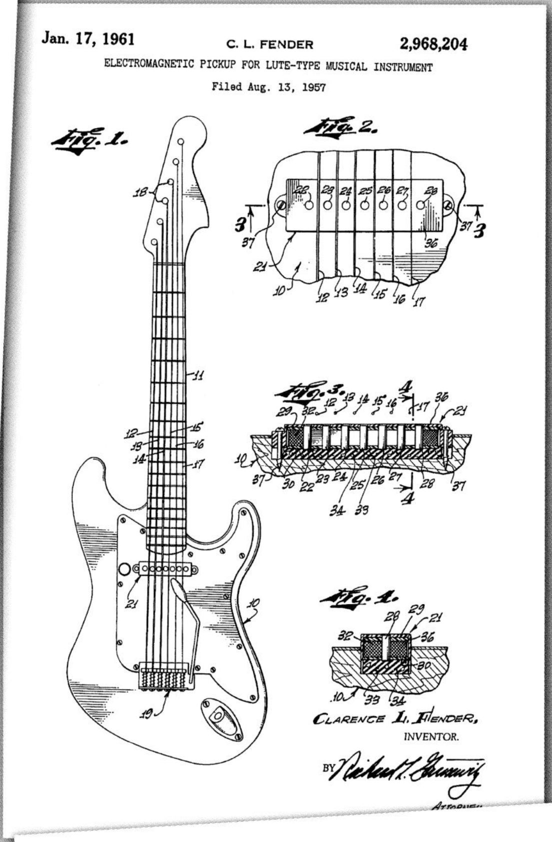

Jan. 17, 1961
C. L. FENDER
2,968,204
ELECTROMAGNETIC PICKUP FOR LUTE-TYPE MUSICAL INSTRUMENT
Filed Aug. 13, 1957
Fig. 1.
Fig. 2.
Fig. 3.
Fig. 4.
CLARENCE L. FENDER,
INVENTOR.
BY

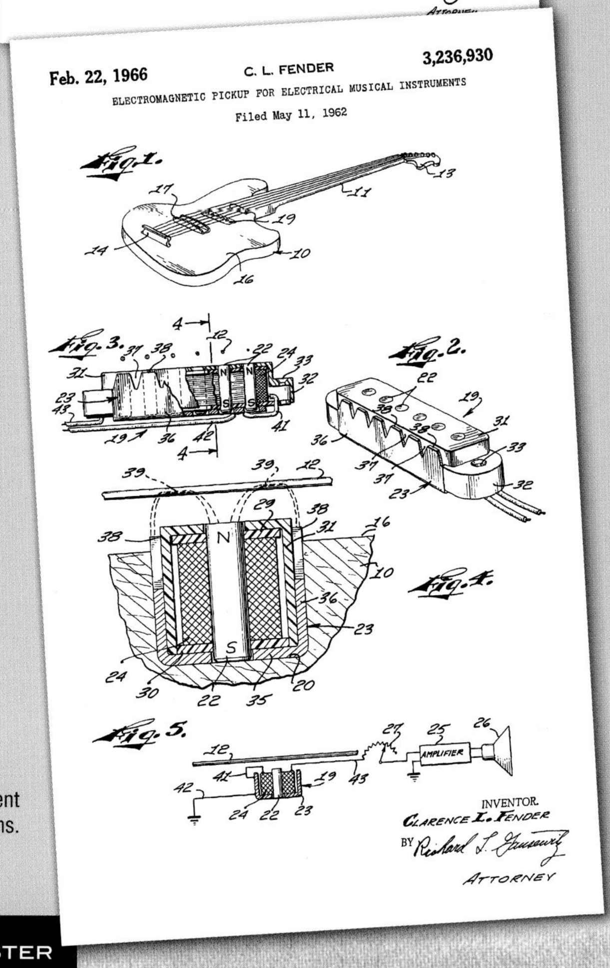

Leo Fender's 1957 and 1962 patent drawings for single-coil pickup designs.

Vibrato Bridge Assembly

Fender called its revolutionary bridge unit the "Synchronized Tremolo," but let's call it what it actually is: a vibrato. Where tremolo fluctuates the volume of a signal, vibrato fluctuates its pitch, which is exactly what this unit did—and still does with great effect. Whatever you call it, though, the bridge hardware developed by Leo, Freddie Tavares, and others on the Fender team was an ingenious piece of engineering for its day, and continues to be among the favorite vibrato units the world over even today. The vibrato's most obvious effect upon the sound of the Stratocaster is heard when it is in use, inducing anything from a gentle shimmer to a deep dive bomb. Leave your hand entirely off the "whammy" bar, though, or even remove the bar altogether, and this clever piece of hardware still makes its mark upon the Strat's tone.

The Stratocaster's lauded Synchronized Tremolo imposes several specific sonic elements upon the guitar's tone, and indeed renders it a very different sounding instrument—in its fine points, at least—than it would be with the strings anchored by any of a number of "hardtail" bridge configurations (just check out the sound of the lesser-seen, so-called "hardtail" Stratocaster to hear the difference for yourself). While the Telecaster's distinctive bridge affects that guitar's tone partly in the way that it interacts with the pickup suspended within it, the Stratocaster's vibrato bridge impacts its tone in multifarious ways primarily according to how its constituent components interact more directly with the guitar's string vibrations and body resonance.

The vibrato bridge's individually adjustable, stamped-steel saddles contribute brightness and clarity to the Strat's tone, as does the steel bridge plate beneath them, to some extent. The truly ingenious element of the design, however, is hidden under all of this, in the form of the solid steel "inertia block" (or "sustain block"). Bolted to the underside of the bridge plate, and drilled with holes through which the strings pass (and into which those strings' ball-ends are anchored), the inertia block was Leo and company's brilliant means of replacing the resonant mass lost by the necessarily flexible coupling of vibrato to guitar body. As such, it provides a great means of retaining adequate—indeed, impressive—sustain in a guitar that has its strings anchored in a moving part. Stratocaster aficionados swear by the original, heavy, cold-rolled steel inertia blocks used on the guitars made between 1954 and 1971, as well as the many high-quality reproductions of such that are out there on the market. The less-dense, die-case Mazak block introduced later in 1971, and others made with softer, sonically inferior alloys, are said to thin out the tone and inhibit the guitar's sustain. All in all, though, the bridge and its original sustain block are impressive for their contributions of warmth, sustain, and low-end solidity that might otherwise be absent. These elements are crucial components of the Stratocaster's overall tonal picture, which can be characterized as ringing chime and jangle with a slightly silky sizzle in the highs, an air of gentle compression, and a somewhat scooped midrange, coupled to a firm bass response.

In addition to the sonic elements contributed by the bridge and inertia block, the springs that help it perform its stated vibrato function add considerably to the playing feel of this guitar. Bend a Strat's G-string hard, for example, and you will note how the bridge plate tips forward slightly. Pick an open high-E string and bend the G-string (without picking it) and note how the pitch of that E dips with the upward bend. That's a clear indication that there's some give in the Strat's vibrato, and your fingers are aware of this elasticity when they play a vibrato-equipped Stratocaster. This "give" can make a Stratocaster feel easier to play than, for example, a Telecaster, which has the same scale length. Many players will also tell you that the sympathetic "reverberation" of the vibrato's springs, set in motion by the vibrations transferred when you pick a note or a chord, also contribute to the sonic brew of the Stratocaster. You can certainly hear this when you play a Stratocaster unplugged, although it might be more difficult to detect once you're amped up.

Pickups

We might infer something about Leo Fender's integrity as a designer from the fact that he didn't merely rejig the mounting arrangement of the existing Telecaster bridge pickup, add a cover, stick it on the new guitar, and call it a Stratocaster pickup. Certainly the newly designed pickups used on the Strat were similar to those that the Tele carried at the time—even once you stripped the Tele pickup from its bridge and base plate—but were different in enough ways to make them an entirely new unit in the Fender camp. A traditional Telecaster bridge pickup is made from fiber top and bottom plates that form a "bobbin" of sorts that is wider than that of the similarly constructed Stratocaster pickup (which is the same in all three positions). The wider Tele pickup bobbin is capable of holding a greater number of turns of 42 AWG wire than that of the Stratocaster pickup, an average, in the early years, of around 9,200 or more turns of wire in the Tele pickup to the Strat pickup's average of around 8,350 turns. The thinner profile of this pickup, and the fewer turns of wire it holds, both contribute to a notable difference in tone. It might be subtle, and most players would still certainly describe both as characteristic of "the Fender sound," but it's a difference worth noting.

Most readers will be familiar with what we call "the single-coil tone" in the general sense, but even among that breed of pickup there's a great variety of sounds according to shape and design. Working from what we just explored in the Stratocaster design, the thinner the pickup (to some extent, at least), and in particular, the narrower and more tightly focused its "magnetic window," the brighter and tighter its sound. Simultaneously, less coil wire wound around a similar bobbin, in relative terms, also enhances clarity and focus. Meanwhile, the fact that Fender continued to use alnico rod magnet sections as pole pieces also enhanced brightness, note definition, and a certain tautness in the tone (compared, on the other hand, to a Gibson P-90 pickup, which gains a certain thickness and edginess from having steel pole pieces in contact with bar magnets below the coil and a much wider coil besides).

The sonic elements of Leo's design goals with the Stratocaster and with his Fender electric guitars, *et al.*, have been discussed several times in this book, and elsewhere: namely, he wanted the clarity, brightness, and definition needed to help guitarists cut through the erstwhile mud on the average bandstand or recording of the day. Having established the tonal significance of scale length, body and neck wood selection, and construction methods, and the sonic impact of the Synchronized Tremolo bridge, it's clear that the design of the Stratocaster pickups also furthered Leo's ends. Hang these narrow, relatively low-output pickups in their "floating" mountings in the Strat's plastic pickguard (where they don't contact any resonating body wood directly), and you have a bright, clear, somewhat glassy, twangy, and jangly guitar, and one that is particularly well suited to the demands of the music scene at the time of its arrival.

What comes across as twangy and jangly from the Stratocaster's bridge pickup, however, translates as warm and juicy from the neck pickup. Move the exact same pickup approximately 4 1/2 inches forward from the bridge toward the neck, and it is now "hearing" the strings at a wider vibrational arc and transmitting that as a fatter and often louder-sounding signal. While many Tele players claim they can never quite achieve the same meat and muscle from a Strat's bridge pickup as they get from a Tele's bridge pickup, most will concede that they'd kill for a Strat's neck pickup tone in their Telecaster. As we have already seen, though, there are so many factors contributing to that final tone that you really can't "fake it" through a pickup swap.

In addition to the effort put into the pickups' design, Leo Fender, Freddie Tavares, and the team put considerable thought into their placement. To some extent, the inclusion of three pickups might first have been largely a USP (unique selling proposition) for the sales team—as quoted in *The Fender Stratocaster* by A. R. Duchossoir, Tavares said, "Leo said it's quite a thing to have two pickups now, so let's have three!"—but the trio would considerably enhance the guitar's versatility (even to an extent, as below, that wasn't yet fully realized). More consciously utilitarian, though, was the decision to slant the bridge pickup in relation to the others, a trick that was already performing well on the Telecaster. Tavares to Duchossoir once more: "The rear pickup is slanted for a very important reason. That was because when you pluck the instrument way back near the bridge, everything is more brilliant, but you lose the depth. So the reason for the slant was to get a little more vitality, or 'virility,' into the bass strings and still maintain all the brilliance that we wanted."

Stratocaster pickups were wound with Formvar-coated 42 AWG wire throughout most of the 1950s, until Fender switched to plain enamel-coated wire in the early 1960s. Strat aficionados will swear by their preferences for one type or the other, and authorities on the fine points will often declare that there is a difference in sound between the two. The thicker Formvar insulation made for fatter coils that were also, at times, wound slightly more loosely as a result; whereas, the enamel-coated wire could be packed in more tightly. Whatever the wire, though, great music has undoubtedly been made on guitars carrying pickups wound with both types, so this can get into rather nitpicky territory. In a more cosmetic alteration, if one that often remains unseen, Fender changed from black fiber pickup-bottom plates to dark gray bottom plates around the end of 1964, then used lighter gray plates from 1968 onward.

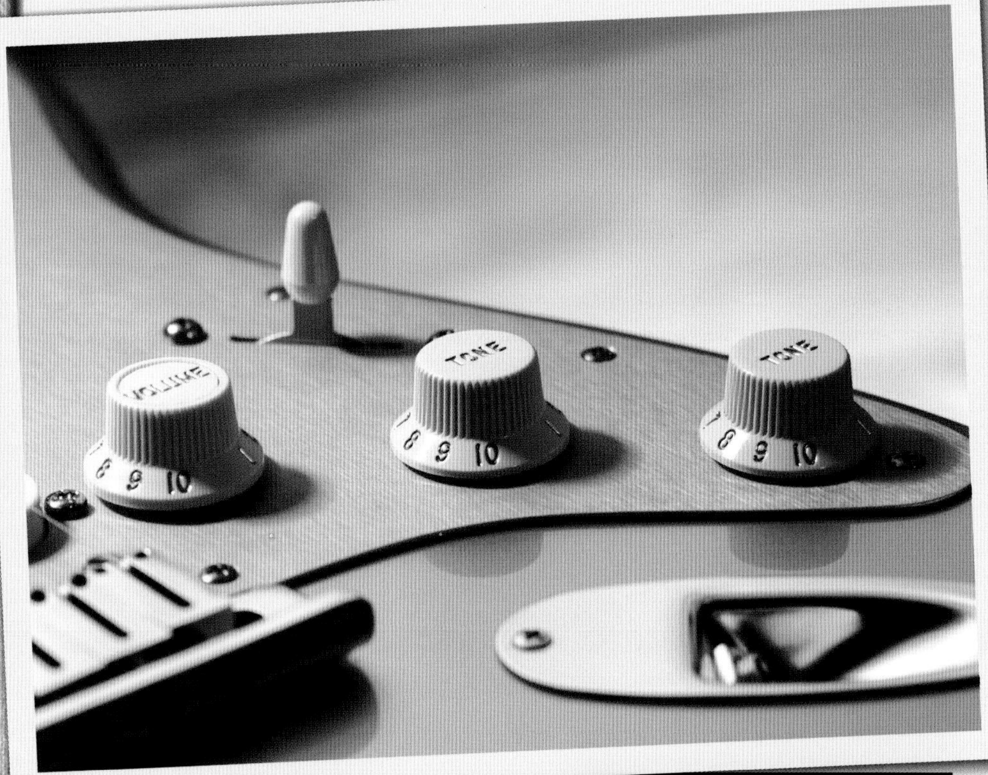

The Stratocaster's classic controls and switch layout remains on the updated 2012 Aztec Gold American Deluxe Stratocaster FSR. *Fender Musical Instruments Corporation*

Classic features of the first Stratocasters live on today on a 2009 Custom Shop 1958 Candy Apple Red Stratocaster. *Fender Musical Instruments Corporation*

Controls and Switching

The original Stratocaster switching layout, and the one honored by traditional "reissue" style Strats today, offered a master volume control, individual tone controls for the neck and middle pickups, and a three-way switch that enabled selection of each pickup alone, but not in combination. Most players today, if faced with an incomplete complement of tone controls, would prefer to have one on the bridge pickup at least, to tame the potentially over-bright tone from that pickup, and many rewire their Strats in that way. But "bright" was the rule of the day, and routing the bridge pickup straight through with a no tone pot provided a means of ensuring maximum treble from that position.

As for the use of a three-way switch on a guitar that would prove to offer so many more potential pickup selections in combination, well, as Leo told Tom Wheeler in *Guitar Player* magazine in 1978, "There weren't too many convenient styles of switches back then. It wasn't a matter of what we would like so much as . . . of what we could get." Regardless of the implied limitations of the switch, players soon discovered that they could find the usefully funky "in between" pickup sounds of the bridge and middle or middle and neck together by simply balancing the switch carefully between its intended positions. Noticing this trend, component manufacturers soon offered an aftermarket five-way switch, and Fender finally began installing one at the factory in 1977.

Put them all together—and put them together *right*—and these constituent parts coalesce into the sublime whole that we have come to know as the Fender Stratocaster, simply the most influential electric guitar ever produced.

Robert Cray and his Strat.
Joby Sessions/Guitarist Magazine/Getty Images

While his style is often pigeonholed as straight-up blues, Robert Cray's music is really an amalgam of classic genres that he has blended into something all his own—part soul, part R&B, and yes, part blues. Whatever you call it, though, most would agree that his tone is seminal Stratocaster at its best. "Every time somebody asks me about where my music comes from, I give them five or six different directions," the guitarist says on Robertcray.com, "a little rock, soul, jazz, blues, a little gospel feel. Then there are some other things that maybe fall in there every once in a while, like a little Caribbean flavor or something." Cray adds, "When I first started playing guitar, I wanted to be George Harrison—that is, until I heard Jimi Hendrix. After that, I wanted to be Albert Collins and Buddy Guy and B. B. King."

Robert Cray was born in Columbus, Georgia, in 1953. His family moved often to follow his father's military career. They were a musical household, and wherever they went Cray was continually exposed to his parents' broad tastes, absorbing everything from pop to rock 'n' roll, to jazz to blues, to gospel and soul. Cray started playing the guitar in his early teens, joined his first band while still in junior high school in Newport News, Virginia, and moved to the Northwest at the age of 21, where he soon formed the Robert Cray Band in Eugene, Oregon. Several years of paying dues all along the West Coast led to a deal with Mercury Records in 1982, but Cray's star truly ascended in 1986 with the release of his third album, *Strong Persuader*, which earned him a Grammy Award. Since then, Cray has gone on to earn another four Grammy Awards, fifteen nominations, and sold more than twelve million records.

From the start, Cray was drawn to the Stratocaster, and for many listeners, his

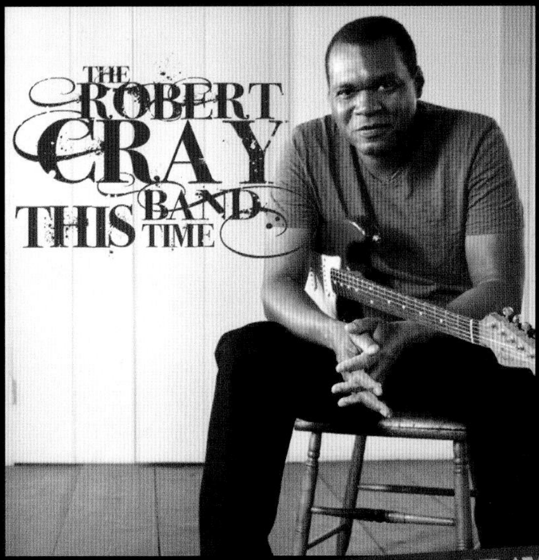

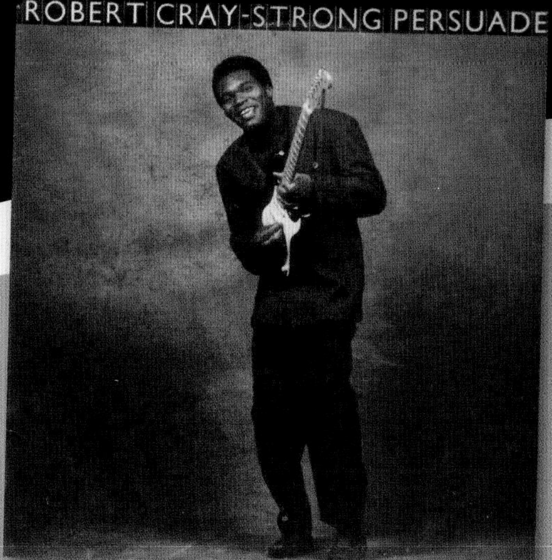

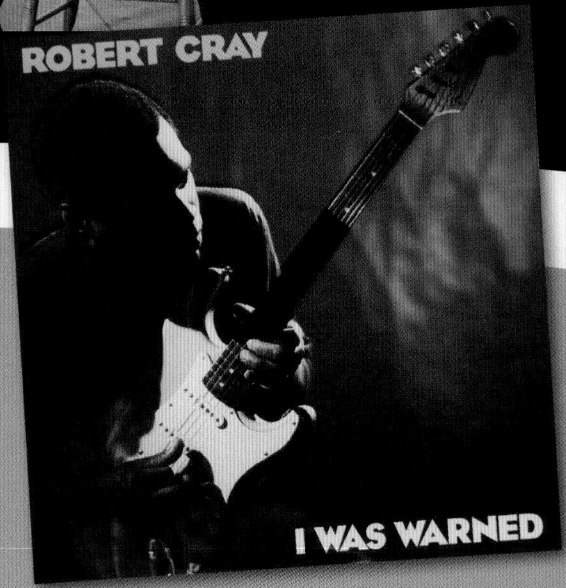

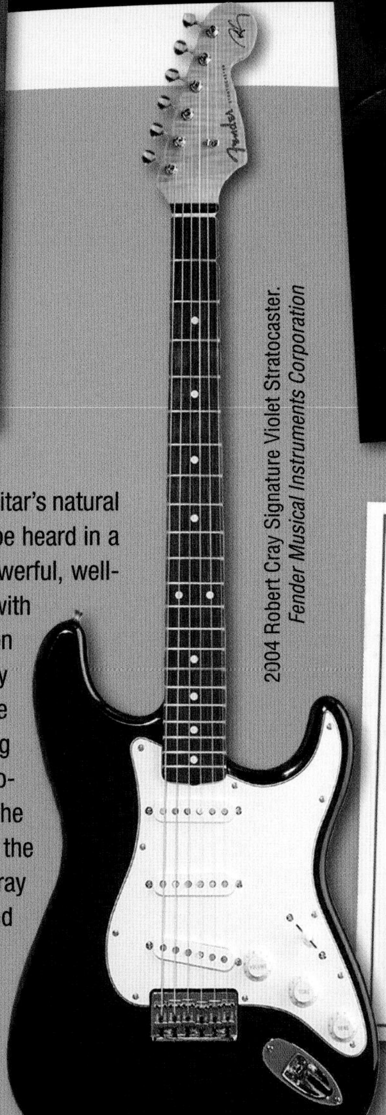

2004 Robert Cray Signature Violet Stratocaster. *Fender Musical Instruments Corporation*

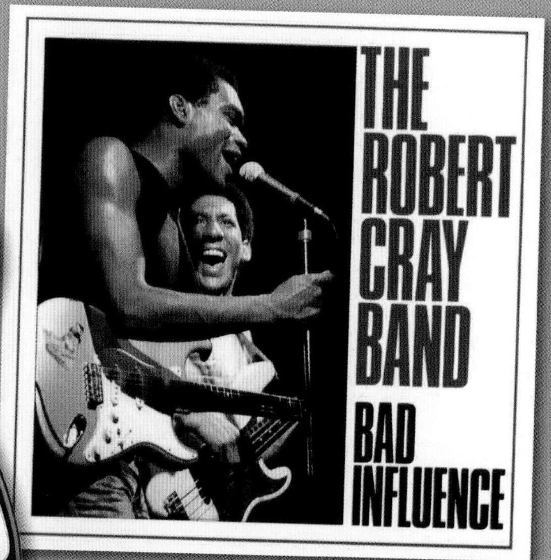

playing has come to define the clean-yet-rich nature of the guitar's natural voice. His spare, tasteful playing style enables that guitar to be heard in a pure setting too—classy enough to make do with a few powerful, well-landed notes where less mature players might assault you with a blizzard of riffage, Robert Cray's playing is a virtual lesson in elegant restraint, yet manages to be utterly moving every time. His intimate technique is enhanced by his use of the bare flesh of his right-hand thumb rather than a pick and running it all through both a Matchless Clubman and a Fender Vibro-King set relatively clean, with just an edge of breakup when he picks hard. Rather than using the Strat's vibrato (he removes the bar from his own guitars or chooses hardtail variations), Cray induces an emotive shake in his tone, using a classic left-hand finger vibrato, although he is also fond of bringing in the Vibro-King's tremolo to assist in some classic retro tones. Fender released the Custom Shop Robert Cray Signature Stratocaster in 2003, a hardtail model with vintage-wind pickups and Cray's favorite Inca Silver finish, which is flanked by the more affordable standard-run Robert Cray Stratocaster.

The Edge and Bono onstage during the Lovetown tour in Australia in 1989. *Bob King/Redferns/Getty Images*

In the alternative punk and new wave scenes of the late 1970s and early 1980s, the Stratocaster was often seen as a square traditionalist, the conventional weaponry of classic rockers and bluesers like Jimi Hendrix, Ritchie Blackmore, Yngwie Malmsteen, and Eric Clapton. As such, for a time there at least, it just wasn't much in favor with what you might call the "hip crowd"—players who were taking up the big names' alternatives like the Jazzmaster and Jaguar, the Les Paul Special and Junior, and other "second-tier" electrics. In using a 1970s Stratocaster to log many of his most notable tones, however, U2's the Edge (a.k.a. Dave Evans) helped drag this seminal Fender toward indie's cutting edge, making it once again acceptable to a younger, up-and-coming generation of players.

While the Edge is reported to own more than 200 guitars and commonly takes more than 40 on tour at any time, Stratocasters take up a bigger chunk of his collection than any other model. As is the way with so many struggling musicians, though, the Strats that peppered the most notable early U2 recordings weren't the prized pre-CBS models. In the early days, he plied his trade on several workaday 1970s Stratocasters with large headstocks, three-bolt necks, and bullet-head truss rod adjustment nuts and forged an instantly recognizable signature sound in the process. Some of the earliest U2 photos from around 1977 and 1978 show the guitarist wielding a mid-'70s Stratocaster with sunburst finish, and a black '73 Strat was often his main squeeze through the 1980s, when the '76 Gibson Explorer was resting. And if an Electro-Harmonix Deluxe Memory Man delay pedal and Vox AC30 give a certain homogeneity to many of the early recordings, the Stratocaster's bright, glassy cutting power can certainly be heard amid the whirl of much of it.

Where the Stratocaster had previously been known primarily as a lead instrument, the Edge took its percussive rhythmic capabilities to new heights. Neither a "lead" nor a "rhythm" player, *per se*, he established a rhythmic momentum on the instrument that allowed U2's early songs, in particular, to display plenty of air and space, while retaining a compelling forward motion and simultaneously eliminating any real need for solos or chord parts in the traditional sense. Listen, for example, to his churning, bouncing performance on "Where the Streets Have No Name" from 1987's *The Joshua Tree*, and hear how well Leo's goal for a "bright, cutting" tone works in a context he could in no way have envisioned when designing the guitar in 1953 and 1954. In its own way, and for its time, it was as fitting a tribute to the traditional that the alternative could make.

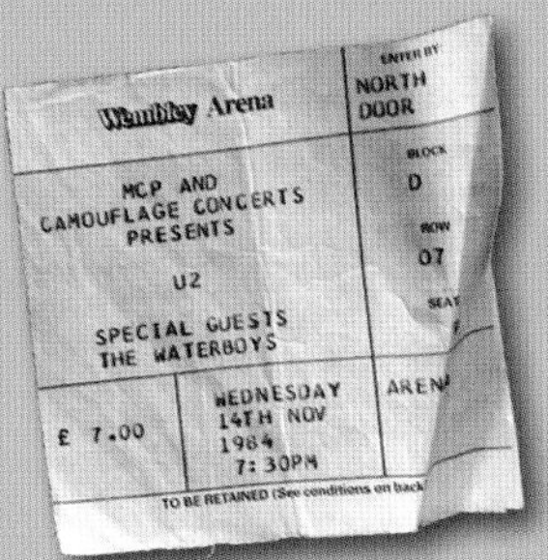

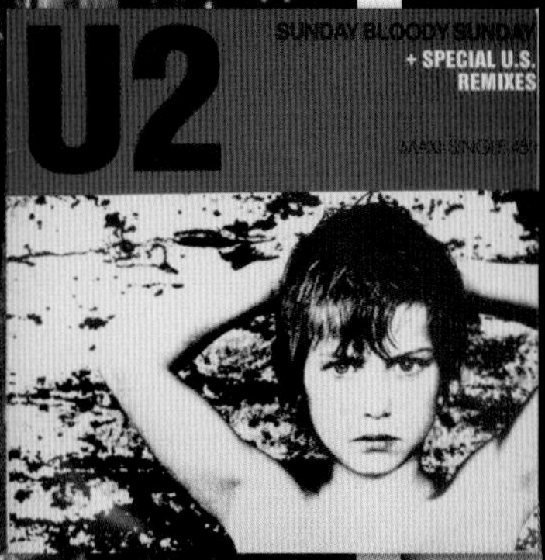

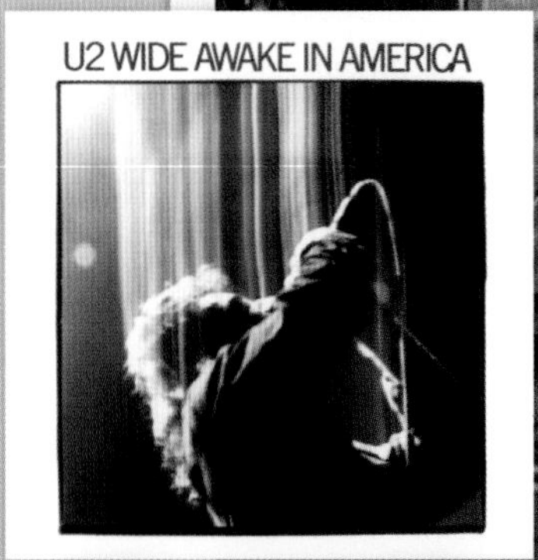

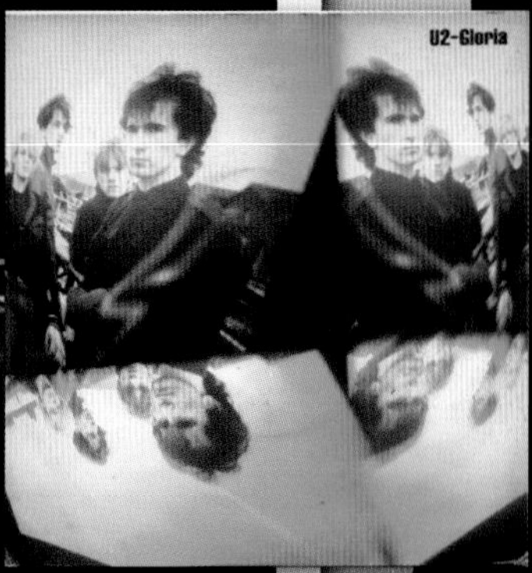

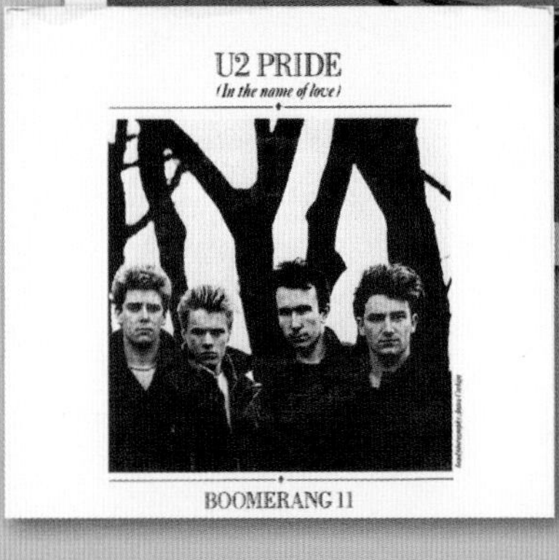

One of the Edge's vintage Strats, backstage during a recent tour. *Rick Gould*

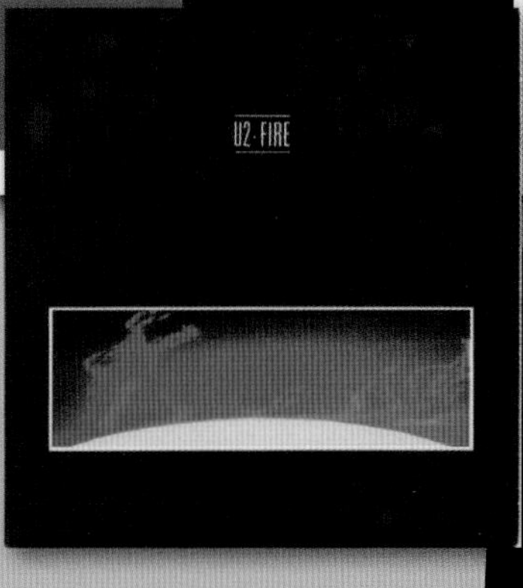

Sonny Landreth

Sonny Landreth slides on his Strat. *Jack Spencer*

Sonny Landreth is famed for his slide guitar mastery, a virtuosic style of slide that he usually plays on Stratocasters. He developed a style of playing bottleneck with his pinky finger, but also fretting the guitar behind the slide at the same time, creating more developed chords, variegated sounds, and complex voicings. Landreth is also known for his right-hand technique, combining slapping, tapping, and picking with all of his fingers.

Born in Canton, Mississippi, in 1951, he settled in Breaux Bridge in southern Louisiana. Throughout his career, he's drawn on the musical traditions of the region in crafting his own, unique sound.

"When I first started listening to Delta blues, I didn't even know what a slide was," Landreth told *Vintage Guitar* magazine in 2012. "I had learned a right-hand finger-style approach from Chet Atkins, so when I listened to the Delta players and discovered a lot of them like to slide, putting the two of those together set me on my path. Looking back on it I realize that my jazz heroes who played trumpet and my blues heroes with a guitar were all seeking to emulate a human voice and to have that character in their playing. I think that really helped me a lot: Slide lends itself to that, but even more so [than fretted playing]."

Landreth has always been faithful to the Stratocaster. His main guitar is a 1966 sunburst Strat that's appeared on most of his albums since his 1981 debut with *Blues Attack*. He also uses several modern Strats, including a '57 Reissue Strat with Lindy Fralin Vintage Hot pickups, his own Signature Strat with Michael Frank-Braun noiseless single coils, and his main touring Strat road Strat with a DiMarzio DP181 Fast Track 1 bridge pickup and DiMarzio Virtual Vintage neck pickup. "I like the idea of changing the pickups," he explains. "I wanted to create different colors and have different voices." —*Michael Dregni*

Black Hen Music
at the Electric Owl
Featuring...
SONNY LANDRETH
"...Probably the most underestimated musician on the planet." - Eric Clapton
Wednesday, January 30
Doors 6 P.M.
Show 8 P.M.
Come Early For Dinner and best seating!
Join us for an evening of spontaneous, unique and unforgettable music!
A different artist each month playing with
Steve Dawson and the Black Hen House Band.
Tickets: $25 (Advance), $27 (Door - Cash Only)
Box Office: 604.990.7810 capilanou.ca/nscucentre

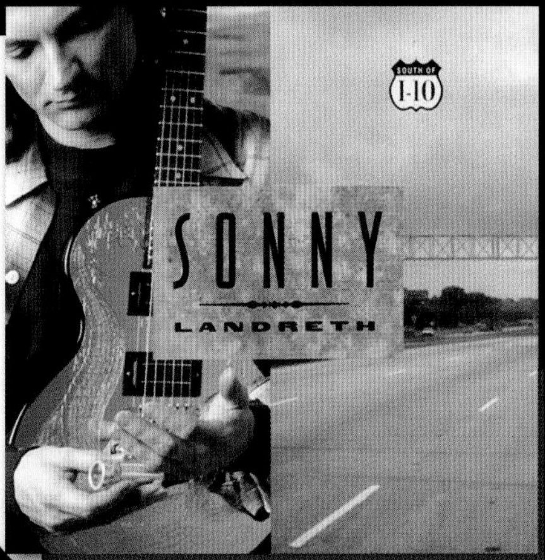
SOUTH OF
I-10
SONNY
LANDRETH

サニー・ランドレス
ダウン・イン・ルイジアナ
Sonny
LANDRETH
DOWN IN
LOUISIANA
epic.
定価¥2,000

SUNSHINE
BLUES
FESTIVAL
ON SALE NOW!
TWO STAGES • ALL DAY MUSIC FESTIVAL
TEDESCHI TRUCKS BAND
DR. JOHN* • WALTER TROUT
SONNY LANDRETH • JOE LOUIS WALKER
JAIMOE'S JASSSZ BAND • MATT SCHOFIELD
THE WOOD BROTHERS
BIG SAM'S FUNKY NATION
SEAN CHAMBERS • BOBBY LEE RODGERS
FORT MYERS
CENTENNIAL PARK
FRIDAY, JANUARY 18
BOCA RATON
MIZNER PARK AMPHITHEATER
SATURDAY, JANUARY 19
ST. PETERSBURG
VINOY PARK
SUNDAY, JANUARY 20
SUNSHINEBLUESFESTIVAL.COM
WORLD OF BEER
*St. Petersburg and Boca Raton Only
Charge By Phone: 800.745.3000. All dates, acts and ticket prices subject to change without notice. Ticket prices subject to applicable fees.
BUY TICKETS AT

SONNY Landreth
MISSISSIPPI BLUES

Sonny
Landreth
Blues Attack

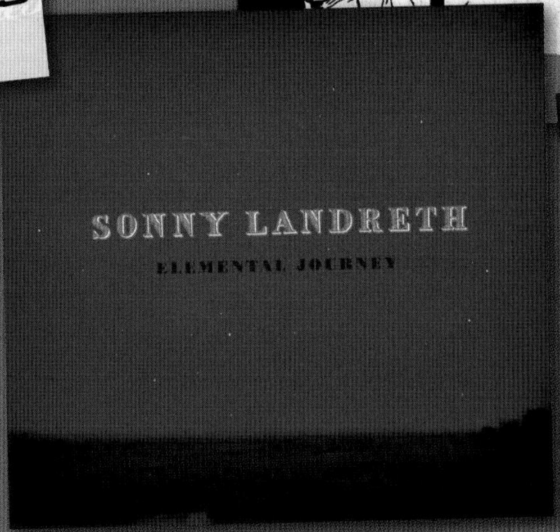
SONNY LANDRETH
ELEMENTAL JOURNEY

SONNY LANDRETH
GRANT STREET

John Mayer

John Mayer swears by his Signature Stratocaster backstage at the Hard Rock Calling festival in London on June 28, 2008. *Joby Sessions/Guitarist Magazine/ Getty Images*

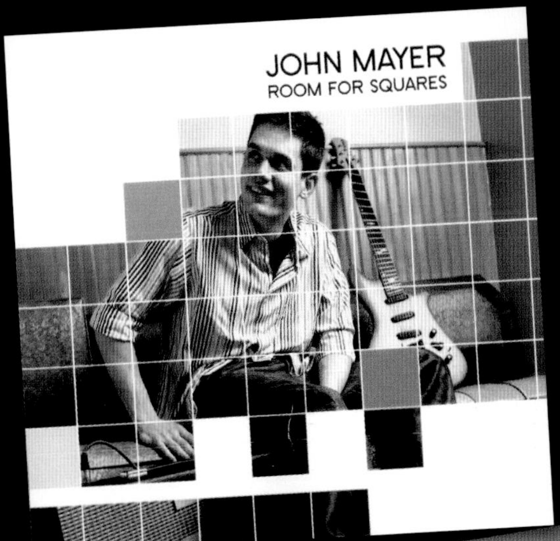

One of the leading lights of a new breed of popular guitar hero, emerging just when it seemed that maybe guitar heroes had forever fallen from popular music, John Mayer has proven he can hang with the likes of Eric Clapton, Buddy Guy, and Robert Cray on stage at the Crossroads Festival and still make adolescent fans swoon with his next chart-topping hit. Peel away the tabloid stories about the latest heartbroken starlet left in the heart-throb's wake, and Mayer, at his core, is really just a guitar player and one that has long favored Fender's seminal Stratocaster.

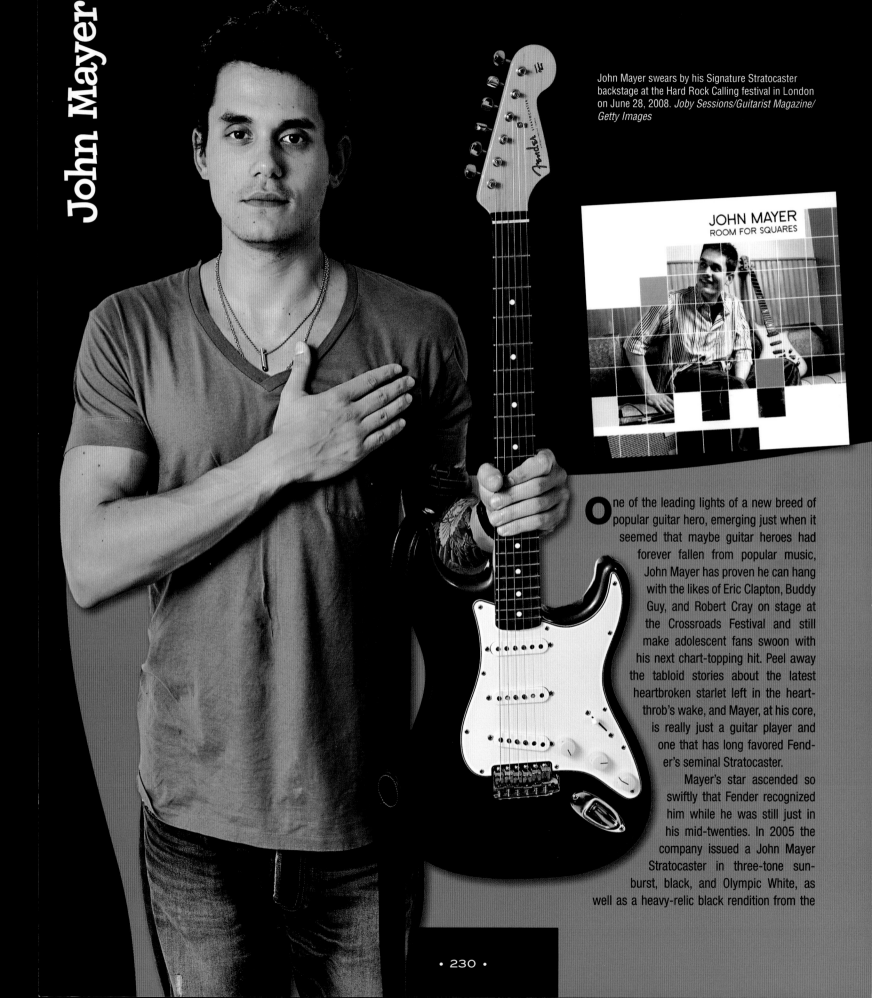

Mayer's star ascended so swiftly that Fender recognized him while he was still just in his mid-twenties. In 2005 the company issued a John Mayer Stratocaster in three-tone sunburst, black, and Olympic White, as well as a heavy-relic black rendition from the

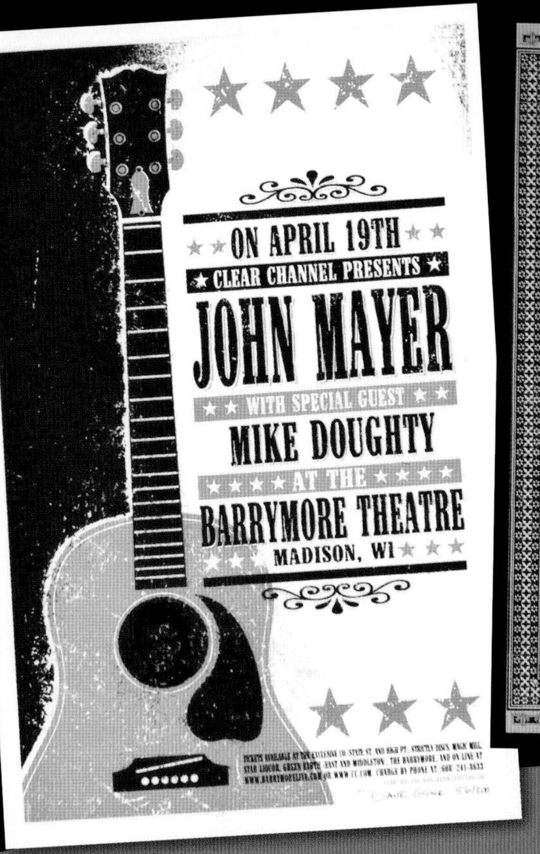

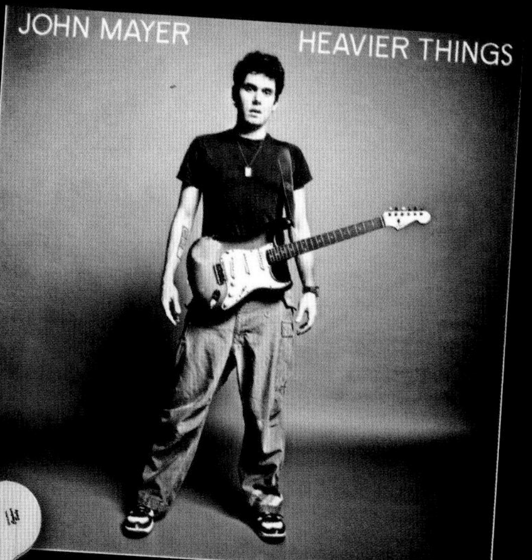

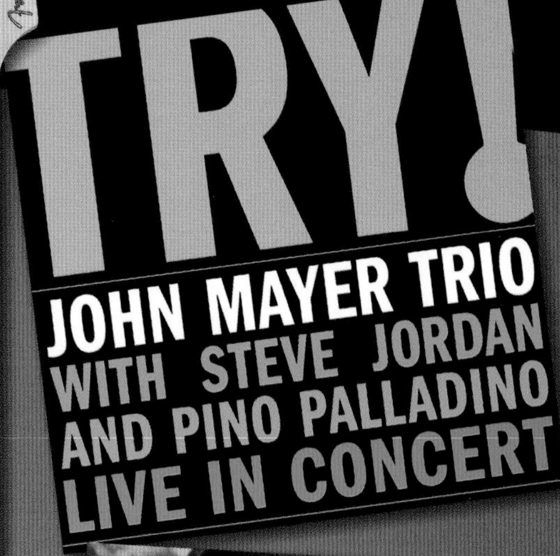

Custom Shop, but Mayer launched his own career on the back of an earlier Artist Series guitar from the hallowed California maker, a Stevie Ray Vaughan Stratocaster that he purchased with money saved from his job at a gas station. He boasts an extensive guitar collection today, but still takes his signature models and contemporary Strats out on the road, alongside other newer gems such as a Custom Shop rosewood Stratocaster.

John Mayer was born in Bridgeport, Connecticut, in 1977 and was raised in nearby Fairfield. His early musical skills were given a bump at Boston's Berklee College of Music, although he left that estimable institution after just two semesters, moved to Atlanta, and set about igniting his musical career. After a notable performance at Austin's SXSW music festival in March 2000, Mayer signed first to Aware Records and then to Columbia, which rereleased his previously Internet-only debut album *Room For Squares* to major commercial and critical success. Alongside the singles "No Such Thing" and "Why Georgia," the album track "Your Body Is a Wonderland" earned Mayer a Grammy Award in 2003, his first of seven Grammies earned from nineteen nominations.

When fully amped with Strat in hand, John Mayer has a playing style that exhibits classic blues tendencies, laced with a versatility that signals his contemporary pop sensibilities. At other times, though, he can be far more adventurous than this mélange might imply. Check out, for example, his use of an AdrenaLinn sequencer pedal to create the stirring arpeggiated guitar part in "Bigger than My Body," along with his collaborations with everyone from jazzer Herbie Hancock to hip hop artist Kanye West. For some tabloid-minded fans, John Mayer might be a household name more for his romances with Jessica Simpson or Jennifer Aniston, but music clearly fuels his fire, and he has certainly helped to bring the Stratocaster back into the Top Forty nearly sixty years after it first hit the scene.

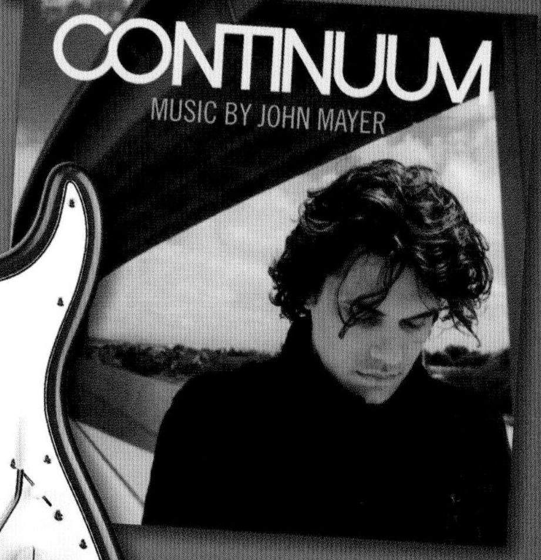

2006 John Mayer Signature Cypress Mica Stratocaster. *Fender Musical Instruments Corporation*

INDEX

Bold numbers indicate artist profiles. *Italics* indicate photos.

First published in 2013 by Voyageur Press, an imprint of MBI Publishing Company, 400 First Avenue North, Suite 400, Minneapolis, MN 55401 USA

ISBN-13: 978-0-7603-4484-2

Library of Congress Cataloging-in-Publication Data

Hunter, Dave, 1962-
Fender stratocaster : the life & times of the world's greatest guitar & its players / Dave Hunter ; foreword by Randy Bachman.
pages cm
ISBN 978-0-7603-4484-2 (hardback)
1. Stratocaster--History. I. Title.
ML1015.G9H8613 2013
787.87028'8--dc23
2013022975

Editors: Michael Dregni and Dennis Pernu
Design Manager: Cindy Samargia Laun
Designer: John Barnett/4 Eyes Design

Printed in China

10 9 8 7 6 5 4 3 2 1

FRONTIS: A well-traveled case with a jewel inside. *Chicago Music Exchange, www.chicagomusicexchange.com*

TITLE PAGE: Buddy Guy plays the blues on his early Stratocaster in London, 1965. *Val Wilmer/Redferns/Getty Images* **INSET:** 2004 '57 Surf Green Stratocaster. *Fender Musical Instruments Corporation*

CONTENTS PAGE: 2009 limited-edition 1958 Candy Apple Red Stratocaster with gold-anodized pickguard. *Fender Musical Instruments Corporation*

LAST PAGE: Marc Bolan of T Rex armed with his Stratocaster in 1972. *Estate of Keith Morris/Redferns/Getty Images*